ACKNOWLEDGMENTS

The Atlanta Braves were kind enough to supply all except one of the photographs in the illustration section.

Nick Manolis performed Herculean duties while the book was being researched at the National Baseball Library in Cooperstown, New York. Jack Redding, Cliff Kachline, Betty McCarthy, and Edith Rumshottel, of that fine institution, were extremely helpful in locating documents for this project. Bob Korch, of the Atlanta Braves' publicity department, provided me with much useful information. At Northeastern University, Bill Fowler, Jack Grinold, and Raymond Robinson provided leads and encouragement. Ken Lewis and Maureen Craft provided clerical assistance, as did Valerie Hawkes-Howat. Art Ballant, my editor at Stein and Day, was most helpful and understanding.

Most important, however, was the support of my family; Maureen, Michael, and Julie sacrificed time and play to allow me to work on this book. My parents, Cynthia and Murray, instilled curiosity and discipline. Thanks to all.

CONTENTS

FOREWORD

I have always had a proprietary interest in the Braves—though not so great a one as Ted Turner now, or the Dovey brothers from 1906 to 1909—because I grew up rooting for the Double-A Atlanta Crackers, a Braves' farm team. Eddie Mathews hit a ball into the Crackers' centerfield magnolia tree, which was a real shot, and soon he was up there with the parent club. I figured I would make the same jump some day, but the next thing I knew, I was a parent, and the Braves were in Atlanta. The Braves have not always played or acted like grownups, as this tidbittersweet history makes clear, but they have been right up there among the big boys since 1876. That, incidentally, was the year (I learn from this book) that Ginger Beaumont was born.

Until I began browsing through these pages, I didn't realize that there were twin-brother Braves in 1915, or that Rico Carty *caught* for the Braves (17 games in 1965), or that the Braves had a "mascot" named Darkhue White, or that there was a Brave named Hubbard (Squash) Perdue, and one named Barbra Chrisley, whose nickname was Neil. (Naming a boy "Barbra" may not be as toughening as the song claims naming one Sue is. Chrisley's lifetime batting average was .210.)

I had never heard of the 1916 Braves' loud-necktie protest, or of the aforementioned Doveys, of South Carolina, who owned the Braves and called them "the Doves." I didn't know about Tommy McCarthy's contribution to the tagging-up-on-a-fly-ball rule, nor did I realize how deep centerfield in old Braves' Field in Boston originally extended (I don't suppose it had a magnolia tree, though).

I knew that Chuck Tanner was born on the Fourth of July, but not that Bobby Malkmus was, also. In fact I had completely forgotten about Bobby Malkmus (average as a Brave: .091), although I used to have his baseball card. I did know that nearly every ballplayer had been a Brave at one time or another, from Cy Young and Babe Ruth, to Rogelio Moret and Jim Bouton . . . and Charley Lau . . . and Joe Pepitone . . . and. . . . I just wish my old parent club would acquire a certain prolific base-stealer currently with the White Sox, so that I could say, "None but the Braves deserve LaFlore."

But if you are or have ever been a Braves' fan, you have by now no doubt pushed bravely beyond these musings on your own, and are looking to see what happened to the Braves on your birthday. Or on Chi Chi Olivo's birthday. Or Virgil Jester's. Have a good time.

ROY BLOUNT, JR.

THIS DATE IN
Braves
HISTORY

DATE SECTION

JANUARY 1*

1869 — Frank Connaughton, 1894; 1906; b.

1912 — Al Moran, 1938–39; b.

1924 — Earl Torgeson, 1947–1952; b.

January 2

1882 — George Jackson, 1911–13; b.

1885 — Chick Autry, 1909; b.

1894 — Bill Wagner, 1918; b.

1905 — Pinky Whitney, 1933–36; b.

1909 — Bobby Reis, 1936–38; b.

January 3

1884 — Kirby White, 1909–10; b.

1891 — Bill McTigue, 1911–13; b.

1894 — Tom Whelan, 1920; b.

1920 — Ed Sauer, 1949; b.

1941 — John Sullivan, 1980–   ; b.

1943 — Adrian Garrett, 1966; b.

January 4

1884 — Al Bridwell, 1906–7; 1911–12; b.

1889 — Rex DeVogt, 1913; b.

1930 — Don McMahon, 1957–62; b.

January 5

1870 — Bill Dahlen, 1908–9; b.

1875 — Izzy Hoffman, 1907; b.

1897 — Art Delaney, 1928–29; b.

---

*The lower case letter *b* at the end of the line identifies the player as having been born in the year that starts the line (on the left).

1899 — Bill Hunnefield, 1931; b.

1944 — Tom Kelley, 1971–73; b.

January 6

1877 — Jack Slattery, 1928; b.

1915 — Chuck Workman, 1943–46; b.

1917 — Phil Masi, 1939–49; b.

1976 — Calling it a "civil venture for the city [of Atlanta] and the South," Ted Turner announced that he had purchased the Braves for approximately $11 million.

January 7

1875 — Kitty Bransfield, 1898; b.

1910 — Johnny McCarthy, 1943; 1946; b.

1922 — Alvin Dark, 1946–49; 1960; b.

1924 — Jim Pendleton, 1953–56; b.

1953 — Roy Hartsfield traded to Brooklyn for Andy Pafko.

1976 — Dave Stegman and Mike Macha chosen in the secondary phase of the free-agent draft.

January 8

1915 — Walker Cooper, 1950–53; b.

1916 — James Gaffney sold the Boston Braves to a local syndicate of bankers including Governor David I. Walsh. George Stallings, the manager, owned some of the club's stock. Percy Haughton, Harvard football coach, was elected president; he served in that capacity until 1918.

1921 — Marv Rickert, 1948–49; b.

1936 — Chuck Cottier, 1959–60; b.

John DeMerit, 1957–59; b.

1937 — Don Dillard, 1963; 1965; b.

1940 — Dick Kelley, 1964–68; b.

1964 — Ernie Bowman was obtained from the Giants to complete a deal begun on December 3, 1963, in which the Braves obtained Felipe Alou, Billy Hoeft, and Ed Bailey in exchange for Bob Hendley, Bob Shaw, and Del Crandall.

January 9

1894 — Ira Townsend, 1920–21; b.

1936 — Julio Navarro, 1970; b.

1955 — Pat Rockett, 1976–78; b.

1974 — Larry McWilliams was selected in the first round (the sixth player chosen) in the free-agent draft.

January 10

1835 — The earliest date on which any Braves' history took place: Harry Wright, the first manager of the Braves, 1876–81, was born.

1873 — Jack O'Neill, 1906; b.

Chick Stahl, 1897–1900; b.

1882 — Johnny Bates, 1906–9; b.

1908 — Bill Swift, 1940; b.

1928 — The Braves obtained Rogers Hornsby from the Giants in exchange for Shanty Hogan and Jimmy Welsh.

Jack Dittmer, 1952–56; b.

1930 — Art "The Great" Shires TKO'd Al Spohrer in a boxing match at the Boston Garden. Shires played 82 games at first for the Braves in 1932, and was a teammate of Spohrer's. Art "The Great" later tried to arrange a bout with Hack Wilson, but was stopped from doing so by Commissioner Kenesaw Mountain Landis.

1973 — The Braves selected Brian Asselstine and Pete Falcone in the secondary phase of the free-agent draft.

January 11

1898 — Gene Lansing, 1922; b.

1937 — Jack Curtis, 1962; b.

1966 — The Braves obtained Red Sox farmhand Jay Ritchie to complete the December 15, 1965, trade in which they obtained Lee Thomas and Arnold Earley for Bob Sadowski and Danny Osinski.

January 12

1876 — George Browne, 1908; b.

1895 — Jack Knight, 1927; b.

1972 — The Braves select Sam Bowen in the secondary phase of the free-agent draft.

1973 — Paul Richards, Vice President for Baseball Operations, is fired, and replaced by Eddie Robinson.

January 13

1904 — Elmer Hearn, 1926–29; b.

1905 — Charles Woodrow Wilson, 1931; b.

1916 — Bama Rowell, 1939–41; 1946–47; b.

1917 — Stan Wentzel, 1945; b.

1944 — Larry Jaster, 1970; 1972; b.

January 14

1856 — Curry Foley, 1879–80; b.

1939 — Sandy Valdespino, 1968; b.

1957 — Tony Brizzolara, 1979–   ; b.

1976 — National League owners unanimously approved the sale of the Braves from the Atlanta–LaSalle Corporation to Turner Communications Corporation.

January 15

1881 — Jess Orndorff, 1907; b.

1891 — Leo Townsend, 1920–21; b.

1897 — Joe Genewick, 1922–28; b.

1943 — Mike Marshall, 1976–77; b.

1965 — The ceremonial ribbon-cutting at the Milwaukee–Atlanta Braves office at the corner of Marietta and Broad Streets, Atlanta, took place.

January 16

1870 — Jimmy Collins, 1895–1900; b.

1880 — Jim Murray, 1914; b.

1907 — Buck Jordan, 1932–37; b.

1921 — Roy Talcott, 1943; b.

1938 — Ron Herbel, 1971; b.

1969 — At the annual stockholders meeting, President Bartholomay announced that the fences in the power alleys would be moved in 10 feet, from 385 to 375, and that the centerfield fence would be moved in 2 feet, from 402 to 400.

January 17

1915 — Luman Harris, 1968–72; b.

1929 — The newly-elected mayor of Revere, Massachusetts, offered the site of the Wonderland Amusement Park to the Braves for Sunday baseball.

January 18

1899 — Eddie Moore, 1926–28; b.

1944 — Carl Morton, 1973–76; b.

January 19

1878 — John White, 1904; b.

1913 — Andy Pilney, 1936; b.

Hugh Poland, 1943–44; 1946; b.

1914 — Al Piechota, 1940–41; b.

1932 — Ed Sadowski, 1966; b.

1943 — Paul Waner and John Cooney were given their unconditional releases.

1954 — The first annual Milwaukee Baseball Writers Diamond Dinner was held at the Pfister Hotel.

January 20

1871 — The Braves' precursor, the Red Stockings of the National Association, was formed at the Parker House in Boston.

1913 — Jimmy Outlaw, 1939; b.

1922 — Sam Jethroe, 1950–52; b.

1936 — Jesse Gonder, 1965; b.

January 21

1895 — Ed Sperber, 1924–25; b.

1927 — Danny O'Connell, 1954–57; b.

1946 — Johnny Oates, 1973–74; b.

1965 — Teams, Inc., a nonprofit organization formed in November 1964 to promote major league sports in Milwaukee, met with National League President Warren Giles to try to persuade him that the Braves should play out the 1965 season before moving to Atlanta.

January 22

1864 — Irv Ray, 1888–89; b.

January 23

1880 — Rip Cannell, 1904–5; b.

1936 — Don Nottebart, 1960–62; b.

1951 — Charlie Spikes, 1979–80; b.

1964 — Warren Spahn signed his 1964 contract, making him, at $85,000, the highest-paid pitcher in baseball.

January 24

1879 — Dave Brain, 1906–7; b.

1901 — Flint Rhem, 1934–35; b.

1904 — Clay Touchstone, 1928–29; b.

1974 — At the 35th Baseball Writers of America award presentations, Henry Aaron was honored with the Judge Emil Fuchs Memorial Trophy for his outstanding contributions to baseball.

January 25

1915 — Dick Culler, 1944–47; b.

1918 — Steve Roser, 1946; b.

1933 — Mel Roach, 1953–54; 1957–61; b.

1936 — Bill Lucas; b.

1948 — Ed Goodson, 1975; b.

1953 — Junior Moore, 1976–77; b.

January 26

1874 — Kaiser Wilhelm, 1904–5; b.

1935 — Bob Uecker, 1962–63; 1967; b.

January 27

1880 — Otis Clymer, 1913; b.

1888 — Al Wickland, 1918; b.

1903 — Earl Williams, 1928; b.

1913 — Stew Hofferth, 1944–46; b.

1915 — Buck Etchison, 1943–44; b.

1847 — George Wright, 1876–78; 1880–81; b.

1884 — Tom Hughes, 1914–18; b.

1887 — Jack Coffey, 1909; b.

1950 — Larvell Blanks, 1972–75; 1980–   ; b.

1967 — The Braves select Kurt Bevacqua in the 6th round of the free-agent draft.

1980 — Henry Aaron refused to accept an award from Commissioner Bowie Kuhn honoring him for his 715th home run, charging that baseball's treatment of retired black ballplayers leaves much to be desired.

1883 — Marty Martel, 1910; b.

1898 — Dick Burras, 1925–28; b.

1919 — Bill Voiselle, 1947–49; b.

1950 — John Fuller, 1974; b.

1888 — Vin Campbell, 1912; b.

1911 — Link Wasem, 1937; b.

1917 — Al Veigel, 1939; b.

1943 — Dave Johnson, 1973–75; b.

1954 — The Braves traded Johnny Antonelli, Don Liddell, and Ebba St. Claire to the New York Giants for Bobby Thomson and Sam Calderone.

1977 — The Braves Board of Directors elected three vice-presidents: Bill Lucas, Major League Personnel Director; Charles Sanders, Business Manager; Bob Hope. Director of Public Relations.

1861 — Al Buchenberger, 1902–04; b.

1862 — Jimmy Manning, 1884–85; b.

1891 — Tex McDonald, 1913; b.

1896 — Pinky Hargrave, 1932–33; b.

1897 — Charlie Robertson, 1927–28; b.

1903 — Abe Hood, 1925; b.

1971 — Donald Davidson received the William J. Slocum Award at the New York Baseball Writers Association dinner for meritorius service to baseball.

FEBRUARY 1

1875 — Billy Sullivan, 1899–1900; b.

1890 — Jim Kelly, 1918; b.

1944 — Hal King, 1970–71; b.

1965 — The Braves traded Ed Bailey to the Giants for Bill O'Dell.

February 2

1874 — Charlie Frisbee, 1899; b.

1908 — Wes Ferrell, 1941; b.

1922 — Sheldon Jones, 1952; b.

1923 — Red Schoendienst, 1957–60; b.

1951 — Leo Foster, 1971; 1973–74; b.

February 3

1881 — Newt Randall, 1907; b.

1882 — Frank Barberich, 1907; b.

1903 — Joe Stripp, 1938; b.

1918 — Sid Schacht, 1951; b.

February 4

1890 — Possum Whitted, 1914; b.

1950 — Max Leon, 1973–78; b.

February 5

1856 — Harry Smith, 1909; b.

1888 — Bill Rariden, 1909–13; b.

1934 — Henry Aaron, 1954–74; b.

1936 — Lee Thomas, 1966; b.

1942 — Braves obtain Tommy Holmes from Yankees for Buddy Hassett and Eugene Moore.

1946 — Vic Correll, 1974–77; b.

   Norm Miller, 1973–74; b.

   Braves obtain Johnny Hopp from the Cardinals for Eddie Joost.

February 6

1895 — Babe Ruth, 1935; b.

1914 — Hal Weafer, 1936; b.

1926 — Sam Calderone, 1954; b.

1928 — Charlie Gorin, 1954–55; b.

1980 — Al Thornwell was named vice-president of the Braves.

February 7

1859 — John Fox, 1881; b.

1876 — Pat Moran, 1901–5; b.

1942 — Ernie Lombardi was purchased from the Cincinnati Reds.

1978 — Craig Skok, who sat out the 1977 season after being released by the Red Sox in December 1976, was signed to a Braves contract.

February 8

1918 — Butch Nieman, 1943–45; b.

1921 — Willard Marshall, 1950–52; b.

1937 — Clete Boyer, 1967–71; b.

1946 — Joe Medwick was given his unconditional release by the Braves.

   Oscar Brown, 1969–73; b.

February 9

1870 — Hi Ladd, 1898; b.

1908 — Buzz Boyle, 1929–30; b.

1945 — Jim Nash, 1970–72; b.

1951 — Buddy Solomon, 1977–79; b.

1954 — Walker Cooper was given his unconditional release by the Braves.

1960 — Stan Lopata was signed by the Braves as a free agent.

February 10

1894 — Cotton Tierney, 1924; b.

1910 — Bob Logan, 1945; b.

1916 — Ralph Hodgin, 1939; b.

1933 — Billy O'Dell, 1965–66; b.

1954 — Vern Bickford was sold to the Baltimore Orioles.

    Larry McWilliams, 1978–   ; b.

February 11

1895 — Joe Shannon and Red Shannon, 1915; b.

1923 — Judge Emil Fuchs, Christy Mathewson, and James MacDonough bought the Boston Braves. Mathewson was elected president and Fuchs the vice-president of the club.

1972 — Ron Herbel was given his unconditional release by the Braves.

February 12

1888 — Joe Connolly, 1913–16; b.

1893 — Earl Sheehy, 1931; b.

1942 — Pat Dobson, 1973; b.

1957 — The Braves obtained Jack Dittmer from the Detroit Tigers for Chick King.

1958 — Ken Smith, 1981–   ; b.

February 13

1887 — Guy Zinn, 1913; b.

1904 — Charlie Fitzberger, 1928; b.

1917 — Norm Wallen, 1945; b.

February 14

1864 — Charlie Getzein, 1890–91; b.

1887 — Mike "King" Kelly released by Chicago to Boston for $10,000.

1897 — Earl Smith, 1923–24; b.

1915 — Red Barrett, 1943-45; 1947; 1949; b.

1940 — Len Gabrielson, 1960; 1963-64; b.

1947 — Jack Zeller signed a contract as chief scout for the Braves.

1968 — Gary Geiger given his unconditional release.

1976 — The Braves sent valentine cards to their season ticket-holders and the media which included the following poem:

> Rose is a Red,
> Morgan's one, too.
> They finished first
> Like we wanted to do.
>
> But last year's behind us
> We're happy to say.
> Now we're tied for first,
> Happy Valentine's Day.

February 15

1905 — Hal Lee, 1933-36; b.

1919 — Ducky Detweiler, 1942; 1946; b.

1979 — Mike Lum, a former member of the Braves, and more recently a member of the Reds, signs another Braves contract as a re-entry free agent.

February 16

1866 — Bill Hamilton, 1896-1901; b.

1880 — Frank Burke, 1907; b.

1886 — Herbie Moran, 1908-10; 1914-15; b.

1947 — Terry Crowley, 1976; b.

1949 — Bob Didier, 1969-72; b.

1953 — The Braves traded Earl Torgeson to the Phillies for Russ Meyer. They then traded Meyer to the Dodgers for Rocky Bridges and Jim Pendleton, whereupon they traded Bridges to the Cincinnati Reds for Joe Adcock.

1980 — The Braves traded Don Collins to the Cleveland Indians for Gary Melson.

February 17

1901 — Eddie Phillipps, 1924; b.

1905 — Ed Brandt, 1928-35; b.

1953 — Jamie Easterly, 1974-79; b.

February 17 (continued)

1954 — Mike Macha, 1979; b.

February 18

1856 — Frank Whitney, 1876; b.

1880 — Dad Hale, 1902; b.

1889 — George Mogridge, 1926–27; b.

1897 — Huck Betts, 1932–35; b.

1959 — Rafael Ramirez, 1980–   ; b.

February 19

1855 — John Morrill, 1876–88; b.

1891 — Larry Chappell, 1916–17; b.

1918 — Tom Earley, 1938–42; 1945; b.

1939 — Bob Sadowski, 1963–65; b.

1952 — Dave Cheadle, 1973; b.

February 20

1921 — Bill Ramsey, 1945; b.

1922 — Jim Wilson, 1951–54; b.

February 21

1867 — Jouett Meekin, 1899; b.

1876 — John Titus, 1912–13; b.

February 22

1931 — Chet Nichols, 1951; 1954–56; b.

1939 — Steve Barber, 1970–72; b.

February 23

1903 — Roy Johnson, 1937–38; b.

1967 — Henry Aaron signed his first $100,000 contract.

1979 — Mike Davey was sold to the Seattle Mariners.

February 24

1896 — Bill Bagwell, 1923; b.

February 25

1854 — Ed Cogswell, 1879; b.

1875 — Johnny Kling, 1911–12; b.

1883 — Jack Hannifan, 1908; b.

1911 — Roy Weis, 1936–39; b.

1921 — Andy Pafko, 1953–59; b.

1939 — Denny Lemaster, 1962–67; b.

1941 — Babe Dahlgren was purchased from the New York Yankees.

February 26

1873 — Bill Banks, 1895–96; b.

1933 — Johnny Blanchard, 1965; b.

1941 — George Kopacz, 1966; b.

February 27

1920 — Connie Ryan, 1943–44; 1946–50; 1975; b.

1935 — Babe Ruth signed a contract with the Braves which made him not only a player, but assistant manager, and second vice-president. The salary was $25,000.

February 28

1872 — Gene McAuliffe, 1904; b.

1948 — Marty Perez, 1971–76; b.

1955 — The Braves were fined $500 for starting their spring training camp before the March 1 starting time announced by the National League office.

Rufino Linares, 1981– ; b.

1973 — Pat Jarvis was dealt to the Montreal Expos for Carl Morton.

February 29

1952 — Al Autry, 1976; b.

MARCH 1

1852 — Paul Hines, 1890; b.

1899 — Ernie Padgett, 1923-25; b.

1915 — Nick Strincevich, 1940-41; b.

1945 — Jim Panther, 1973; b.

March 2
1903 — Art Mills, 1927-28; b.

1913 — Mort Cooper, 1945-47; b.

1917 — Jim Konstanty, 1946; b.

1936 — Don Schwall, 1966-67; b.

1959 — Albert Hall, 1981-   ; b.

March 3

1888 — Art Bues, 1913; b.

1940 — Debs Garms was sold to the Pittsburgh Pirates.

March 4

1862 — Tom Gunning, 1884-86; b.

1876 — Piano Legs Hickman, 1897-99; b.

1883 — Chet Spencer, 1906; b.

1914 — Dick Errickson, 1938-42; b.

1936 — Bob Johnson, 1968; b.

1946 — Danny Frisella, 1973-74; b.

March 5

1888 — Jake Northrop, 1918-19; b.

1897 — Virgil Barnes, 1928; b.

1930 — Del Crandall, 1949-50; 1953-63; b.

1941 — Phil Roof, 1961; b.

March 6

1886 — Bill Sweeney, 1907-13; b.

1933 — Ted Abernathy, 1966; b.

16

1948 — Bama Rowell and Ray Sanders were traded to the Brooklyn Dodgers for Eddie Stanky.

March 7

1881 — Rube Sellers, 1910; b.

1941 — Glen Clark, 1967; b.

1951 — Jeff Burroughs, 1977–80; b.

1981 — Pitcher Carlos Diaz acquired from Seattle for outfielder Jeff Burroughs.

March 8

1875 — Bob Brush, 1907; b.

1879 — Josh Clarke, 1911; b.

1912 — Ray Mueller, 1935–38; 1951; b.

1917 — Bill Salkeld, 1948–49; b.

1924 — Toby Atwell, 1956; b.

1939 — Jim Bouton, 1978; b.

March 9

1890 — George Davis, 1913–15; b.

1893 — Billy Southworth, 1921–23; 1946–51; b.

1917 — Woody Rich, 1944; b.

1932 — Ron Kline, 1970; b.

1948 — Darrell Chaney, 1976–79; b.

March 10

Nothing of importance happened on this date.

March 11

1879 — Joe Stewart, 1904; b.

1974 — Commissioner Bowie Kuhn ordered the Braves to play Henry Aaron in the club's season opener in Cincinnati.

March 12

1892 — Bill James, 1913–15; 1919; b.

1914 — Otto Huber, 1939; b.

1942 — Jimmy Wynn, 1976; b.

March 12 (continued)

1956 — Dale Murphy, 1976-   ; b.

March 13

1879 — Mal Eason, 1902; b.

1886 — Frank Miller, 1922–23; b.

1917 — Joe Walsh, 1938; b.

1918 — Buzz Clarkson, 1952; b.

1925 — Ray Martin, 1943; 1947–48; b.

1940 — Gary Kolb, 1964–65; b.

1942 — Marv Staehle, 1971; b.

1953 — On what was called "Black Friday" by Boston sportswriters, Lou Perini announced that he was going to ask National League owners' permission to move the Braves from Boston to Milwaukee.

1954 — Bobby Thomson suffered a triple fracture of his ankle, which sidelined him until July 14. Taking his place in the outfield, as a regular, was Henry Aaron.

March 14

1900 — Marty McManus, 1934; b.

1954 — Henry Aaron started his first major league exhibition game. He had three hits, including a home run, in a game against the Boston Red Sox.

March 15

1898 — Rosy Ryan, 1925–26; b.

1907 — Lou Fette, 1937–40; 1945; b.

1919 — Whitey Wietelmann, 1939–46; b.

March 16

1865 — Patsy Donovan, 1890; b.

1906 — Lloyd Waner, 1941; b.

1913 — Ken O'Dea, 1946; b.

1969 — Carlos Santeliz, the Venezuelan League Rookie of the Year, en route to the Braves' spring training camp, was one of 140 people killed in a plane crash in Maracaibo. Pablo Torrealba, originally scheduled to take the same flight, missed it and had to take a later one.

March 17

1871 — Chick Fraser, 1905; b.

1876 — John Gammons, 1901; b.

1884 — Bill Collins, 1910–11; b.

1897 — Harry Riconda, 1926; b.

1919 — Pete Reiser, 1949–50; b.

1938 — Jimmie Hall, 1970; b.

1944 — Cito Gaston, 1967; 1975–78; b.

1969 — Joe Torre was traded to the St. Louis Cardinals for Orlando Cepeda.

March 18

1901 — Johnny Cooney, 1921–30; 1938–42; b.

1916 — Elbie Fletcher, 1934–35; 1937–39; 1949; b.

1917 — Ace Williams, 1940; 1946; b.

1918 — Dick Mulligan, 1946–47; b.

1928 — Federico "Chi Chi" Olivo, 1961; 1964–66; b.

1941 — Pat Jarvis, 1966–72; b.

1953 — At 1:33 P.M., Milwaukee time, at the Vinoy Park Hotel in St. Petersburg, Florida, the National League owners voted unanimously in favor of allowing the Braves to move from Boston to Milwaukee.

1963 — The Braves acquired Ty Cline to complete the November 27, 1962, deal in which they traded Joe Adcock and Jack Curtis to the Cleveland Indians for Frank Funk and Don Dillard.

March 20

1885 — Hosea Siner, 1909; b.

1912 — Clyde Shoun, 1947–49; b.

1915 — Ground was broken at the site of Braves Field in Boston. When the project was completed, it was estimated that 750 tons of steel were used to build the park, along with 8.2 million pounds of cement.

1954 — Roy Smalley was obtained from the Cubs for Dick Cole.

March 21

1890 — John Sullivan, 1920–21; b.

19

March 21 (continued)

1906 — Shanty Hogan, 1925–27; 1933–35; b.

1960 — Matt Sinatro, 1981– ; b.

March 22

1854 — Myron Allem, 1886; b.

1864 — Al Schellhasse, 1890; b.

1884 — Bill Chappelle, 1908–9; b.

1898 — Luke Urban, 1927–28; b.

1907 — Johnny Scalzi, 1931; b.

1923 — George Crowe, 1952–53; 1955; b.

1936 — Gene Oliver, 1963–67; b.

1963 — Carlton Willey was sold to the New York Mets.

March 23

1880 — Peaches Graham, 1908–11; b.

1911 — Siggy Broskie, 1940; b.

1927 — Johnny Logan, 1951–61; b.

1938 — Bobby Dews, 1979– ; b.

March 24

1865 — Billy Klusman, 1888; b.

1869 — Al Lawson, 1890; b.

1874 — Roy Thomas, 1909; b.

1893 — George Sisler, 1928–30; b.

1906 — Art Veltman, 1931; b.

1937 — Bob Tillman, 1968–70; b.

March 25

1944 — Jim Britton, 1967–69; b.

1969 — Bob Johnson was traded to the Cardinals for Dave Adlesh.

1974 — Ron Swoboda and Dick Dietz were given their unconditional releases.

1981 — Pitcher Bob Walk acquired from Philadelphia for outfielder Gary Matthews.

March 26

1874 — Gene DeMontreville, 1901–2; b.

1974 — Buzz Capra was purchased from the New York Mets.

Church Goggin was traded to the Red Sox for Vic Correll.

1979 — Bob Horner reported to training camp after a three-week holdout.

March 27

1856 — Jim Tyng, 1879; b.

1924 — Walt Linden, 1950; b.

1932 — Wes Covington, 1956–61; b.

1951 — Dick Ruthven, 1976–78; b.

1973 — Denny McLain was given his unconditional release; Dick Dietz was purchased from the Dodgers.

1975 — Paul Casanova was given his unconditional release.

March 28

1868 — Elmer Smith, 1901; b.

1894 — Lee King, 1919; b.

1901 — Al Hermann, 1923–24; b.

1911 — Clarence Pickrel, 1934; b.

1977 — Robert D. Johnson signed as a free agent.

March 29

1865 — Hank Gastright, 1893; b.

1867 — Cy Young, 1911; b.

1873 — Duff Cooley, 1901–4; b.

1883 — Rube Dessau, 1907; b.

1894 — Dixie Leverett, 1929; b.

1917 — Tommy Holmes, 1942–51; b.

1944 — Denny McLain, 1972; b.

1975 — Jack Pierce traded to the Tigers for Reggie Sanders.

March 30

1874 — Ed Gremminger, 1902–3; b.

1977 — Pablo Torrealba was sold to the Oakland Athletics.

1978 — Buzz Capra, Vic Correll, Craig Robinson, and Tom Paciorek were given their unconditional releases.

1979 — Rod Gilbreath was given his unconditional release.

March 31

1868 — Jack Stivetts, 1892–98; b.

1882 — Big Jeff Pfeffer, 1906–8; 1911; b.

1904 — Red Rollings, 1930; b.

1920 — Dave Koslo, 1954–55; b.

1938 — John Herrnstein, 1966; b.

1939 — The Braves obtained Bill Posedel from the Dodgers for Al Todt.

1958 — Dick Littlefield was purchased from the Chicago Cubs.

1959 — The Braves obtained Stan Lopata, Johnny O'Brien and Ted Kazanski from the Philadelphia Phillies in exchange for Gene Conley, Joe Koppe, and Harry Hanebrink.

1961 — Andre Rogers and Darrell Robertson were traded to the Cubs for Moe Drabowsky and Seth Morehead.

1979 — Dave Campbell was traded to the Montreal Expos for Pepe Frias.

APRIL 1

1904 — Jack Cummings, 1929; b.

1911 — Bob Brown, 1930–36; b.

1913 — Buster Bray, 1941; b.

1915 — Jeff Heath, 1948–49; b.

1917 — Chet Ross, 1939–44; b.

1921 — Red Murff, 1956–57; b.

1939 — Phil Niekro, 1964–   ; b.

1948 — Willie Montanez, 1976–77; b.

1964 — The Braves acquired Mike de la Hoz from the Cleveland Indians to complete an October 1963 deal involving Chico Salmon.

1968 — Stu Miller purchased from the Baltimore Orioles.

1974 — Ivan Murrell bought from the San Diego Padres.

1977 — Steve Kline was given his unconditional release.

April 2

1856 — Tommy Bond, 1877–81; b.

1881 — Joe Stanley, 1903–4; b.

1924 — Bobby Avila, 1959; b.

1972 — Henry Aaron, Rico Carty, and Orlando Cepeda appeared together in a Braves lineup for the first time since 1970. They had not done so for over a year because of injuries.

1975 — The Braves obtained Joe Nolan from the Mets' Tidewater club in exchange for Leo Foster.

April 3

1850 — Charley Jones, 1879; b.

1939 — Hawk Taylor, 1957–58; 1961–63; b.

1957 — The Braves obtained Dick Cole from the Pirates for Jim Pendleton.

1979 — Buzz Capra was given his unconditional release.

April 4

1878 — Jake Volz, 1905; b.

1885 — Bill Dam, 1909; b.

1887 — Bill Cooney, 1909–10; b.

1888 — Bill Upham, 1918; b.

1937 — Gary Geiger, 1966–67; b.

1943 — Tom Fisher, 1967; b.

1974 — Henry Aaron hit the 714th home run of his major league career, tying him with Babe Ruth as the all-time leader. The blast came against Jack Billingham of the Reds in a game in Cincinnati. Ralph Garr and Mike Lum were on base when Aaron hit a 3–1 pitch in the first inning. The Braves lost the game, however, 7–6, in 11 innings, before a crowd of 52,154, the largest opening day crowd in Cincinnati history.

April 5

1876 — Bill Dineen, 1900–1; b.

1921 — Bobby Hogue, 1948–51; b.

1966 — Frank Thomas was released.

1975 — Joe Niekro was sold to the Houston Astros.

1979 — Charlie Spikes signed a free-agent contract with the Braves.

April 6

1863 — Dick Johnston, 1885–89; b.

1871 — The Boston Red Stockings, the Braves' National Association ancestor, won their first game, 41–10.

1890 — Red Smith, 1914–19; b.

1908 — Dick Gyselman, 1933–34; b.

      Ernie Lombardi, 1942; b.

      Joe Mowry, 1933–35; b.

1925 — Hal Schacker, 1945; b.

1976 — Terry Crowley was obtained from the Reds for Mike Thompson.

April 7

1879 — Tom Needham, 1904–7; b.

1893 — Fletcher Low, 1915; b.

1978 — In Bobby Cox's managerial debut, the Braves lost to the Dodgers, 13–4, after holding a 3–0 lead. Rowland Office and Dale Murphy had homers in the game; Phil Niekro took the loss.

The Braves re-signed Tom Paciorek, who had been released March 30.

1979 — Ken Forsch threw a no-hitter against the Braves in Houston. The Astros won, 6–0, as Forsch walked only two. Larry McWilliams was the losing pitcher for the Braves.

April 8

1857 — Bill Crowley, 1881; 1884; b.

1887 — Bill Jones, 1911–12; b.

1888 — Hap Myers, 1913; b.

1914 — Andy Karl, 1947; b.

1953 — Twelve thousand fans met the Braves at a Milwaukee train station. The Braves were arriving from spring training and were making their first official appearance in the city of Milwaukee. Sixty thousand people turned out for a parade later in the day.

1974 — Henry Aaron hit home run No. 715, breaking Babe Ruth's record. It happened in Atlanta, in front of a crowd of 52,870. The record-breaker came against Al Downing in the fourth inning. Aaron hit a 1-0 pitch at 9:07 EDT off the lefty, Downing. The Braves won the game, 7–4. In his first at-bat of the game in the second inning, Aaron walked on five pitches, and later scored his 2,063rd run to set a National League record for most runs scored in a career.

1975 — Henry Aaron played his first game in the American League at Fenway Park in Boston. He went 0-for-3, as the Red Sox won, 5–2. Tony Conigliaro made his first appearance on the comeback trail in front of the home folks. Conigliaro had sat out since playing for the Angels in 1971. He had a hit and a stolen base (his last SB in the majors) on this date.

1977 — On opening day in Houston, Jeff Burroughs made his National League debut memorable by hitting a two-run homer in the first inning. The Braves got no more runs in the game, though, and lost to the Astros, 3–2, in 11 innings.

April 9

1904 — Fred Frankhouse, 1930–35; 1939; b.

1915 — Stan Shemo, 1944–45; b.

1952 — Bob Elliott was traded to the New York Giants for Sheldon Jones.

1956 — George Crowe was traded to Cincinnati for Bob Hazle.

1964 — Bob Uecker was traded to the Cardinals for Jim Coker and Gary Kolb.

1966 — The first game was played in Atlanta–Fulton County Stadium. It was an exhibition game with the Detroit Tigers which the Braves won, 6–3. Felipe Alou had the first hit off Hank Aguirre in the first inning. Tommie Aaron had the first home run, also off Aguirre in the first. Alou, obviously, scored the first run. The first double was hit by Joe Torre in the 8th, the first triple, by Sandy Alomar in the 4th. Denny Lemaster was the first winning pitcher, and Aguirre was the first loser.

1970 — Jumbo Jim Nash made his National League debut in San Diego, beating the Padres, 6–1, for the Braves.

1976 — Darrell Evans began a consecutive-game walk streak that would last for 15 games, through April 27, good for 19 free passes, and the National League record for most consecutive games with at least one walk.

1979 — In the Braves' home opener they lost to the Reds, 9–4. After the game, Barry Bonnell stopped the unannounced entry of two women sportswriters into the clubhouse.

1980 — Tom Seaver came down with the flu, so Frank Pastore substituted, and threw a three-hit shutout at the Braves, the first opening day shutout for the Reds since 1943.

April 10

1930 — Frank Lary, 1954; b.

1949 — Lee Lacy, 1976; b.

   Pete Varney, 1976; b.

1953 — The first baseball game in Milwaukee's major league history since the 1901 season took place, as the Braves and Red Sox played two innings before rain halted the game.

1976 — The Braves signed free-agent Andy Messersmith.

April 11

1882 — Bill McCarthy, 1906; b.

1886 — Al Nixon, 1921–23; b.

1959 — Mickey Vernon was obtained from the Cleveland Indians for Humberto Robinson.

1967 — Eddie Mathews made his first appearance against his Braves teammates since being traded to the Astros, as the Braves lost in the Dome.

1969 — Orlando Cepeda hit his first home run in an Atlanta uniform as the Braves won, 6-4, in Atlanta.

1975 — Henry Aaron got his first American League hit against Jim Perry of the Indians in a game in Milwaukee.

   Dave Johnson was placed on waivers.

April 12

1876 — Vic Willis, 1898–1905; b.

1879 — Fred Brown, 1901–02; b.

1888 — Charlie Pick, 1919–20; b.

1898 — Mickey O'Neil, 1919–25; b.

1930 — Johnny Antonelli, 1948–50; 1953; 1961; b.

1933 — Charlie Lau, 1960–61; 1967; b.

1955 — Chuck Tanner of the Braves became the second major leaguer in history to hit the first pitch ever thrown to him for a home run. He was the first pinch-hitter to accomplish the feat. He came to bat in the eighth inning in a game at Milwaukee and whacked the first pitch to the right-field bleachers. Gerry Staley gave up the blast, and the Braves won, 4-2.

1956 — Jose Alvarez, 1981–   ; b.

1966 — The first regular-season game in Atlanta history resulted in a 3-2 loss to the Pirates, as Willie Stargell hit a homer off of Tony Cloninger to win it in the 13th. Stargell had hit a home run earlier in the game as well. The first home run hit was by Joe Torre against Bob Veale in the fifth inning. All of the runs scored in the game, in fact, resulted from home runs. Jim Pagliaroni hit the other one for the Pirates. Don Schwall got the first regular season win, and Cloninger took the loss.

April 13

1866 — Herman Long, 1890-1902; b.

1902 — Ben Cantwell, 1928-36; b.

1904 — Ken Jones, 1930; b.

1953 — The Milwaukee Braves played their first game. It was on opening day in Cincinnati, and they beat the Reds, 2-0, on a three-hitter by Max Surkont. Rookie outfielder Billy Bruton got the first Milwaukee Brave hit, stolen base, and run. Joe Gordon got the first RBI.

1954 — Braves Field in Boston was re-named BU Field by Boston University, the new owners.

1970 — Henry Aaron hit the first home run by an Atlanta player to the upper level at the Atlanta ball park. It was opening night against the Giants, and Frank Reberger was the victim.

1976 — Opening day in Atlanta: bands, singers, dancing girls, a man in a gorilla suit sweeping the bases between innings, fireworks, balloons—and 37,973 people in the stands. The Braves lost, 6-1.

1979 — Rick Matula got his first major league win as the Braves beat the Dodgers, 2-1, in L.A.

April 14

1886 — Herman Young, 1911; b.

1916 — Johnny Hutchings, 1941-42; 1944-46; b.

1935 — Marty Keough, 1966; b.

1943 — Nanny Fernandez (1942; 1946-47) joined the US Army Air Corps.

1953 — The first game at Milwaukee's County Stadium. Warren Spahn threw a six-hitter as the Braves beat the St. Louis Cardinals, 3-2, in 10 innings. Billy Bruton hit a home run off of Enos Slaughter's glove in the tenth to win it.

1955 — Jim Wilson was sold to the Orioles.

April 15

1877 — Ed Abbaticchio, 1903-05; 1910.

1910 — Eddie Mayo, 1937-38; b.

27

April 15 (continued)

1931 — Ed Bailey, 1964; b.

1947 — Jackie Robinson made his major league debut in a game against the Braves. The Braves lost, 5–3; Robinson went hitless.

1952 — The last home opener in Boston. The Braves lost, 3–2, to the Dodgers. Spahn took the loss, Preacher Rowe took the win. Roy Campanella had a bases-loaded single in the fifth to knock in the go-ahead runs. Sam Jethroe had a homer for the Braves. Attendance was 4,694.

1954 — Opening day in Milwaukee. The Braves ruin the NL debut of Vic Raschi by knocking him out of the box, though Harvey Haddix took the loss. Spahn won it for the Braves, 7–6.

1958 — Pennant Raising at County Stadium. But the Braves lost, 4–3, in the 14th to the Pittsburgh Pirates, as the two clubs tied the National League record for the longest opening day game. It was Milwaukee's first opening day loss; Gene Conley was saddled with the loss.

1962 — The Braves win their first game of the year after an 0–5 start. Hendley got the win as Aaron and Mathews had two RBIs each, to beat Koufax in L.A.

1964 — Ground was broken for Atlanta–Fulton County Stadium.

1965 — Milwaukee's last opening day for the Braves. Sadowski threw a four-hitter as the Braves won, 5–1, before 33,874.

1977 — The Braves retired Henry Aaron's No. 44, thus making Aaron the first man ever to have his number retired by two different clubs (the Brewers had done it the year before). The Braves won the ball game, too, as Jeff Burroughs, making his Atlanta debut, hit a two-run HR in his first at-bat to power the Braves to a 4–3 win.

April 16

1903 — Paul Waner, 1941–42; b.

1935 — Babe Ruth hit his first National League home run, and his first as a Brave. It was the 709th of his career, and it came in Boston against the Giants' Carl Hubbell.

1946 — Johnny Sain made his first appearance since 1942 beating the Dodgers, 5–3, while scattering 10 hits in a game at Boston.

Sandy Sanders bought from the Cardinals.

1955 — Braves' pitchers tied a National League record for most home runs in a game, one club, no other runs, as they gave up five homers to the Reds in Cincinnati. Jablonski hit two, and Semenick, Thurman, and Post each hit one for the Reds. But Del Crandall, Joe Adcock, and Johnny Logan had homers for the Braves and the Braves beat the Reds, 9–5.

1957 — Warren Spahn retired the last 14 men he faced to get a 4–1 opening day win over the Cubs in Chicago.

28

1966 — The New York Mets beat the Braves, 3–1, in New York to reach the .500 mark for the first time in Mets' history.

1968 — The Braves lost to the Cardinals for the eighth straight time, 6–2.

Stu Miller called up from the minors.

1969 — Henry Aaron hit home run No. 512 off the Astros' Denny Lemaster at the Astrodome. The homer tied him with Eddie Mathews on the all-time home run list.

1971 — The Braves signed Luis Tiant as a free agent. Tiant was 7–3 with the Minnesota Twins in 1970, but was released at the end of spring training in 1971. The Braves assigned him to their Richmond farm club and released him on May 15, 1971.

1976 — Tommy John made his first National League appearance since July 1974, but the Braves beat him, 3–1, in Atlanta. Darrell Evans had a three-run homer, and Rogelio Moret had his first major league save. (Ruthven got the win.)

April 17

1878 — Judge Emil Fuchs, 1923–35; b.

1890 — The Braves' Charlie Smith became the first player in baseball history to face a pitcher six times in a game without earning an official at-bat. He walked five times, and was hit by a pitch.

1917 — Stan Andrews, 1939–40; b.

1945 — Opening day in Boston. The Giants beat the Braves, 11–6, as Mel Ott set six National League records: twentieth season with one club; two walks gave him 1,631 (the NL high); he had an RBI to give him 1,778 (an NL high); he had a double, to give him 1,026 extra base hits and 2,076 extra bases (NL highs); and he scored three runs to give him 1,787 (another NL record).

1947 — Jackie Robinson got his first major league hit off the Braves' Glenn Elliott as the Dodgers beat Boston, 12–6, in Brooklyn.

1953 — The Milwaukee Braves lost their first game, 10–9, to the Reds, but Billy Bruton had three hits to give him 8 for his first 14 at-bats.

1971 — Earl Williams hit his first two major league home runs as the Braves beat the Phillies, 6–2, in Philadelphia.

1975 — Minor league pitcher Jimmy Freeman was traded to the Baltimore Orioles for Earl Williams.

1977 — The umpiring crew walked off the field to protest the showing of a controversial call on the instant replay screen, as the Braves won, 5–4, over the Astros in Atlanta. In the fourth inning, after Bob Watson scored on a passed ball on a close call at the plate, the replay was shown on the scoreboard, and the crowd responded with resounding boos. Braves' executive Bill Lucas had to persuade the umpires to return, and promised that no more close calls would be shown on the replay screen.

1892 — Jack Scott, 1917; 1919–21; b.

1893 — Bill Marriott, 1925; b.

1899 — Harry Hulihan, 1922; b.

1918 — Rip Conway, 1918; b.

1947 — John Beazley purchased from the Cardinals.

1948 — Ron Schueler, 1972–73; b.

1950 — The first black player ever to wear a Boston uniform, Sam Jethroe, made his appearance. He had two hits in four times at bat, including a home run, two runs scored, and two RBI's, as the Braves beat the Giants, 11–4, in New York.

Bob Chipman purchased from the Cubs.

1957 — The Braves won their fifth home opener in a row in Milwaukee, this time by a 1–0 score over the Cincinnati Reds. Lew Burdette threw the six-hit shutout for his eighth straight win over the Reds since June 26, 1955.

1968 — Joe Torre, just returning from a finger fracture injury that kept him out of the lineup since April 12, was beaned by the Cubs' Chuck Hartenstein. Torre suffered a minor fracture of the left cheekbone.

1972 – Tommy John's first National League appearance, in Atlanta, resulted in his first NL win as he beat the Braves 3–1, giving up four hits in seven innings.

1976 — Jimmy Wynn had his first home run and RBI in a Braves uniform, as the Braves beat Wynn's old mates, the Dodgers, 7–6. Wynn hit a three-run homer off of Charlie Hough. Andy Messersmith made his Braves' debut against his former mates, hurling four innings.

1980 — The Braves won their first game of 1980, and the Reds took their first loss of the year, breaking nine game streaks for both clubs.

April 19

1886 — Scotty Ingerton, 1911; b.

1887 — Jack Martin, 1914; b.

1900 — The Braves opened the twentieth century by giving up a record number of runs. They lost to the Phillies, 19–17, in 10 innings. No team had ever scored that many runs on opening day. The total of 36 for the two clubs was also a record for opening day runs by two clubs. In the 9th inning, three Boston pinch-hitters not only got on base, but scored, establishing another major league record (equalled five times since) for most runs scored by pinch-hitters in one inning: three.

1909 — Bucky Walters, 1931; 1950; b.

1938 — The Braves signed John Cooney, released by the Cardinals.

1946 — Max West was traded to the Reds for Jim Konstanty.

1948 — The Brooklyn Dodgers returned Ray Sanders (obtained in a March 6 swap for Eddie Stanky), taking $60,000 instead.

1949 — The Boston Braves bought Al Lakeman from the Milwaukee (American Association) Braves.

1963 — Henry Aaron hit home run No. 300 off Roger Craig against the Mets at the Polo Grounds.

1978 — Dick Ruthven tied the National League record for most putouts by a pitcher in a nine-inning game: five.

April 20

1891 — Dave Bancroft, 1924–27; b.

1896 — The Braves rapped out 28 hits versus Baltimore, tying the major league record for most singles in a game.

1898 — Johnny Wertz, 1926–29; b.

1902 — Frank Wilson, 1902; b.

1949 — The Braves beat the Phils, 6–5, as Phillie third baseman Willie "Puddin' Head" Jones tied a National League record by hitting four consecutive doubles.

1964 — Bob Sadowski struck out five straight times to tie the National League record held by only eight others at the time.

1966 — Henry Aaron hit the 400th home run of his career against Bo Belinsky of the Phillies in the 9th inning. He had hit No. 399 in the first inning off of Ray Culp. The Braves won, 8–1.

1970 — Dick Farrell signed as a free agent.

April 21

1855 — Hardy Richardson, 1889; b.

1929 — What would have been the first Sunday game in Boston history was rained out. The Red Sox took that honor on April 28, as they lost to the Philadelphia Athletics, 7–3. The Braves got another chance on May 5, and they lost to Pittsburgh, 7–2.

1935 — Babe Ruth hit his second Braves' home run, and the 710th of his career against the Brooklyn Dodgers. Ray Benge was the Dodger pitcher. This was Ruth's first NL homer in Boston.

1950 — Boston fans saw the first black man to wear a Boston uniform when Sam Jethroe made his Hub debut, going one-for-three in a 2–2 game with Philadelphia (called because of a thunderstorm).

1970 — The Reds hit seven homers and the Braves hit three to give the two clubs a share of the NL record for most homers by two clubs in a nine-inning night game. (The two clubs also hit ten homers on August 18, 1956.) Six different Reds had homers, tying another NL record for most players (one or more home runs, nine-inning game). That, combined with the three different players who hit homers for the Braves, gave the two clubs a share of yet another NL record: most players, one or more homers, both clubs. For the Reds, Pete Rose, Bobby Tolan, Bernie Carbo (2), Johnny Bench, Dave Concepcion, and Tony Perez hit them. For the Braves, it was Felix Millan, Orlando Cepeda, and Rico Carty.

1976 — Andy Messersmith had his first save as a Brave as the Braves beat the Giants, 3–0, in Atlanta.

1978 — Gaylord Perry notched his first National League win since 1971 as his San Diego Padres beat the Braves, 9–3, in San Diego.

1980 — The Braves announced that Bob Horner had been optioned to Richmond.

April 22

1876 — The Braves' very first game. They beat Philadelphia, 6–5, in the first National League game ever. In an error-ridden game in Philadelphia (Phils had 13, Braves 7), Jim O'Rourke got the first hit ever in the National League, Tim McGinley scored the first run, John Manning had the first run-batted-in, Tim Murnane had the first stolen base, and McGinley was the first strikeout victim. The Braves lineup for their first game ever, and the first ever in the National League, was as follows:

SS George Wright	1B Tim Murnane	RF John Manning
2B Andy Leonard	3B Harry Schaefer	LF William Parks
CF Jim O'Rourke	C Tim McGinley	P Joseph Borden

1898 — James Hughes of Baltimore threw the first 60′ 6″ no-hitter at the Braves in Baltimore, winning by an 8–0 score.

Bob Smith, 1923–30; 1933–37; b.

1902 — Ray Benge, 1936; b.

1908 — Fabian Kowalik, 1936; b.

1910 — The Braves and Phillies combined for a major league record: fewest official at-bats—game, both clubs, nine innings: 48 (25 and 23, respectively).

1918 — Mickey Vernon, 1959; b.

1964 — Warren Spahn, Phil Roof, and six others were arrested for drinking after hours in a Houston bar. Each paid $10 fines for drinking after the 1:00 A.M. closing time at the Show Biz Lounge.

1966 — The Braves win their first game in Atlanta, 8–4, over the Mets behind Tony Cloninger.

1971 — Willie Stargell of the Pirates tied the major league record for home runs in the month of April, with his 10th in a game against the Braves that the Pirates won, 7–4.

1979 — Larry McWilliams tied a National League record by striking out twice in one inning.

1981 — Gaylord Perry recorded his first win as a Brave as he beat the Reds 7–3.

April 23

1906 — Ray Starr, 1933; b.

1921 — Warren Spahn, 1942; 1946–64; b.

1946 — Ed Head of the Brooklyn Dodgers threw a no-hitter at the Braves, winning 5–0. It was the first no-hitter in the majors since 1944.

1954 — Henry Aaron hit his first major league home run off of Vic Raschi at Sportsman's Park, St. Louis.

1961 — On his 40th birthday, Warren Spahn won his 289th game, beating the Pirates.

1975 — Pablo Torrealba optioned to Richmond.

1978 — The Padres beat the Braves, 5–4, in 12 innings in San Diego, giving them their first four-game sweep since 1976.

April 24

1894 — Braves pitchers gave up 14 runs in the ninth inning of a game against Baltimore, establishing a major league record which has not been broken: most runs given up in ninth inning.

1906 — Red Worthington, 1931–34; b.

1945 — Ivan Murrell, 1974; b.

1947 — Johnny Mize of the Giants hit three consecutive home runs off of the Braves' Johnny Sain. Mize thus became the first major leaguer to hit three consecutive home runs, five times. The Braves won the game, 14–5.

1948 — Bob Beall, 1975; 1978–80; b.

1976 — Donald Davidson was fired by the Braves, ending a 30-year association which began when Davidson was a batboy for the Boston club.

April 25

1866 — Dick Conway, 1887–88; b.

1869 — Jim Sullivan, 1891; 1895–97; b.

1886 — Ralph Good, 1910; b.

1898 — Fred Haney, 1956–59; b.

Arthur Shay, 1924; b.

1917 — John Dagenhard, 1943; b.

April 25 (continued)

1943 — Bob Johnson, 1977; b.

Lew Krausse, 1974; b.

1948 — The Braves lost a doubleheader to the Giants, 6–2, and 6–0. In the first game, Bobo Newsom made his Giant debut (his ninth club), but was knocked out of the box with a groin injury.

1976 — In a game with the Phillies, Darrell Evans drew a walk for the 13th consecutive game, setting a National League record. The Braves won, 3–2.

1977 — Braves pitchers Phil Niekro, Jamie Easterly, and Mike Beard tied a National League record for most runs given up, fifth inning, when they let the Reds get 12 in a 23–9 loss in Atlanta. Braves' pitchers shared the record, in fact. The staff gave up the same number of runs to the Giants on September 3, 1926.

1978 — Phil Niekro won his 179th game as a Brave, tying him with Lew Burdette for most wins by a righthanded pitcher.

April 26

1895 — Buzz Murphy, 1918; b.

1951 — Johnny Sain won his 100th major league game, a six-hit shutout over the Giants in New York. Roy Hartsfield's and Sam Jethroe's homers accounted for all of the game's runs.

1962 — Tommie Aaron hit his first major league homer (and single and triple) as the Braves beat the Phillies, 10–4.

1974 — Henry Aaron hit his 15th career grand slam, setting an NL record, and putting him ahead of Gil Hodges and Willie McCovey.

April 27

1896 — Rogers Hornsby, 1928; b.

1916 — Enos Slaughter, 1959; b.

1943 — The Braves obtained Connie Ryan and Hugh Poland from the New York Giants in exchange for Ernie Lombardi.

1944 — The Braves' Jim Tobin threw a no-hitter against the Dodgers at Braves Field, winning 2–0. He walked Paul Waner to start the game, and with two outs in the ninth, walked him again. Tobin also had a home run, thus becoming the first man to hit a home run and throw a no-hitter in the same game.

1957 — Despite being under heavy scrutiny by players, coaches, and slow-motion cameras because of accusations (by Cincinnati manager Birdie Tebbetts) that he threw spitballs, Lew Burdette beat the Reds, 5–4, at Cincinnati, as Aaron and Adcock homered.

1971 — Henry Aaron hit the 600th home run of his career against Gaylord Perry of the Giants. The Giants won, however, 6–5, in 10 innings.

1973 — Henry Aaron and Darrell Evans hit home runs on consecutive pitches by Tom Seaver in the fourth inning of a game in Atlanta, which the Braves won, 2–0. Pat Dobson threw a three-hit shutout for the Braves.

1975 — Henry Aaron, now with the Milwaukee Brewers, tied Babe Ruth's career RBI record of 2,209 when he knocked in two runs in a game against the Yankees at Shea Stadium.

April 28

1902 — Red Lucas, 1924–25; b.

1929 — The Boston Red Sox played the first Sunday game in Boston history, but they played it at Braves Field because of the protests of a few members of a church near Fenway Park. The Braves had been scheduled to play the first Sunday game on April 21, but it was rained out. The Red Sox lost to Philadelphia, 7–3. The Braves played their first Sunday game on May 5, losing to Pittsburgh, 7–2.

1948 — Pablo Torrealba, 1975–76; b.

1961 — Warren Spahn threw the major leagues' only no-hitter of 1961, against the Giants. It was the first time that a San Francisco major league team was a no-hitter victim.

1969 — Henry Aaron hit his 513th career home run, moving him past Eddie Mathews into sixth place on the all-time list.

1972 — Jim Hardin signed a Braves contract as a free agent.

April 29

1876 — The Boston Braves participated in the first extra-inning game in major league history, losing to the Hartford Blues, 3–2, in 10 innings, in Boston.

1916 — Art Kenney, 1938; b.

1917 — Bob Whitcher, 1945; b.

1946 — Si Johnson was obtained from the Phillies.

1947 — Tom House, 1971–75; b.

1953 — Joe Adcock hit a 465-foot home run off of Giants hurler Jim Hearn. It landed in the tenth row of the left-centerfield bleachers, the first ball to reach that part of the Polo Grounds since its remodeling in 1923. The Braves beat the Giants, 3–2.

1962 — Roman Mejias's 9th inning HR off Don McMahon gave the Colt .45s a 3–2 win over the Braves.

1968 — In his starting debut as a Brave, Tito Francona went four-for-four against the Giants' Juan Marichal, with two RBIs, 3 singles, a home run, and two stolen bases. The Braves won, 7–2.

April 30

1939 — Bob Hendley, 1961–63; b.

1953 — Bobby Thomson's ninth-inning, 280-foot homer at the Polo Grounds gave the Giants a 1–0 win over Vern Bickford and the Braves.

1955 — Roy Smalley sold to Philadelphia.

1961 — Braves pitchers gave up eight home runs to the San Francisco Giants, tying a National League record held by an earlier Braves team, the 1956 squad, which yielded eight homers to the Reds on August 18.

1962 — Bob Buhl was traded to the Cubs for Jack Curtis.

1968 — Stu Miller given his unconditional release.

1970 — Rico Carty extended his hitting streak to 20 games by hitting his first career grand-slam homer off Ferguson Jenkins of the Chicago Cubs, in a game in Atlanta which the Braves won, 9–2.

1977 — Mike Marshall was traded to the Texas Rangers for cash and a player to be named later.

1981 — Mike Lum was given his unconditional release.

MAY 1

1889 — Fuller Thompson, 1911; b.

1903 — Fritz Knothe, 1932–33; b.

1909 — Bill Dunlap, 1929–30; b.

1917 — Tom Nelson, 1945; b.

1920 — The Braves and the Dodgers played the longest game ever in the major leagues, a 26-inning, 1–1 tie. Both pitchers went all the way. Joe Oeschger of the Braves had to learn how to brush his teeth lefthanded because he couldn't raise his pitching arm, and Leon Cadore of the Dodgers spent the 36 hours immediately following the game in bed.

1949 — In his first major league start, Johnny Antonelli got his first win by a 4–2 score in a game in Boston.

1975 — Henry Aaron took over the all-time lead in runs-batted-in when he knocked in Sixto Lezcano with a single, giving him 2,210 RBIs.

1979 — Phil Niekro's 200th win was recorded in a 7-hit, 5–2 Braves victory over the Pirates in Pittsburgh. The Braves scored three runs in the top of the ninth, beginning with Garry Matthews's home run.

May 2

1886 — Larry Cheney, 1919; b.

1892 — Zip Collins, 1915–17; b.

1941 — Clay Carroll, 1964–68; b.

1943 — Walt Hrniak, 1968–69; b.

1975 — The Braves gave the Phillies permission to negotiate with Dick Allen after having failed to get waivers on him.

1977 — Willie Montanez was placed on the 15-day disabled list.

1980 — The first victory on the road in nine games, a 6–1 win over the Pirates.

May 3

1895 — Bobby Lowe scored six runs in a game to grab a share of the NL record for most runs scored in a nine-inning game.

1916 — Ken Silvestri, 1967; b.

1975 — Gary Nolan of the Reds beat the Braves, 6–1. It was his first win in the majors since October 3, 1972, when he beat the Braves by the same score. Pete Rose made his first appearance at third base since 1966.

May 4

1912 — The Braves purchased Dick Rudolph from Toronto for Buster Brown and $4,000.

1914 — Harl Maggert, 1938; b.

1926 — Bert Thiel, 1952; b.

1953 — Lew Burdette recorded his first win in a Milwaukee uniform when, in relief of Antonelli, he beat the Dodgers, 9–4, to break a six-game Brooklyn winning streak.

1954 — The Braves beat Pittsburgh, 6–1, and moved out of last place. Spahn gave up only six hits, and fanned 12. Max Surkont, in his first appearance against his former Brave teammates, was rapped for seven hits and four runs. The game was held up for 12 minutes because of snow. Milwaukee's temperature dropped to 37° during the game.

1963 — Wycliffe "Bubba" Morton purchased from the Detroit Tigers.

1973 — Ralph Garr tied the major league record for most at-bats and most plate appearances in an extra-inning game when he had 11 of both in a 20-inning affair in Philadelphia which the Braves lost, 5–4. The game took 5 hours and 16 minutes to complete. In the 13th inning, it was 2–2; Darrell Evans hit a two-run homer to put the Braves ahead, but the Phillies came back to tie it at four. It was the longest game played by an Atlanta club in its history (through 1980). The Braves left 27 men on base, another major league record for most men left on in an extra-inning game.

May 5

1857 — Lee Richmond, 1879; b.

1871 — Jimmy Bannon, 1894–96; b.

May 5 (continued)

1929 — The Braves played the first Sunday game in their history, losing to the Pirates, 7–2. An unusual triple play highlighted the contest. With Heinie Mueller on third, and Rabbit Maranville on first, Al Spohrer bounced a ball back to Pirate pitcher Burleigh Grimes, Mueller getting caught in a rundown between third and home for the first out. Spohrer rounded first during the rundown, and was nailed trying to take second. Maranville was then cut down trying to score.

1935 — Babe Ruth faced Dizzy Dean for the first time and struck out, walked, and grounded out twice.

1954 — Gene Conley got his first major league win as he beat the Pirates, 4–1, in Milwaukee.

1964 — Warren Spahn shut out the Mets, 6–0, thus giving him the rare distinction of having shut out every National League team at least once in his career.

1979 — Bill Lucas, Vice President and Director of Operations, died in Atlanta three days after a brain hemorrhage.

1980 — Bill Hahorodny broke up a no-hit bid by Lefty Carlton.

May 6

1864 — Bill Stemmyer, 1885–87; b.

1882 — In a game against Troy, Joseph Hornung of the Braves had two triples in one inning, a feat accomplished by only eight others since then. The Braves had a total of four triples in the inning, and no club has exceeded that total since.

1890 — Walton Cruise, 1919–24; b.

1917 — Mike McCormick, 1946–48; b.

1926 — Dick Cole, 1957; b.

1950 — The Braves hit five homers in a 15–11 rout of the Reds, increasing their three-game total to 13 homers, breaking the Giants' 1947 record for homers in a three-game series. In this game, the circuit clouts were clocked by Luis Olmo, Earl Torgeson, Bob Elliott, Willard Marshall, and Sid Gordon.

1951 — Clifford Chambers of the Pirates threw a no-hitter at the Braves in Boston in the second game of a doubleleader, the first Pirate no-hitter since 1907. Boston won the first game of the doubleheader behind Spahn, 6–0.

1952 — Johnny Klippstein won his fifth straight game against the Braves since coming up from the minors in 1950, this time on a two-hit shutout in Chicago which took only 1 hour and 38 minutes to complete.

1970 — Dick Farrell was released.

1974 — "Welcome Home Henry Night" in Milwaukee as the Braves played the Brewers in an exhibition game. Aaron hit a 398-foot HR.

1975 — Dick Allen and Johnny Oates were traded to the Phillies for Barry Bonnell, Jim Essian, and a player to be named later.

1976 — Terry Crowley was released.

1979 — Cubs 14, Braves 13. Glenn Hubbard had four hits, three of them doubles. In the ninth, the Braves tied the score at 13, but in the bottom half of the inning, leftfielder Charlie Spikes failed to pursue a leadoff fly ball by Tim Blackwell, thinking that it would drop foul. It didn't. Blackwell had a leadoff triple, and the Cubs won.

May 7

1889 — Cyril Collins, 1913–14; b.

1896 — Tom Zachary, 1930–34; b.

1913 — Art Doll, 1935–36; 1938; b.

1937 — Claude Raymond, 1961–63; 1967–69; b.

1941 — Nick Strincevich was traded to the Pirates for Lloyd Waner.

1942 — Jim Wallace, nearly denied entrance by the gatekeeper, who thought that the skinny 21-year old wasn't a big-leaguer, threw a six-hitter at the Pirates, winning 7–1, his only win of 1942.

1972 — Mike Fiore had his first National League hit for the Cardinals, and his first NL game-winning RBI as Reggie Cleveland and the Cards beat the Braves, 5–3.

May 8

1850 — Ross Barnes, 1881; b.

1858 — Dan Brouthers, 1889; b.

1901 — The Braves beat Brooklyn, 7–6, in 12 innings in front of a crowd which included most of the schoolboys from the English and Latin schools, who had been admitted free.

1907 — The Braves' Frank Pfeffer pitched a no-hitter against the Cincinnati Reds in Boston. The Braves won, 6–0.

1926 — The National League's Golden Jubilee celebration was held at Braves Field before the Braves beat Chicago, 5–2.

1953 — The first night game played in Milwaukee resulted in a 2–0 win for the Braves over the Cubs. Johnny Antonelli recorded the shutout.

1963 — The Braves obtained Humberto Chico Fernandez from the Detroit Tigers for Sweet Lou Johnson.

1964 — Roy McMillan was traded to the Mets for Jay Hook.

1981 — Rick Mahler recorded his first major league decision as the Braves beat the Cubs 4–3.

May 9

1854 — Joe Borden, 1876; b.

1919 — Carl Lindquist, 1943–44; b.

1940 — Herb Hippauf, 1966; b.

1961 — Frank Thomas obtained from the Cubs in exchange for Mel Roach.

1962 — Don McMahon was sold to the Houston Colt .45s.

The Braves beat Pittsburgh, 4–2, in front of the smallest crowd in Milwaukee Brave history. The 38° weather kept the crowd down to 3,673, who saw Jack Lamabe and Tom Sturdivant work for Pittsburgh on the mound, Dick Schofield and Dick Stuart toil for Pittsburgh in the infield, and Hank Fischer pitch for the Braves. What did they all have in common? They were either past or future members of the Boston Red Sox.

1975 — Biff Pocoroba had his first big league hit, driving in two runs in the second inning, as the Braves won, 3–1.

1976 — The Braves dropped their thirteenth straight game, 5–2, to the Pirates.

May 10

1863 — Chippy McGarr, 1890; b.

1872 — John Malarkey, 1902–03; b.

1899 — Freddie Maguire, 1929–31; b.

1913 — Roland Gladu, 1944; b.

1917 — Chet Clemens, 1939; 1944; b.

1929 — Braves' centerfielder Earl Clark set a major league record which has never been broken: 12 putouts by a centerfielder in a nine-inning game.

1938 — Merritt Ranew, 1964; b.

1953 — The first doubleheader in Milwaukee Braves history. The Braves swept the Cubs, 6–2, and 4–1. In the first game, Max Surkont got his fourth win in as many decisions as Billy Bruton and Johnny Logan each went three-for-five. In the second game, Don Liddle made his first big league start and tossed a two-hitter, as Bruton extended his hitting streak to nine games.

1956 — Howard Valentine obtained from the Reds to complete the April 9 deal in which the Braves got Bob Hazle in exchange for George Crowe.

1957 — Juan Pizarro earned his first major league win and hit his first home run as well, as the Braves beat the Cardinals, 10–5, in St. Louis. Logan and Mathews also had homers for the Braves.

1962 — Cold weather kept fans away for the second night in a row as the Braves dropped a 4–3 decision to the Pirates. A new low in attendance, 2,746, was set.

1967 — Henry Aaron hit his first home run against Jim Bunning, an inside-the-park job in Philadelphia.

1975 — Jim Essian was sent to the Chicago White Sox to complete a December 1974 deal involving Dick Allen.

May 11

1939 — Milt Pappas, 1968–70; b.

1946 — The first night game at Braves Field drew the largest crowd in 13 years: 35,945. The Giants beat the Braves, 5–1.

1948 — Dan Litwhiler was traded to the Cincinnati Reds for Marvin Rickert.

1954 — Gene Conley threw his first major league shutout, a 2–0 win in Brooklyn.

1957 — Johnny Logan's eight-game hitting streak ended as the Braves lost, 8–7, in St. Louis.

1960 — Bob Giggie traded to the A's for George Brunet.

1976 — The Braves break a 13-game losing streak, coming up with a run in the bottom of the ninth to beat the Mets, 8–7. The losing streak, the longest in Atlanta history, began on April 26, and ended when Rowland Office knocked in Marty Perez to give Elias Sosa the win.

1977 — The Braves lost their 17th straight game, their first loss under manager Ted Turner, who had given regular manager Dave Bristol a vacation. NL President Chub Feeney called Turner the following day to cite Rule 20, Section A, which says that no player or manager could own stock in the club.

1979 — Jeff Burroughs broke up Bob Forsch's no-hitter with a home run in the seventh. Atlanta won the game, 3–0.

May 12

1897 — Joe Dugan, 1929; b.

1900 — Phil Voyles, 1929; b.

1935 — Felipe Alou, 1964–69; b.

1951 — Joe Nolan, 1975; 1977–80; b.

1953 — The Braves come up with their second straight two-hit performance by a rookie pitcher making his first major league start, as Bob Buhl beat the Giants, 8–1, in Milwaukee.

41

1962 — The New York Mets won the first doubleheader in their history, and the Braves were the victims. Hobie Landrith and Gil Hodges hit 9th-inning home runs in the first and second games, respectively, to help their team win by scores of 3–2 and 8–7. Craig Anderson won both games in relief. His win in the second game was his last in the major leagues. He went on to lose 16 straight during the rest of 1962; he lost two without winning in 1963 and was 0–1 in 1964.

1964 — Gus Bell was released.

1966 — In the first game ever at Busch Stadium, St. Louis, the Braves lost to the Cardinals, 4–3. Felipe Alou hit two homers (the first at Busch) to raise his season total to eight.

1970 — Rico Carty extended his hitting streak to 30 games as the Braves dropped a 4–3, 11-inning decision to the Cubs at Wrigley Field. Ernie Banks hit his 500th career homer.

1977 — The Braves' 17-game losing streak stopped in Pittsburgh as they beat the Pirates 6–1, thus snapping an 11-game Buc win streak at the same time. Vern Benson was the man at the helm for the Braves. Dave Bristol had not yet returned from a vacation ordered by Ted Turner.

1979 — Ted Turner named John Mullin general manager.

May 13

1897 — Hugh Canavan, 1918; b.

1918 — Carden Gillenwater, 1945–46; b.

1942 — The Braves' Jim Tobin became the only National League pitcher ever to hit three home runs in a game, hitting three in a row. This feat also gave him the record for total bases in a game by a pitcher, 12. No American League pitcher ever hit more than two in a game, and the last man to do that was Boston's Sonny Siebert on September 2, 1971.

1951 — The Browns sold Sidney Schacht to the Braves and bought Bob Hogue.

1978 — Phil Niekro recorded his 2,000th career strikeout, but lost to Montreal's Steve Roger's three-hit shutout (in Montreal).

1980 — Doyle Alexander notched his first National League win since 1971 as the Braves won, 7–3.

May 14

1881 — Ed Walsh, 1917; b.

1894 — A fire at the Braves' Congress Street Grounds in Boston caused $1M damage. It started in a rubbish pile beneath the rightfield bleachers during the third inning of a game with Baltimore. The bleachers and the grandstands were destroyed by the fire, which then spread to nearby buildings, gutting 170 of them. No lives were lost in the blaze.

1913 — Johnny Babich, 1936; b.

1927 — Braves pitchers yielded five runs in the 18th inning of a game with the Cubs, thus establishing a record for most runs given up, 18th inning, a record not liable to be broken soon.

1946 — Ernie White purchased from the Cardinals.

1947 — Frank McCormick, unconditionally released by the Phillies, signed a Braves contract, and went on to lead the league in pinch-hits in 1947.

1957 — The Braves moved into sole possession of first place by beating the Brooklyn Dodgers, 3–2, in Milwaukee; Bob Buhl walked nine, but hung on to get the win.

1966 – The Braves gave the Cardinals their first Busch Stadium loss, as Denny Lemaster threw a four-hit shutout to win, 3–0.

1973 — Bob Didier was traded to the Detroit Tigers for Gene Lamont.

May 15

1895 — Jimmy Smith, 1918; b.

1915 — Don Manno, 1940–41; b.

1919 — Ed Wright, 1945–48; b.

1944 — Clyde Shoun of Cincinnati threw a no-hitter at the Braves in Cincinnati, winning 1–0. The Braves were involved in the only other 1944 no-hitter, Jim Tobin's, on April 27. Tobin was the only baserunner on this date, having drawn a walk.

1951 — The Braves tied the major league record for fewest official at-bats—game, one club, nine innings (as they had 24 against the Reds in Cincinnati)—as Ewell Blackwell tossed a one-hit shutout at them. Vern Bickford of the Braves wasted a two-hitter.

1953 — John Mullin was named farm director of the Braves.

1962 — Denis Menke's first major league home run, a grand slam, was not enough as the Pirates beat Milwaukee, 5–4, in Pittsburgh, breaking a six-game losing streak.

1964 — Jeoff Long hit the only home run of his major league career, and Julian Javier added a grand slam as the Cardinals beat the Braves, 10–6, in St. Louis.

1970 — Rico Carty hit in his 31st consecutive game.

1971 — The Braves organization released Luis Tiant, who had been signed on April 16 as a free agent and sent to Richmond.

1974 — Ron Reed was hit on the hand by a line drive from the bat of San Diego's Bobby Tolan, and had to leave the game in the fourth inning. Buzz Capra came on in relief, threw six shutout innings, got credit for the 3–0 win, and went on to win eight more in a row (an Atlanta record), before he was stopped on July 7.

May 15 (continued)

1975 — Jim Essian, obtained from Philadelphia on May 7 along with Barry Bonnell, in exchange for Dick Allen and Johnny Oates, was sent to the White Sox to complete the deal in which the Braves obtained Allen from the White Sox for $50,000 and a player to be named later.

May 16

1859 — Steve Dignan, 1880; b.

1875 — George Barclay, 1904–5; b.

1928 — Billy Martin, 1961; b.

1933 — Bob Bruce, 1967; b.

1946 — Mort Cooper was married before the game and was pulled for a pinch-hitter in a three-run sixth inning, but Jeff Cross of the Cardinals stole home in the 10th with two out, to give the Braves a loss in Boston.

1953 — Curt Simmons gave up a first-pitch single to Billy Bruton to start the game, and then retired the next 27 Braves in a row as the Phillies won, 3–0, snapping a six-game Brave winning streak, and dropping them to second place.

1954 — Johnny Antonelli beat his former mates, the Braves, 9–2, in his first appearance against them since the trade.

1970 — Jim McGlothlin threw a five-hit shutout, beating the Braves, 2–0. Rico Carty had none of the five hits, and thus saw his 31-game hitting streak come to an end.

1977 — The Braves overcame a nine-run deficit to beat the Cardinals, 15–12. Barry Bonnell had a bases-clearing single to knock in the winning run.

1978 — Free-agent Jim Bouton signed a Braves contract, and was assigned to Savannah.

1979 — Tony Brizzolara was called up from Richmond; Mike Macha was sent down.

May 17

1910 — Mike Balas, 1938; b.

1932 — Billy Hoeft, 1964; b.

1948 — After having been shut out for 39 consecutive innings, the Braves exploded for an 18-hit, 12–3 win in Brooklyn.

1960 — Ray Boone was traded to the Red Sox for Ron Jackson.

1970 — Henry Aaron recorded his 3000th hit, a first-inning single in the second game of a doubleheader against the Reds' Wayne Simpson. The Braves lost both games, 5–1, and 7–6, in 15 innings.

1971 — Ralph Garr tied the major league record for most home runs in extra innings as he hit one against Tom Seaver in the 10th inning, and another against Ron Taylor in the 12th. The Mets won, 4–3.

1977 — Phil Niekro recorded his first win of the year, a relief stint against the Expos. Biff Pocoroba hit a pinch-hit, two-out, grand slam in the ninth, with the Braves down, 6–5.

May 18

1977 — Jamie Easterly notched his first win of the year in a 10–8 victory over the Expos. Andre Dawson hit his first major league homer for Montreal.

1979 — Dale Murphy hit three home runs in a 6–4 win over the Giants in Atlanta, bringing his season's total to 13. Murphy hit homers against Vida Blue in the first and third innings, and one off Tom Griffin in the seventh, thus becoming the first Brave to have three home runs in a game since Mike Lum did it in 1970.

May 19

1874 — Pop Williams, 1903; b.

1891 — Dixie Carroll, 1919; b.

1910 — Tommy Thompson, 1933–36; b.

1917 — Skippy Robert, 1941–42; 1946; b.

1948 — Vern Bickford's major league starting debut resulted in a victory for him as the Braves won, 4–1.

Al Santorini, 1968; b.

1973 — Joe Pepitone was obtained from the Cubs in exchange for Andre Thornton.

1979 — Tony Brizzolara started his first major league game, against the Giants.

May 20

1889 — Ted Cather, 1914–15; b.

1947 — All 22 hits in Pittsburgh's 4–3 win over the Braves (12 by the Pirates, and 10 by Boston), were singles.

1953 — Braves attendance after their 13th game of the year surpassed all of 1952's attendance of 281,278.

1954 — The organ at Milwaukee was played for the first time in an exhibition game against the Chicago White Sox.

1962 — The Braves lost their second straight doubleheader to the New York Mets, by scores of 7–6 and 9–6 in games played in Milwaukee. Former Brave Frank Thomas had two hits in each game, and five RBIs for the day. Ken MacKenzie, also a former Brave, won the first game for the Mets in relief. In the second game, the Mets had a six-run 7th, with homers by Thomas, Charley Neal, and Felix Mantilla (another former Brave). (Note that the Mets won all of 40 games in 1962.)

May 20 (continued)

1965 — Warren Spahn made his first Mets appearance against the Braves after his trade, and lost, 7-1, as Wade Blasingame threw a one-hitter. Eddie Mathews hit a grand slam off of Spahn.

1973 — The Dodgers' Walter Alston intentionally walked Darrell Evans in the 10th inning to pitch to Henry Aaron. Aaron singled home the winning run.

1975 — Vic Correll hit his fifth home run in five games, a grand slam, as the Braves won, 9-4.

May 21

1891 — Bunny Hearn, 1918; 1926-29; b.

1902 — Earl Averill, 1941; b.

1932 — Earl Hersh, 1956; b.

1935 — Babe Ruth hit his first road home run as a Brave, and his third in a Braves' uniform (No. 711 lifetime) off of Tex Carleton of the Cubs.

1941 — Bobby Cox, 1978-81; b.

1952 — Milwaukee acquired Gene Mauch from the Cardinals and assigned him to the minor leagues.

1958 — Paul Runge, 1981- ; b.

1961 — Joe Torre made his major league debut in a doubleheader against the Reds, going three-for-eight, with a double and a home run. He also threw out three would-be base stealers: Vada Pinson, Frank Robinson, and Eddie Kasko.

1962 — The Braves obtained Gus Bell from the Mets to complete a November 28, 1961, swap involving Frank Thomas.

1966 — Henry Aaron hit the first pinch-hit home run by an Atlanta Brave in a game against the Cubs in Atlanta.

1968 — Rookie Jim Britton's 16-inning scoreless string ended in Atlanta, as he was touched for a first-inning homer in a 6-4 Braves' loss.

May 22

1884 — Tom McCarthy, 1918-19; b.

1886 — Charlie Maloney, 1908; b.

1902 — Al Simmons, 1939; b.

1935 — The Braves dropped into the cellar, a position they would not leave in 1935. They finished 61½ games behind the Cubs.

Ron Piche, 1960-63; b.

1949 — Mike Eden, 1976; b.

1969 — After 9,015 at-bats, Henry Aaron was lifted for a pinch-hitter, in a game against New York in Atlanta. Earlier in the game, Aaron hit home run No. 519 which moved him ahead of Ted Williams on the all-time extra-base-hit list. In his next at-bat, he singled, moving ahead of Charlie Gehringer in career hits with 2,840. Then, in the seventh inning, Mike Lum pinch-hit for Aaron, and doubled. The Braves won, 15-3, thus administering the Mets' worst defeat since the Braves beat them, 17-1, on June 16, 1966.

1971 — Henry Aaron was intentionally walked three times in an 8-7 loss to the Mets at Shea Stadium, thus tying the major league record for most free passes in a game.

1973 — Connie Ryan was named to the Braves coaching staff.

1976 — Rogelio Moret notched his first National League win as the Braves beat the Giants, 3-2, at Candlestick Park.

1981 — Claudell Washington hit his first HR in a Braves uniform as the Braves lost to the Padres 5-2.

May 23

1878 — Dave Shea, 1909-1910; 1912; b.

1919 — Hank Gowdy Day in Boston. The first man to enter World War I from baseball's ranks appeared in his first game since his enlistment. He hit the first pitch thrown to him for a single.

1924 — Clyde King, 1974-75; b.

1945 — Red Barrett was traded to the Cardinals for Mort Cooper.

1965 — Lee Maye was traded to the Astros for Ken Johnson.

1978 — Tom Paciorek was released.

1979 — Tony Brizzolara chalked up his first big league win as the Braves scored five runs in the eighth inning to win, 6-5.

May 24

1857 — Bill Annis, 1884; b.

1876 — Fred Jacklitsch, 1917; b.

1891 — Joe Oeschger, 1919-1923; b.

1895 — Gus Felix, 1923-25; b.

1898 — Leo Mangum, 1932-35; b.

1941 — Paul Waner, released by the Dodgers earlier in the month, was signed by the Braves.

May 24 (continued)

1958 — Bob Hazle was sold to the Detroit Tigers.

Billy Bruton played in his first game since his July 11, 1957, collision with Felix Mantilla. He had missed 105 straight regular-season games.

1962 — Bob Buhl of the Cubs, making his first appearance against his former Brave mates, beat them, 4–3, in Milwaukee.

1968 — Ron Reed beat the Mets for the second time of the year. In the sixth inning, though, he accidentally swallowed a bug and had to summon the Braves' trainer. When asked what kind of bug it was, Reed replied, "It tasted like a roach."

1977 — Buddy Solomon was purchased from the Cardinals.

May 25

1916 — Frank Drews, 1944–45; b.

1918 — Johnny Beazley, 1947–49; b.

1925 — Don Liddle, 1953; b.

1935 — Boston Brave Babe Ruth hit the last three home runs of his career against the Pirates at Forbes Field. Ruth hit No. 712 against Red Lucas, and Nos. 713 and 714 off of Guy Bush.

1947 — Shortstop Buddy Kerr of the New York Giants made his first error in 69 games (286 chances) as the Giants beat the Braves, 9–3, in Boston.

1950 — John Montefusco, 1981– ; b.

1953 — Max Surkont set a major league record for most consecutive strikeouts by a pitcher as he mowed down eight Reds in the second game of a doubleheader which the Braves won, 10–3. He struck out the last man to face him in the second, and then got the side on strikes in the third and fourth innings. The game was then halted for 38 minutes because of rain, but Surkont struck out Andy Seminick to begin the fifth inning. He struck out a total of 13, and he won his sixth straight decision in front of a home crowd.

1979 — The Braves obtained Bo McLaughlin from the Astros for Frank LaCorte.

May 26

1874 — Dave Pickett, 1898; b.

1902 — Herb Thomas, 1924–25; 1927; b.

1912 — Jim McClosky, 1936; b.

1929 — Les Bell, a pinch-hitter for the Braves, and Pat Crawford, a pinch-hitter for the Giants, hit grand slam home runs, the only time in baseball history that two pinch-hitters from different clubs hit slams in the same game.

48

1931 — Jim Frey, 1950–56 (minor leaguer); b.

1935 — Eddie Haas, 1958; 1960; b.

1947 — Darrell Evans, 1969–76; b.

1956 — Johnny Klippstein, Joe Black, and Hersh Freeman combined for a 9 2/3-inning no-hitter against the Braves, but lost it in the 10th, 2–1, in a game at Milwaukee.

1959 — Harvey Haddix of the Pittsburgh Pirates pitched 12 perfect innings but lost the game in the 13th inning to the Braves in Milwaukee. In the 13th, Felix Mantilla reached first on Don Hoak's error, was sacrificed to second by Eddie Mathews, and stayed there as Henry Aaron was intentionally walked. Joe Adcock hit one out of the park, but while Mantilla scored, Aaron stopped running at second base, and Adcock passed him and went on to touch home. Umpire Dascoli ruled that the Braves had won, 2–0, but NL President Giles later ruled that the Braves won by a 1–0 score. The Braves still hold the record for fewest hits in an extra-inning game: one.

1967 — The Mets beat the Braves, 1–0, in New York as Jerry Buchek hit a 410-foot home run into the wind in the second inning.

1969 — Chief No-ka-homa's tepee caught on fire after a Clete Boyer home run against the Cardinals. Earlier in the game Henry Aaron hit his 500th career double, joining Babe Ruth and Ted Williams as the only players to have 500 doubles and 500 home runs.

1972 — Henry Aaron stroked his 3,300th hit, home run No. 646, as the Braves beat the Giants 9–4.

May 27

1916 — John Dudra, 1941; b.

1925 — Donald Davidson, 1947–1976; b.

1945 — Mort Cooper made his first start for the Braves and shut out the Reds, 4–0, in the first game of a doubleheader. Buck Walters, who began and ended his career with the Braves, returned the favor in the second game and shut out the Braves, 5–0, on a three-hitter.

1947 — Don Padgett was dealt to the Phillies for Anton Karl.

1962 — Tommie Aaron tied the major league record for most double plays started by a first baseman: three.

1971 — Tom Kelley, in his first major league start since 1966, threw a four-hit, nine-strikeout performance, for his first National League win, and first in a Braves uniform.

1977 — Rookie Barry Bonnell went five-for-five, but the Braves lost, 4–3, in 10 innings in San Francisco.

May 28

1881 — King Brady, 1912; b.

1886 — Jim Thorpe, 1919; b.

1951 — Willie Mays slapped his first major league hit in the first inning of a game against the Braves, a home run off of Warren Spahn. Mays had been hitless in his first 12 major league at-bats. The Braves won, though, 4–1, in New York.

1960 — Warren Spahn threw his second career no-hitter, this one against the Giants in Milwaukee.

1962 — Warren Spahn lost his 200th career game, 2–1, to the Cubs in Chicago, despite giving up only four hits.

1966 — Lee Thomas was traded to the Cubs for Ted Abernathy. The Braves and Cubs then played a game: the Cubs won, 8–5, in 12 innings, and the loser was Ted Abernathy, who gave up a three-run homer to Ron Santo in the bottom of the 12th.

1975 — Ron Reed was traded to the Cardinals (with a player to be named later) for Elias Sosa and Ray Sadecki. Wayne Nordhagen was sent to the Cards on June 2 to complete the deal.

1981 — The Dodgers' Fernando Valenzuela suffered his first major-league shellacking as the Braves pounded him for seven runs in the fourth. Atlanta fans watched the majors' oldest pitcher, Gaylord Perry, beat the NL's youngest by a score of 9–4.

May 29

1929 — Roberto Vargas, 1955; b.

1945 — Blue Moon Odom, 1975; b.

1954 — St. Louis stopped a 10-game Braves winning streak, beating them, 12–7, in Milwaukee, in front of the club's first 40,000 crowd, a Milwaukee record for attendance.

1966 — Mack Jones stole two bases in one inning, the first time that that was accomplished by an Atlanta Brave. The Cubs won the game, however, 3–2, in 10 innings, despite Eddie Mathews' inside-the-park homer, a rarity for both Mathews and Wrigley Field.

Marty Keough was traded to the Cubs for John Herrnstein.

1971 — Darrell Evans hit his first major league home run as the Braves lost, 8–7, in St. Louis.

1976 — Joe Niekro of the Astros hit his first major league home run to tie the game in the seventh inning, and the Astros went on to win, 4–3, in the Astrodome. The loser, and the victim of Joe Niekro's HR, was none other than brother Phil.

May 30

1878 — Mike Donlin, 1911; b.

1894 — The Braves' Bobby Lowe became the first man in major league history to hit four home runs in one game. He hit his consecutively; no National Leaguer has matched that feat in a nine-inning game. He also had a single in the game. Elton Chamberlain was the pitcher; Cincinnati outfielders watched the balls fly out of the Congress Street Grounds in Boston.

1936 — Ed Rakow, 1967; b.

1947 — Jackie Robinson made his Boston debut, his first Hub appearance since his 1945 tryout with the Red Sox. The Braves took two from Brooklyn, 6–3, and 3–0. In the first game, Braves first baseman Earl Torgeson tied a major league record by playing the entire game without a putout.

1956 — The Braves tied a major league record for most consecutive home runs in an inning, when they hit three against the Cubs in the first inning of the first game of a twin bill. Eddie Mathews, Henry Aaron and Bobby Thomson hit them. When Billy Bruton came up to bat, Cub pitcher Russ Meyer hit him with a pitch; Bruton charged the mound, and both players were ejected. The Braves lost that first game, 10–9, but won the second, 11–9. In the doubleheader, the Braves had a total of nine homers, and the Cubs had six; the grand total of 15 was the major league record for most home runs by two clubs in a doubleheader.

1976 — The Braves dropped a twin bill to the Astros in Atlanta, 5–2, and 16–2. In the second game, the Astros set a club record with 25 hits, and Rogelio Moret suffered his first National League loss. The 16 runs and the 25 hits were highs for the Braves staff of 1976.

May 31

1896 — Socks Seibold, 1929–33; b.

1897 — Fred Tenney of the Braves went six-for-eight; the Braves infield had 18 hits, the most ever by a National League infield.

1947 — The Braves were shut out, 5–0, by Ralph Branca of the Dodgers before 23,275, the largest weekday crowd in Boston since 1933, the size of which was attributed in large part to the presence of rookie Jackie Robinson in the Dodger lineup.

1952 — Tommy Holmes was fired as Braves manager and was replaced by Charlie Grimm.

1955 — Larry Owen, 1981– ; b.

1956 — The Braves hit five home runs as they beat the Cubs, 15–8, in Chicago, giving them 16 in four games, tying their own National League record for homers in a four-game span; they also set a new record with 14 in three games. Joe Adcock had two, and Del Crandall, Billy Bruton, and Eddie Mathews had one each.

1958 — Henry Aaron, Eddie Mathews, and Wes Covington hit consecutive home runs in the first inning. The same three men accomplished exactly the same feat on June 26, 1957.

1967 — Ty Cline was sold to the Giants and Charlie Lau was purchased from the Baltimore Orioles.

May 31 (continued)

1970 — Rico Carty hit three home runs in a game in Atlanta.

1972 — Henry Aaron hit home run No. 648, tying him with Willie Mays for second place on the all-time list. The Braves won, 5–4, in Atlanta. Fred Norman of the Padres was the victim.

1976 — With 2,994 fans on hand, in the middle of the eighth inning, Braves' owner Ted Turner grabbed the microphone at Atlanta Fulton County Stadium after an error by Marty Perez had opened the gates for six San Diego runs. "Nobody's going to leave here a loser tonight," said Turner. "If the Braves don't win, I want you people to come back tomorrow night as my guest (cheers). We're going to be in big league baseball for a long, long time, and we appreciate your support."

1978 — Brian Asselstine broke his leg and dislocated his ankle; he would not return to the Braves' lineup in 1978.

1980 — Bill Naharodny hit his first National League home run as the Braves won, 6–5, in Los Angeles.

JUNE 1

1846 — Andy Leonard, 1876–78; b.

1901 — Lou Legett, 1929; b.

1911 — Lou Tost, 1942–43; b.

1944 — Johnny Sain was commissioned as an ensign in the Naval Air Corps.

1946 — The Cubs beat the Braves, 6–3. The Braves had men on in every inning, but hit into four double plays; three were started by the Cub pitcher, tying a league record. The last NL pitcher to start three double plays in one game was Gene Conley of the Braves on July 19, 1957.

1952 — Charlie Grimm's managerial debut was spoiled, briefly, as the Braves lost the first game of a doubleheader, 1–0, in Cincinnati. They won the second game, however, by a 9–4 score.

1961 — Billy Martin was traded to the Minnesota Twins for Billy Consolo.

1966 — Willie Mays hit the first inside-the-park HR of his career—against the Braves.

1968 — The Braves moved into a first place tie, the first time an Atlanta club sat that high in the National League standings.

June 2

1917 — Hank Gowdy, the first major league baseball player to enlist for World War I, joined the 4th Ohio Militia, which later became the 166th Infantry.

1928 — Lester Bell of the Braves hit three homers in a game at Braves Field.

1935 — Babe Ruth announced at a press conference that he was going onto the voluntary retired list.

1948 — Jack Pierce, 1973-74; b.

1951 — The 75th anniversary of the National League was the subject of a celebration at Braves Field, Boston. The two oldest teams in baseball, the Chicago Cubs and the Braves, faced each other for the 1,112th time. The Braves lost, 7-5.

1952 — Mike Davey, 1977-78; b.

1953 — The Braves stopped Brooklyn's 10-game winning streak (after stopping an eight-game Dodger streak earlier in the year) by beating them, 4-3, at Ebbets Field. Burdette was the winner in relief.

1968 — The Braves and the Pirates combined for 55 hits in a doubleheader in Pittsburgh.

1971 — Clete Boyer was released.

1975 — Wayne Nordhagen was sent to the Cardinals to complete the May 28 Ron Reed deal.

June 3

1897 — Thomas Tucker was sold to Washington.

1946 — Mike McCormick was bought from the Reds.

1950 — Sid Gordon hit his second grand slam in three games as the Braves won, 10-6, in Pittsburgh, thus making Johnny Sain the first eight-game winner in either league.

1955 — Del Rice was obtained from the St. Louis Cards in exchange for Pete Whisenant.

1975 — Ron Reed made his first appearance in a Cardinal uniform, and beat his former mates, 4-2.

1978 — The Braves and Cubs used seven pitchers each in an 8-6 Cub win at Wrigley Field, tying the major league record for pitchers used in one game by both teams. The Braves' pitchers were Phil Niekro, Craig Skok, Buddy Solomon, Adrian Devine, Jamie Easterly (who got the loss), Dave Campbell, and Rick Camp.

June 4

1849 — Bill Parks, 1876; b.

1873 — George Yeager, 1896-99; b.

1882 — Pete Burg, 1910; b.

1888 — Orlie Weaver, 1911; b.

1892 — George Twombly, 1917; b.

1911 — The Cincinnati Reds had 13 different players cross home plate, a major league record, as they swamped the Boston Braves.

June 4 (continued)

1913 — Amby Murray, 1936; b.

1952 — Willard Marshall was sold to the Reds.

1954 — The first Girls' Knot Hole Club in the major leagues, a takeoff on the old Knot Hole Gang which began in Boston and made fans out of a lot of people, including my father, was started in Milwaukee.

1964 — The Braves executed a triple play, but lost to the Reds, 6–3. Tony Cloninger walked Gerry Coleman and Frank Robinson in the second inning. Leo Cardenas lined to Mike de la Hoz, who threw to Denis Menke at second to trap Coleman; Menke relayed to Gene Oliver to nail Robinson.

1971 — Ferguson Jenkins of the Cubs won his 100th game, beating the Braves, 11–0, in Atlanta, on a three-hitter. Joe Pepitone went four-for-five with a homer and three RBIs for the Cubbies.

1975 — Glenn Hubbard was selected in the 20th round of the free-agent draft; Larry Whisenten was selected in the second.

1976 — Andy Messersmith threw a one-hit shutout at the Montreal Expos.

1979 — Bill Lee won his 100th career game, beating the Braves, 8–1, on a four-hitter in Atlanta.

June 5

1852 — Tim Murnane, 1876–77; b.

1878 — Fred Mitchell, 1913; 1921–23; b.

1896 — Wade Lefler, 1924; b.

1903 — Billy Urbanski, 1931–37; b.

1905 — Owen Kahn, 1930; b.

1916 — Eddie Joost, 1943; 1945; b.

1918 — Al Javery, 1940–46; b.

Dave Odom, 1943; b.

1949 — The Cardinals beat the Braves, 8–1, in Boston as seven fans ran onto the field and forced the umpires to threaten a forfeit unless they left; they left.

1966 — Denis Menke had the first five-hit game ever in Atlanta Stadium, as the Braves shellshocked the Cardinals, 14–4.

1969 — Mickey Rivers was selected in the secondary phase of the free-agent draft.

1973 — In the free-agent draft, the Braves selected Pat Rockett in the first round (the tenth player chosen), Terry Harper in the 16th, and Larry Bradford in the 19th.

1974 — Henry Aaron hit his 16th career grand slam as the Braves won in Philadelphia, 7-3. It was Aaron's 731st homer, including World Series and All-Star games, and moved him ahead of Babe Ruth who had 730, all told.

In the free-agent draft, the Braves selected Dale Murphy in the first round (the fifth player chosen), Joey McLaughlin in the 2nd, and Mickey Mahler in the 10th.

1977 — Barry Bonnell hit his first big-league homer, a grand slam in the 7th; however, the Braves lost, 10-9, in San Francisco.

June 6

1894 — Braves pitchers gave up 12 runs to Pittsburgh in the third inning, and then gave up nine in the fourth. The 21 runs in two consecutive innings was a major league record which still stands.

1931 — Carlton Willey, 1958-62; b.

1940 — Warren Spahn signed a contract with the Boston Braves.

1945 — Larry Howard, 1973; b.

1953 — Philadelphia 6, Milwaukee 2. Robin Roberts chalked up his 100th win, retiring the first fifteen men to face him. The Braves got their runs when Harry Hanebrink hit a pinch-hit homer, his first homer in the major leagues. He would not hit another until 1958.

1966 — Frank Duffy was selected in the third round of the free-agent draft.

1967 — Ralph Garr was selected in the third round of the free-agent draft.

1972 — Preston Hanna was selected in the first round of the free-agent draft (the 11th man chosen).

1978 — The Braves selected Bob Horner first in the free-agent draft. Horner was the first player chosen in the 1978 draft.

1979 — Jamie Easterly was loaned to the Montreal Expo organization. He was returned on August 31.

June 7

1882 — Hubbard Perdue, 1911-14; b.

1948 — Jim Russell became the only Brave ever to have switch-hit homers in one game.

1967 — Gene Oliver was traded to the Phillies for Bob Uecker.

1973 — Pat Dobson was traded to the Yankees for Frank Tepedino, Wayne Nordhagen and two players to be named later.

1975 — Roric Harrison was traded to the Indians for Blue Moon Odom.

1977 — Robert D. Johnson was released. Tim Cole was selected in the first round of the free-agent draft. Tony Brizzolara was taken in the 2nd.

June 7 (continued)

1979 — Bullpen coach Bobby Dews, 41, made his pitching debut, throwing a perfect ninth inning as the Braves beat their Richmond farm club, 12–6.

June 8

1913 — Earl Reid, 1946; b.

1919 — Damon Phillips, 1944; 1946; b.

1928 — Manager Rogers Hornsby benched Ed Brown, ending his 618 games-played streak.

1930 — Phil Paine, 1951; 1954–57; b.

1935 — George Brunet, 1960–61; b.

1949 — Nels Potter pitched 9 1/3 innings of scoreless relief, striking out eight, as the Braves beat Cincinnati, 8–7, in 15 innings.

1957 — Chuck Tanner was sold to the Chicago Cubs.

1961 — Eddie Mathews, Henry Aaron, Joe Adcock, and Frank Thomas hit consecutive home runs, the only time that four straight homers have been hit in the NL.

1965 — Joe Torre, Eddie Mathews, Henry Aaron, and Gene Oliver hit four home runs in one inning, but not consecutively.

1966 — Henry Aaron hit his first grand slam in an Atlanta uniform, against Jack Fisher in New York.

1971 — In the free-agent draft, the Braves selected Jamie Easterly (2nd round), Dennis Lewallyn (3rd), Junior Moore (11th), and Biff Pocoroba (17th).

1976 — The Braves picks in the free-agent draft were Kenny Smith (first round, third player chosen), Bruce Benedict (5th), Ricky Peters (12th), and Rick Matula (14th).

1979 — Bobby Horner had a four-hit game against the Phillies.

June 9

1879 — Bill Lauterborn, 1904–5; b.

1883 — Jim Whitney became the first National Leaguer to score six runs in one game as the Braves won.

1887 — Clarence Kraft, 1914; b.

1911 — Frank McCormick, 1947–48; b.

1926 — Roy Smalley, 1954; b.

1946 — Dan Litwhiler was purchased from the Cardinals.

1949 — Bob Elliott was benched for the first time in his career; he was in the middle of a 0–20 slump.

1975 — "Blue Moon" Odom started his first National League game, getting knocked out in the fifth inning of a 5–4 Braves loss in Atlanta.

June 10

1880 — Charley Jones of the Braves became the first man ever to hit two home runs in a game.

1883 — Ernie Lindeman, 1907; b.

1900 — Garland Braxton, 1921–22; b.

1910 — Frank Demaree, 1941–42; b.

1950 — Elias Sosa, 1975–76; b.

1953 — Rick Camp, 1976–78; 1980–   ; b.

1961 — Bob Boyd purchased from the Athletics.

1969 – Willie Smith of the Cubs hit the first upper-level home run at Atlanta Stadium, against Ron Reed.

1972 — Henry Aaron moved ahead of Willie Mays into second place on the all-time home run list when he hit No. 649, his 14th grand slam, against the Phillies in Philadelphia.

June 11

1884 — Allie Strobel, 1905–6; b.

1906 — Third baseman Dave Brain set a major league record with five errors in a nine-inning game. The rest of the team chipped in with six more.

1929 — Frank Thomas, 1961; 1965; b.

1938 — Johnny Vander Meer threw his first of two consecutive no-hitters. The Braves were the victims of the first one, in Cincinnati, by a 3–0 score.

1975 — Craig Robinson was dealt to the Giants for Ed Goodson.

June 12

1857 — Joe Hornung, 1881–88; b.

1928 — Jack Cusick, 1952; b.

1936 — Braves pitchers yielded two bases-loaded triples to Chicago Cubs batters, tying the major league record for most in one game.

1941 — Lloyd Waner was traded to the Reds for John Hutchings.

June 12 (continued)

1946 — The Braves purchased Don Padgett from the Brooklyn Dodgers.

1949 — Charlie Grimm ended 13 years as manager of the Braves as the club split a doubleheader with the Cubs, losing the first game, 6–2, and winning the second, 2–0. The 19,802 fans in attendance gave Grimm a long standing ovation during his last appearance between the coaching box lines. Grimm moved into a vice-presidential position with the Braves.

1954 — Jim Wilson threw the first no-hitter by a Milwaukee Brave, a 2–0 whitewashing of the Phillies and Robin Roberts in Milwaukee. It was the only no-hitter in either league in 1954.

1957 — Eddie Mathews hit his 200th career homer, breaking Wally Berger's club record. The Braves lost, however, 11–9, in Brooklyn.

1962 — Lew Burdette recorded his first win against the Dodgers in Milwaukee since June 13, 1956. The Braves pounded LA, 15–2.

1967 — Henry Aaron swatted the 2,500th hit of his career. Dick Farrell of the Phils was the pitcher.

Tito Francona was purchased from the Phils.

1969 — Walt Hrniak, Van Kelly, and Andy Finley were sent to the San Diego Padres for Tony Gonzalez.

Garry Hill appeared in his only game ever with the parent club as the Braves lost to the Cubs, 12–6, in Atlanta.

1975 — Milwaukee Brewer Henry Aaron hit his first home run in Milwaukee's County Stadium since September 30, 1965. This blast was the 739th of his career.

June 13

1871 — Fred Klobedanz, 1896–99; 1902; b.

1895 — Emilio Palmero, 1928; b.

1934 — William Urbanski of the Braves tied the major league record for most-times-faced-pitcher—game, no official at-bats: six. He walked four times, and had two sacrifice hits, thus becoming the last man, through 1980, to have six appearances and no at-bats.

1945 — The Braves beat the Phillies, 8–3, in the first game of a doubleheader in Boston, thus extending Philadelphia's losing streak to 16 games, a club record. In the second game, however, the Phils ended their streak with a 5–4, 15-inning win, thanks (in part) to eight Braves' errors.

1947 — Bill Voiselle was obtained from the Giants for Mort Cooper.

1952 — Charlie Grimm's Boston debut as manager of the Braves. (He took over the club at the beginning of the month while they were on the road.) Bob Rush of the Cubs threw a three-hit shutout at the Braves, though, to spoil it for Grimm.

1957 — The Braves beat the Dodgers, 8–5, in Brooklyn, and moved into the league lead for the first time since May 15. Carl Sawatski's HR was the difference. Billy Bruton had two homers as well. After his second one, Don Drysdale of the Dodgers hit Johnny Logan, prompting Logan to charge the mound. Both players were ejected.

1958 — Carl Sawatski was traded to the Phillies for Joe Lonnett.

1962 — Sandy Koufax hit his first major league home run (half of his career total) as the Dodgers beat the Braves and Warren Spahn, 2–1, in Milwaukee. Spahn's record dropped to 6–7; the loss was his fifth by one run in 1962.

1976 — Darrell Evans and Marty Perez were traded to the Giants for Willie Montanez, Mike Eden, Jake Brown, and Craig Robinson.

1978 — Preston Hanna hit his first major league home run as the Braves won, 12–1, in Atlanta.

June 14

1861 — Charles Buffinton, 1882–86; b.

1876 — In a game against St. Louis, the Braves made 24 errors, 17 by the infield. Andy Leonard set a National League record with nine; he had made two on June 10—the 11, for two consecutive games, was also a record.

1887 — Walt Tragesser, 1913; 1915–19; b.

1900 — Dave Harris, 1925; 1928; b.

1933 — Jim Constable, 1962; b.

1940 — John Hassett of the Braves whacked his tenth straight hit, giving him a share of the National League record for most consecutive hits with six others. Only one man has duplicated the feat since.

Al Lopez was traded to the Pirates for Ray Berres.

1945 — Clyde Kluttz was dealt to the Giants for Joe Medwick and Ewald Pyle.

1952 — Braves scout Dewey Griggs signed Henry Aaron to his first major league contract after Aaron's Indianapolis Clowns contract was purchased from that Negro American League club for $10,000. Meanwhile, back at the ranch, Warren Spahn pitched 15 innings, struck out 18 men, hit a home run, but lost, 3–1, to the Cubs in front of 3,053 Boston fans.

1953 — Warren Spahn was credited with the win as the National League beat the American League, 5–1, in the All-Star Game.

1961 — Bill Robinson signed as a free agent.

June 15

1863 — Jerry Hurley, 1889; b.

June 15 (continued)

1866 — Nick Wise, 1888; b.

1876 — Charlie Dexter, 1902–3; b.

1891 — Lou North, 1924; b.

1912 — Babe Dahlgren, 1941; b.

1937 — The Braves obtained Wally Berger for Frank Gabler in a deal with the New York Giants.

1939 — Ty Cline, 1963–67; b.

1940 — Tony Cuccinello was sent to the New York Giants for Manny Salvo and Alben Glossop.

1941 — Babe Dahlgren was sold to the Cubs on his birthday.

1943 — Alan Closter, 1973; b.

1946 — The Braves obtained Billy Herman from the Dodgers for Stew Hofferth.

Ken Henderson, 1976; b.

1949 — Dusty Baker, 1968–75; b.

1957 — The Braves obtained Red Schoendienst from the Giants for Ray Crone, Danny O'Connell, and Bobby Thomson.

Brett Butler, 1981– ; b.

1961 — Sammy White was purchased from the Boston Red Sox.

Johnny Logan was dealt to the Pirates for Gino Cimoli.

1963 — Lew Burdette was sent to the Cardinals for Bob Sadowski and Gene Oliver.

1965 — Eddie Mathews rapped his 2,000th hit as the Braves won, 12–7.

1966 — Hank Fischer was obtained from the Reds for Joey Jay.

1967 — Claude Raymond was obtained from the Astros for Wade Blasingame.

1972 — The Braves traded Jim Nash and Gary Niebauer to the Phillies for Andre Thornton and Joe Hoerner.

1977 — Steve Hargan was obtained from the Texas Rangers for a player to be named.

1978 — Dick Ruthven was traded to the Phillies for Gene Garber.

1979 — Craig Swan beat the Braves on a two-hitter, 2–1, at Shea Stadium. Swan was almost hit by a pitch while trying to bunt in the fifth; in the eighth inning he hit Phil Niekro in the head with a pitch.

60

1883 — Al Mattern, 1908–12; b.

1888 — Jay Kirke, 1911–13; b.

1889 — Wynn Noyes, 1913; b.

1916 — Thomas Hughes threw a no-hitter at the Pittsburgh Pirates in Boston.

1922 — Fred Nicholson, Braves' outfielder, made four errors in a nine-inning game, a National League record that still stands.

Max Surkont, 1950–53; b.

1924 — Ernie Johnson, 1950; 1952–58; b.

1957 — Lew Burdette threw a one-hitter, but lost to Philadelphia, 1–0, in Philly.

1965 — Pat Corrales hit his first major league homer—off of the Braves' Denny Lemaster. The Braves lost to the Phillies, 6–2, in Milwaukee.

1975 — The Braves obtained Rob Belloir from the Indians to complete the Roric Harrison/Blue Moon Odom deal.

Ricky Mahler signed as a free agent.

1978 — Bob Horner made his professional debut in Atlanta. In his third at-bat he hit a two-run homer off of Bert Blyleven; the Pirates won the game, 9–4.

1979 — Mickey Mahler pitched 5 1/3 no-hit innings before Doug Flynn's HR broke the ice for the Mets at Shea Stadium; the Mets won, 2–0.

June 17

1887 — The Braves scored 10 runs in the 10th inning to beat New York, the most runs ever scored in the 10th inning by any club in the National League.

1891 — Zeb Terry, 1918; b.

1915 — Joe Burns, 1943; b.

1951 — Chet Nichols threw his first major league shutout in the second game of a doubleheader in Cincinnati, winning, 5–0. The Braves lost the first, 2–1.

1956 — Fred Haney's first game at the helm of the Braves. They won two from the Dodgers at Ebbets Field. Joe Adcock had three homers, one of them a shot over the leftfield roof, which was 350 feet from home plate, and 83 feet high.

1964 — The Braves acquired Adrian Garrett from the Mets to complete the May 8 deal involving Jay Hook and Roy McMillan.

1970 — Jim Gosger hit his first National League home run off of Jumbo Jim Nash; the Braves won, 6–5, in Montreal.

June 18

1862 — Charlie Ganzel, 1889-97; b.

1933 — Taylor Phillips, 1956-57; b.

1947 — Ewell Blackwell of the Reds fired a no-hitter at the Braves in Cincinnati.

1952 — Warren Spahn, who in his previous outing struck out 18 men and lost, struck out 11 men and lost, this time 3-1, to the Reds in Boston.

1962 — Henry Aaron became only the second man in history to hit a ball to the deepest part of the leftfield bleachers at the Polo Grounds (duplicating Joe Adcock's 1953 feat) as the Braves beat the Mets, 7-1.

1967 — Don Wilson of the Houston Astros threw the first no-hitter versus an Atlanta team; Astros 2, Braves 0, at the Dome.

1972 — Rico Carty had an 18-game hitting streak stopped by Mike Torrez of the Expos.

June 19

1935 — Dan MacFayden was claimed on waivers from Cincinnati.

1938 — Bob Aspromonte, 1969-70; b.

1942 — Paul Waner lashed his 3,000th hit (against Rip Sewell of the Pirates), the seventh man in major league history to accomplish that feat. Big Poison played 15 of his 20 seasons with the Pirates; he played for the Braves in 1941 and 1942.

1951 — In Billy Southworth's last game as manager of the Braves, Bob Rush of the Cubs shut the Braves out at Wrigley Field.

1955 — In a game against the Braves, Willie Mays was benched for the first time in his career after "slumping" to .279. The Braves beat the Giants, 8-7, in Milwaukee as Whitey Lockman filled in for Mays in centerfield.

1962 — The Mets beat Milwaukee, 6-5, at the Polo Grounds, their sixth win in 10 games with the Braves. At that point in the season, the Mets' record was 17-45; more than one-third of their wins had come against the Braves.

1969 — The Southern League All-Stars beat the Braves, 7-1, in Birmingham, Alabama, in a game marred by torrential rain, lightning, a power failure, and heavy winds.

1973 — Joe Pepitone was released.

1977 — Steve Carlton racked up his 100th victory as a member of the Phillies, beating the Braves, 4-2, in Philadelphia. Steve Hargan, making his first Braves appearance, took the loss.

June 20

1879 — Jim Delahanty, 1904-5; b.

1883 — Samuel Wise became the first Brave to have six hits in a game.

1912 — Boston scored 10 runs and New York scored seven to set a National League record for most runs scored by two teams in one inning. In addition, the Giants had the distinction of having 13 different men score runs, a major league record.

1951 — Tommy Holmes's managerial debut was a pleasant one. Warren Spahn threw a five-hitter at the Cubs, went three-for-four (including his first home run of the year), and the Braves won, 9-0, in Chicago.

1967 — Don Schwall was released.

1976 — In the first Sunday night game ever played at Atlanta Stadium, Dick Ruthven threw a four-hit shutout at the Cubs, and Steve Renko. The Braves won, 5-0, as Rowland Office extended his hitting streak to 25 games.

June 21

1900 — Red Barron, 1929; b.

1905 — Randy Moore, 1930-35; b.

1950 — Mike Beard, 1974-77; b.

1952 — Vinegar Bend Mizell threw his first major league shutout, a four-hitter, 9-0, at the Braves in Boston.

1963 — Mike Lum signed as a free agent.

1966 — Henry Aaron hit his 24th homer of the year to give him a tie for the record for most home runs through the end of June.

1967 — Bob Uecker knocked in five runs, four of them on his first career grand slam, as the Braves won, 9-2, in San Francisco.

1971 — Mike Lum, Hal King, Henry Aaron, and Darrell Evans hit home runs in the eighth inning, thus making the Braves the 13th NL club to have that many in one inning.

1979 — Gary Matthews recorded his 1,000th hit.

June 22

1888 — Bert Whaling, 1913-15; b.

1894 — The Braves pitching staff allowed Washington to score in each of their nine innings, only the second time that happened in NL history. (The Braves did it first, on August 15, 1889.) The Braves scored in six different innings of their own on this date, giving the two clubs 15 total scoring innings, a major league record which still stands.

1944 — Jim Tobin threw a five-inning perfect game against the Phillies in Boston and won, 7-0.

1956 — The Braves won their seventh straight game under new manager Fred Haney by beating the Giants, 3-1, in New York, thus increasing their first-place cushion to one full game.

June 22 (continued)

1964 — Bobby Bragan signed on to manage through 1965; the Braves dropped their seventh straight, 10–9.

1970 — Ron Kline was released.

1971 — The Braves beat the Expos, 4–0, in Atlanta behind Ron Reed's three-hit shutout. Steve Renko of the Expos yielded three walks and three wild pitches (the latter tied an NL record for most in one inning) in the third when the Braves got all of their runs.

June 23

1884 — Dick Egan, 1915–16; b.

1890 — Bill Calhoun, 1913; b.

1895 — Jack Smith, 1926–29; b.

1912 — Gene Ford, 1936; b.

1933 — Dave Bristol, 1976–78; b.

1953 — Warren Spahn threw a two-hitter at the Pirates in Milwaukee, but lost, 1–0.

1956 — The Braves won their eighth straight under new manager Fred Haney by beating the Giants, 2–1, in New York.

1958 — An eventful day. Carlton Willey made his first major league start and threw a six-hit shutout over the Giants in Milwaukee; Willie Mays had his 1,000th hit; Joe Adcock made his first putout in leftfield since 1952 as he made a spectacular catch, climbing the fence; and the Braves became the first team in baseball to provide transportation from the bullpen to the mound, with a chauffeur-driven motor scooter and sidecar. Don McMahon of the Braves was the first passenger.

1976 — Rowland Office hit in his 29th straight game.

Mike Marshall obtained from the Dodgers in exchange for Elias Sosa and Lee Lacy.

June 24

1864 — Jack Clements, 1900; b.

1865 — Billy Nash, 1885–89; 1891–95; b.

1892 — George Harper, 1929; b.

1953 — Joey Jay signed a Braves contract, thus becoming the first Little League product to make it to the major leagues.

1956 — The Braves extended their winning streak to 10 games under manager Fred Haney who had yet to taste defeat. The Braves took two from the Giants in New York, 6–2, and 7–1, behind the pitching of Lew Burdette and Gene Conley.

1969 — Bob Tillman hit a grand-slam homer to beat Don Drysdale and the Dodgers, 9–5, in Atlanta.

1976 — Don Stanhouse of the Expos stopped Rowland Office's 29-game hitting streak in Atlanta; the Braves won, 2–1.

1977 — The Braves won a wild one from the Padres in Atlanta, 9–8, in 10 innings. The Braves tied the game up in the bottom of the ninth at 6–6. Montanez knocked in two with a double, and Junior Moore singled him home. The Padres went up, 8–6, in the top of the tenth; but in the bottom of the inning Darrell Chaney singled, Vic Correll hit a home run, Gary Matthews singled, stole second with one out and stayed there while Tom Paciorek struck out, and Jeff Burroughs was intentionally walked. Moore doubled Matthews home to win it for Rick Camp.

June 25

1914 — The Braves moved out of the cellar for the first time in 1914.

1930 – Humberto Robinson, 1955–56; 1958; b.

1955 — New manager Fred Haney's record went to 11–0, as the Braves beat the Phillies, 8–5, getting three runs in the top of the ninth. Bob Buhl got the win with relief help from Spahn. The 11-game streak was the longest since the club moved to Milwaukee.

1966 — Paul Richards was named Director of Player Development.

1971 — The Braves beat Cincinnati, 8–6, in Atlanta, and tied the National League record for fewest assists in one game, one.

June 26

1908 — Debs Garms, 1937–39; b.

1914 – After one day out of the cellar, the Braves dropped back in and stayed there for three more weeks.

1918 — Elmer Singleton, 1945–46; b.

1941 — Gil Garrido, 1968–72; b.

1943 — Bill Robinson, 1966; b.

1956 — The Braves lost to Robin Roberts in Philadelphia, 4–2 (Fred Haney's first loss as Braves manager after 11 wins).

1957 — Henry Aaron, Eddie Mathews, and Wes Covington hit consecutive home runs in the fifth inning of a game with Brooklyn which the Braves won, 13–9, behind Gene Conley.

1964 — Warren Spahn started his 693rd game, more than any other lefty, against the New York Mets.

1978 — Adrian Devine got his first major league hit and first game-winning RBI as he beat the Dodgers, 5–2.

June 27

1868 — Bill Daley, 1889; b.

1930 — Bob Trowbridge, 1956–59; b.

1946 — Warren Spahn suffered his first loss, a 3–1 decision to the Brooklyn Dodgers.

June 28

1868 — John Taber, 1890; b.

1911 — Jim Hitchcock, 1938; b.

1969 — George Stone of the Braves and Don Wilson of the Astros collided on the first-base line during a bunt try, triggering a minor brawl which featured Dave Rader against Orlando Cepeda. Atlanta won, 5–1, at the Astrodome.

1974 — Frisbee Day in Atlanta. The Braves lost the first game, 6–5, and won the second, 1–0, in 10 innings. The first game was stopped twice in the fourth inning when the crowd littered the field with frisbees after an umpire's call went against the Braves.

June 29

1876 — Patsy Flaherty, 1907–08; 1911; b.

1925 — Nippy Jones, 1957; b.

1933 — Bob Shaw, 1962–63; b.

1951 — Jimmy Freeman, 1972–73; b.

1952 — Tommy Holmes, who was fired as manager on May 31 (and later traded), hit a pinch-hit single in the seventh inning of a game in Brooklyn, to help the Dodgers beat the Braves, 6–5, the 11th straight win for the Dodgers over the Braves in 1952.

1957 — Felix Mantilla hit his first major league homer, and Henry Aaron and Del Crandall chipped in with circuit clouts of their own, as the Braves beat Pittsburgh, 13–6, in Milwaukee to maintain their ½ game lead.

Eddie Miller, 1978–   ; b.

1958 — Henry Aaron hit the first of many home runs against Don Drysdale, a grand slam. Drysdale gave up more home runs to Aaron than any other pitcher.

1970 — The Braves bought Jimmie Hall from the Cubs.

1972 — Orlando Cepeda was sent to the Oakland Athletics for Denny McLain and cash.

June 30

1873 — George Stultz, 1894; b.

1913 — Manny Salvo, 1940–43; b.

1949 — The Braves swept the Giants in New York, 3–0, and 6–2. In the second game, Alvin Dark and Bob Elliott had inside-the-park home runs.

1951 — Tommy Holmes' first appearance as Braves manager in front of the home crowd. The Braves beat the Giants, 19–7, getting eight runs in the seventh, and seven runs in the eighth to beat Sal Maglie. Earl Torgeson had seven RBIs in those two innings to tie the NL record for most RBI's in consecutive innings. Vern Bickford took the win.

1960 — Don Nottebart was recalled from the minor leagues.

1970 — Henry Aaron hit the first home run at Riverfront Stadium in an 8–2 win over the Reds. It was the first game at Riverfront.

1975 — Bruce Dal Canton was purchased from the Kansas City Royals.

1978 — The Braves won a doubleheader from the Giants, 10–9, and 10–5. Ten home runs were hit in the twin bill, five by the Giants in the first game alone. Willie McCovey hit his 500th career homer off of Jamie Easterly, and Mike Ivie of the Giants hit his second pinch grand slam of the year.

JULY 1

1861 — John Clarkson, 1888–92; b.

1870 — Charlie Nice, 1895; b.

1902 — Kent Greenfield, 1927–29; b.

1913 — Frank Barrett, 1946; b.

1919 — Rabbit Maranville became the first major leaguer to hit two inside-the-park home runs in one game.

1952 — Earl Torgeson attacked Giant catcher Sal Yvars in the Giant dugout at Braves Field during a 6–3 Braves loss. In the first inning, Torgeson hit Yvars on the shin with his backswing; they exchanged words; Torgeson singled; Yvars broke Torgeson's bat on home plate. Torgeson was stranded on the bases and remained in the field for the Giants' half of the inning. At the end of the frame, however, Torgeson went into the dugout after Yvars and punched him in the face. Torgeson was ejected as was Vern Bickford, who argued that Yvars should have been, too.

1962 — Ken Aspromonte was purchased from the Cleveland Indians.

July 2

1909 — Gil English, 1937–38; b.

1949 — Del Crandall hit his first two major league homers, solo shots, as the Braves lost to Philadelphia, 3–2, in Boston.

1952 — Rookie Jack Dittmer hit his first major league homer to beat the Giants, 2–1, in Boston. Warren Spahn's four-game losing streak and the Braves' six-game losing streak came to an end.

1969 — Five Braves' batters were hit by Cincinnati Red pitches, the most-hit batsmen in a game since 1896. Gerry Arrigo hit Henry Aaron and Felix Millan; Pedro Ramos hit Millan, Bob Aspromonte, and Clete Boyer. No warnings were issued; however, Milt Pappas was ejected for yelling unkind things at the umpires.

July 3

1869 — George Cuppy, 1900; b.

1883 — Cliff Curtis, 1909–11; b.

1911 — Bill Sweeney hit in his 31st consecutive game, thus extending his club record. Hugh Duffy had hit in 26 games in 1894. Sweeney's mark held up until Tommy Holmes broke it in 1945 with a 37-game streak.

1920 — Al Montgomery, 1941; b.

1953 — Hank Small, 1978; b.

1956 — Larry Whisenton, 1977–78; b.

1960 — Henry Aaron hit the 200th homer of his career off Ron Kline in St. Louis.

1963 — Warren Spahn pitched 15 1/3 innings, giving up nine hits, and one walk. Juan Marichal pitched 16 innings, giving up eight hits, and striking out 10. The Giants won, 1–0, in a game that took 4:10 to complete at Candlestick Park.

1966 — Tony Cloninger hit two grand slams in one game, the only National Leaguer ever to accomplish that feat. He knocked in one other run to give him the major league record for most RBI's by a pitcher in one game, too. The slams came against Jerry Priddy in the first inning, and Ray Sadecki in the fourth, in a game in San Francisco which the Braves won, 17–3.

1967 — The Cubs hit three homers and the Braves hit two, all in the first inning, thus enabling the two clubs to tie the major league record for most home runs in an inning by two clubs.

1970 — Mike Lum hit three homers as the Braves beat San Diego, 8–1, in the first game of a doubleheader in Atlanta. Jim Nash ran his record to 10–2. The Braves won the second, too, 9–4.

1972 — Henry Aaron became the first National Leaguer to hit the 2,000 plateau in RBIs as he hit a three-run homer in a 13–9 win over the Astros at the Dome.

July 4

1915 — Joe Mack, 1945; b.

1929 — Chuck Tanner, 1955–57; b.

1931 — Bobby Malkmus, 1957; b.

1948 — Eighteen-year-old Johnny Antonelli made his major league debut in the eighth inning of a 7–2 loss to the Phillies, giving up one run on two hits. The Braves also lost the second game of the doubleheader.

1950 — Sid Gordon hit his fourth grand slam of the year to tie the major league record for most slams in a year, set by Frank Schulte of the Cubs in 1911.

1956 — Jim Frey was traded to the Brooklyn Dodgers for Ray Shearer.

1961 — Johnny Antonelli was purchased from the Indians on the anniversary of his major league debut with the Braves.

1971 — Mike Lum's outstanding throw from right field nailed Cleon Jones at the plate, and gave the Braves a rare Shea Stadium sweep of the Mets. Lum also made a circus catch off the bat of Jerry Grote. Phil Niekro won his fifth straight game, beating Tom Seaver.

1972 — Paul Casanova hit his first National League homer as the Braves beat the Cubs and Juan Pizarro, in the first of two in Atlanta. In the second game, Denny McLain made his National League debut, but got no decision as the game ended in a 3–3 tie because of rain in the 8th.

1973 — The Astros swept the Braves in Atlanta, 11–4 and 12–8, as the two teams pounded out 56 hits and 10 home runs between them.

1979 — Pepe Frias's fake steal of home in the eighth inning caused Gary Lavelle to balk, thus helping the Braves to a 7–6 win over the Giants.

July 5

1866 — Lee Viau, 1892; b.

1880 — Harvey Aubrey, 1903; b.

1886 — Beals Becker, 1908–09; b.

1897 — Tom Miller, 1918–19; b.

1940 — Braves pitchers gave up four runs in the top of the 20th inning of a game with the Dodgers. No team has ever given up more runs in the 20th inning.

1950 — Gary Matthews, 1977–80; b.

1970 — The Braves signed free-agent veteran Steve Barber.

July 6

1890 — Lefty Gervais, 1913; b.

1916 — Bill Donovan, 1942–43; b.

1934 — Harold Lee of the Braves hit three home runs in a road game.

1936 — The Braves claimed Rabbit Warstler off the waiver wire.

July 6 (continued)

1945 — Tommy Holmes hit in his 33rd and 34th consecutive games as the Braves beat the Pirates, 13–5 and 14–8. Holmes had three hits in each game.

1950 — Jackie Robinson sat out of a game for the first time since June 2, 1948, a 340-game streak. Brooklyn beat the Braves, 8–3, in Boston.

1951 — The Braves and Giants combined for five homers in the third inning of a 12–10 Giants' win in New York. Willard Marshall and Walker Cooper hit them for Boston; Wes Westrum, Bobby Thomson, and Don Mueller hit them for New York.

1970 — Felix Millan went six-for-six, the first time anyone had six hits in one game in Atlanta. The Braves beat the Giants, 12–4.

July 7

1868 — Willard Mains, 1896; b.

1873 — Oscar Streit, 1899; b.

1909 — Billy Herman, 1946; b.

1928 — Sammy White, 1961; b.

1936 — The National League won its first All-Star Game, after losing the first three. The game took place in Boston. Lefty Grove was the losing pitcher; Carl Hubbell was the winner. Joe Medwick's RBI single in the fifth inning was the deciding run in a 4–3 game. Lou Gehrig and Augie Galan hit home runs.

1945 — Chuck Goggin, 1973; b.

1946 — Rick Kester, 1968–70; b.

1953 — Joe Adcock hit the first inside-the-park homer at Milwaukee's County Stadium, as the Braves and Antonelli beat Chicago, 4–1, in front of a record crowd of 37,113.

1974 — Buzz Capra's nine-game winning streak was stopped in Chicago as the Cubs won, 4–3. Henry Aaron had HR No. 725 for the Braves. The nine-game streak was, and is, a record for Braves pitchers.

July 8

1872 — Frank Sexton, 1895; b.

1890 — Rowdy Elliott, 1910; b.

1898 — The Braves were the victims of a no-hitter for the second time of the 1898 season, this time by Frank Donohue in Philadelphia, 5–0.

1926 — Gene Tunney Patton, 1944; b.

1946 — The Braves bought Ken O'Dea from the St. Louis Cardinals.

1965 — Mike de la Hoz was the hero as the Braves won, 9–8, in 12 innings. De la Hoz hit a pinch homer in the eighth inning, singled to tie the game in the ninth when the Braves got three runs, and in the 12th, singled, went to second on a sacrifice, and scored on a single by Frank Bolling.

July 9

1885 – Buck Herzog, 1910–11; 1918–19; b.

1938 — Tony Cuccinello, Max West, and Elbie Fletcher hit consecutive HRs in the third inning of a Braves game.

1944 — Sonny Jackson, 1968–74; b.

1946 — George Stone, 1967–72; b.

1970 — Chief No-ka-homa was joined by long-lost cousin Chief Round-the-Horn, but it didn't work, as the Giants beat the Braves, 7–6, in 11.

1971 — Leo Foster's major league debut was one to remember. He made an error on the first ball hit to him, hit into a doubleplay in the fifth, and hit into a triple play in the seventh. After Jackson and King singled, Foster hit into an around-the-horn TP, Hebner to Cash to Robertson.

1972 — Denny McLain recorded his first NL decision, a loss, as the Braves fell to the Pirates, 7–4, despite Henry Aaron's 657th career home run.

July 10

1855 — Jim Hart, 1889; b.

1867 – Bob Allen, 1897; b.

1868 — Bobby Lowe, 1890–1901; b.

1888 — Jack Spratt, 1911–12; b.

1901 — The Braves rapped out 15 hits in 12 innings, but scored no runs, losing to Pittsburgh, 1–0, thus establishing the NL record for most hits—extra innings, no runs. They did it again, if fact, on August 1, 1918.

1903 — Johnny Niggeling, 1938; 1946; b.

1926 — Harry MacPherson, 1944; b.

July 11

1873 — Jimmy Slagle, 1901; b.

1889 — Billy Burke, 1910–11; b.

1898 — Jim Batchelder, 1923–25; b.

1956 — Joey McLaughlin, 1977; 1979; b.

1957 — Felix Mantilla and Billy Bruton collided going after a popup in Pittsburgh. Mantilla missed 19 games; Bruton was out for almost a year.

1968 — Phil Niekro threw a four-hit, 1–0 shutout at the Dodgers in the Braves' shortest game of the year; it took 1 hour and 42 minutes.

1970 — Orlando Cepeda rapped his 2,000th hit, but the Braves lost to the Reds, 7–6, in Atlanta.

1972 — Henry Aaron walked five times in a 15-inning game against the Cardinals which the Braves won, 5–4. The five walks tied a major league record.

July 12

1891 — Hank Schreiber, 1917; b.

1940 — Mike Page, 1968; b.

1945 — Tommy Holmes's hitting streak, a Cubs winning streak, and Chicago's Claude Passeau's personal winning streak all came to an end in Chicago, as the Braves split a twin bill with the Cubs, 1–6, 3–1. Holmes's batting streak stopped at 37, the Cubs won their 11th in a row in the first game, and Passeau was beaten in the second game after nine consecutive wins.

1946 — Johnny Sain just missed a perfect game in Cincinnati. In the first inning, Grady Hatton's popup dropped among three Braves fielders in back of third base for a double. No one else got on. The Braves won, 1–0.

1953 — Eddie Mathews hit his first major league grand slam while going four-for-five in the first game of a doubleheader which the Braves swept from the Cardinals, 10–1, and 4–3, in St. Louis.

1964 — Henry Aaron slapped his 2,000th base hit in the second game of a doubleheader against the Phillies in Milwaukee. Wade Blasingame and Billy Hoeft won for the Braves, 4–3 and 6–2.

1970 — Bob Didier was sent to Richmond to make room for recently-obtained Don Cardwell.

July 13

1874 — Wiley Piatt, 1903; b.

1905 — Tiny Chaplin, 1936; b.

1940 — Jack Aker, 1974; b.

1948 — Rob Belloir, 1975–78; b.

1961 — Mack Jones had four hits in his first major league game, tying a National League record for most hits in a first game.

1964 — The Braves made an unscheduled stop in Cleveland, en route home from

Philadelphia. Their United Airlines DC 6B made a precautionary landing after one engine lost power.

July 14

1915 — Don Hendrickson, 1945–46; b.

1945 — Bill Lee was sold to the Braves on waivers by the Phillies.

1946 — Warren Spahn won his first major league game by beating the Pirates, 4–1.

1948 — Pepe Frias, 1979; b.

Earl Williams, 1970–72; 1975–76; b.

1954 — The Braves became the first team to hit the million mark in attendance, but lost, 2–1, to the Dodgers in 12. Gil Hodges had his 1,000th hit in the Brooklyn 11th inning.

1968 — Henry Aaron hit the 500th HR of his career, a three-run job off Mike McCormick in Atlanta, the game-winner in a 4–2 Braves victory. It was his 19th HR of the season and his 2,700th hit.

July 15

1872 — Dan McGann, 1896; 1908; b.

1891 — Dick Crutcher, 1914–15; b.

1954 — A record crowd of 43,633 saw the Braves sweep a doubleheader behind a Bob Buhl shutout in the first game, and a come-from-behind, six-runs-in-the-bottom-of-the-ninth, 9–8 win behind Joey Jay.

1978 — The Braves turned a triple play and three double plays to beat the Phils in Atlanta, 3–2, behind Rick Camp. In the seventh, with Garber on the mound, Luzinski and Hebner walked. Cardenal grounded to Horner, who threw to Hubbard, who threw to Murphy: TP.

July 16

1936 — Al Lopez reached first base three times on errors, the third man in major league history to accomplish that feat.

1939 — Eddie Miller, obtained in the off-season for five players, broke a leg and sat out the year.

1950 — Ted Beard hit an eighth-inning home run over the rightfield stands at Forbes Field (a feat last accomplished before him by Babe Ruth in 1935) in a 6–5 loss to the Pirates.

1962 — Joey Jay of the Reds lost his first game to his former teammates after beating them five times. Braves, 3–0, behind Bob Hendley.

1978 — Larry McWilliams's first major league start resulted in his first major league win, a 3–0 combined shutout (with Gene Garber) over the Mets in Atlanta.

July 17

1891 — Eddie Brown, 1926–28; b.

1924 — Jesse Harris of the Cardinals threw a no-hitter at the Braves in St. Louis.

1930 — Roy McMillan, 1961–64; b.

1938 — Deron Johnson, 1968; b.

1956 — Joe Adcock chased Ruben Gomez off the mound after Gomez hit Adcock with a pitch in an 8–6, 12-inning, Giant win in Milwaukee, ending a 7-game Braves winning streak. Both men were ejected by Umpire Bill Jackowski.

1965 — Ron Reed signed as a free agent.

July 18

1863 — Charlie Parsons, 1886; b.

1903 — Hod Kibbie, 1925; b.

1916 — Johnny Hopp, 1946–47; b.

1940 — Joe Torre, 1960–68; 1982–   ; b.

1956 — NL President Warren Giles fined Joe Adcock $100 for the Gomez incident of the day before.

July 19

1887 — Butch Schmidt, 1913–15; b.

1895 — Snake Henry, 1922–23; b.

1914 — The Braves swept Cincinnati. In the second game they came up with three runs in the top of the ninth to win, 3–2, and left last place for good on their way to the "Miracle Pennant."

Ben Geraghty, 1943–44; b.

1943 — Tony Cuccinello was released.

1955 — The Braves turned a triple play, but lost, 4–3, in Pittsburgh. With Toby Atwell on second and Frank Thomas on first, the Pirates' Johnny O'Brien lined to Eddie Mathews at third. He relayed to Henry Aaron at second to nip Atwell, and Aaron gunned a throw to Joe Adcock at first to nail Thomas.

1958 — Phil Niekro signed as a free agent.

1972 — Henry Aaron hit his 659th career home run, tying Babe Ruth's record for most home runs with one club. (In addition to the 659 he hit for the Yankees, Ruth hit 49 for the Red Sox, and six for the Braves.)

1974 — Henry Aaron tied Ty Cobb with 3,033 games, good for first on the all-time list.

July 20

1900 — Hunter Lane, 1924; b.

1957 — Del Crandall, playing rightfield because of injuries to Aaron, Bruton, and Pafko, dropped a fly ball in the eighth, opening the way for five unearned Giant runs. The Braves held on to win, though, 7–5, in NY.

1974 — On Henry Aaron Day in Atlanta, Aaron broke Ty Cobb's record for games played as he appeared in his 3,034th. The Braves lost, 7–6, in 11.

July 21

1877 — Irv Young, 1905–08; b.

1881 — Johnny Evers, 1914–17; 1929; b.

1891 — Ray Keating, 1919; b.

1915 — Connie Creedon, 1943; b.

1923 — Paul Burris, 1948; 1950; 1952–53; b.

1935 — Moe Drabowsky, 1961; b.

1940 — Denis Menke, 1962–67; b.

1941 — Frank Demaree was obtained from the Giants for the waiver price.

1949 — Al Hrabosky, 1980–   ; b.

1959 — Bobby Avila was purchased from the Red Sox.

1973 — Henry Aaron hit his 700th HR in the third inning of an 8–4, Braves loss in Atlanta. Aaron hit a 1–1 fastball off the Phillies' Ken Brett.

July 22

1885 — Elmer Knetzer, 1916; b.

1915 — Butch Sutcliffe, 1938; b.

1926 — Braves pitchers gave up four triples in the second inning of a game with Cincinnati, tying the NL record for most triples given up in one inning.

1943 — Johnny McCarthy fractured an ankle while sliding, and was out for the year.

1959 — Bobby Avila, in his first game as a Brave, hit a ninth-inning, two-run HR to give the Braves a 5–4 win.

1972 — Denny McLain's first victory as a Brave, a 10-inning, 8–7 win over the Cardinals in Atlanta, was secured in the 10th when Dusty Baker hit a HR against former Brave Tony Cloninger.

1973 — The Braves made a club-record seven errors in the second game of a doubleheader they lost in Atlanta to the Phillies, 6 5, 5 1. Garr, Casanova, Morton, Jackson (2), Tepedino, and Johnson made the errors.

July 23

1876 — Ginger Beaumont, 1907–09; b.

1879 — Hod Ford, 1919–23; 1932–33; b.

1896 — Art Rico, 1916–17; b.

1912 — Al Glossop, 1940; b.

1927 — Virgil Jester, 1952–53; b.

1950 — Red Schoendienst extended his own consecutive errorless-chances streak record to 285, as the Cardinals beat the Braves, 8–4, in St. Louis. Stan Musial extended his hitting streak to 28 games, and Buck Walters made his first mound appearance since 1948, getting the side in order.

1951 — The Braves beat the Pirates, 15–14, in Pittsburgh. The 29 runs and 34 hits by the two clubs were NL game highs for 1951.

1979 — Phil Niekro grounded into his second career triple play in the second game of a doubleheader with Pittsburgh. He threw a two-hit shutout to win, however, after the Braves lost the opener, 7–1.

July 24

1864 — Tommy McCarthy, 1885; 1892–95; b.

1893 — Joe Schultz, 1912–13; b.

1921 — Clint Conaster, 1948–49; b.

1940 — Ethan Blackaby, 1962–64; b.

1962 — The Mets' Robert G. Miller made a one-pitch National League debut. Del Crandall hit the one pitch for a HR in the bottom of the 12th to give the Braves a 5–4 win in New York.

1974 — Clyde King was named interim manager, replacing Eddie Mathews, who was fired.

1976 — Earl Williams was dealt to the Expos for a player to be named.

July 25

1953 — Biff Pocoroba, 1975–   ; b.

1969 — After whacking a first-inning double for his 2,900th hit, Henry Aaron slammed his 536th career HR, tying him with Mickey Mantle on the all-time list.

1972 — In the All-Star Game in Atlanta, a record Atlanta crowd of 53,107 saw the National League win, 4–3, as Henry Aaron hit a home run off Gaylord Perry in the bottom of the sixth to put the NL up, 2–1.

1974 — Clyde King's managerial debut in Atlanta resulted in a 1–0 win over San Diego.

July 26

1853 — Phil Powers, 1880; b.

1886 — Roy Witherup, 1906; b.

1904 — Bill Dreesen, 1931; b.

Doc Gautreau, 1925–28; b.

1920 — Sibby Sisti, 1939–42; 1946–54; b.

1923 — Hoyt Wilhelm, 1969–71; b.

1962 — Warren Spahn broke the all-time record for HRs by a pitcher when he hit the 31st of his career off of Craig Anderson of the Mets. The Braves won the game, 6–1. It was the 11th straight loss for New York. Spahn's HR broke Jack Stivetts' record.

1964 — Chi Chi Olivo won his only two games of 1964 by getting credit for the victories in a doubleheader drubbing of the Mets, 11–7, and 15–10, in New York.

1970 — Cha Cha Cepeda hit three consecutive HRs in an 8–1 win in Chicago.

1977 — Pitcher Steve Kline was released.

July 29

1880 — Chief Meyers, 1917; b.

Ed Donnelly, 1911–12; b.

1891 — Fred Smith, 1913; b.

1895 — Sterling Stryker, 1924; b.

1934 — Felix Mantilla, 1956–61; b.

1948 — Big Bill Voiselle got his fifth hit of the year, raising his batting average to .097, one point higher than his uniform number, and beat the Pirates, 2–1, in Boston.

1968 — Wayne Causey was purchased from the Angels.

1977 — Phil Niekro tied a major league record by striking out four Pirates in one inning while getting his tenth win, 5–3, in Pittsburgh. He whiffed Dave Parker and Bill Robinson to open the sixth; Al Oliver doubled; Rennie Stennett fanned but got to first base on a passed ball; Omar Moreno then K'd, making Niekro the 15th pitcher in history to strike out four men in an inning.

July 29 (continued)

1978 — Bob Horner hit two home runs for the second day in a row as the Braves beat Montreal, 9–6, at Atlanta Stadium.

July 30

1870 — Bill Merritt, 1893–94; 1899; b.

1890 — Casey Stengel, 1924–25; 1938–43; b.

1895 — Bill Cunningham, 1924; b.

1906 — Johnnie Tyler, 1934–35; b.

1952 — Mickey Mahler, 1977–80; b.

1953 — Boston University purchased Braves Field for $500,000.

1958 — Warren Spahn beat the Dodgers for the first time since September 25, 1951.

1966 — Gene Oliver hit three home runs in a game against the Giants.

1969 — Bob Tillman hit three consecutive home runs, and Denis Menke and Jimmy Wynn hit grand slams, as the Braves pounded the Expos, 19–0, in Atlanta.

1978 — Atlanta pitchers Boggs, Skok, and Mahler allowed 13 different Expos to get hits, tying a National League record for most different players allowed hits in one game. Eight of the hits were home runs, the most ever allowed by an NL staff.

July 31

1892 — Art Nehf, 1915–19; b.

1912 — John M. Ward resigned as president of the Boston club.

1916 — Billy Hitchcock, 1966–67; b.

1935 — Terry Fox, 1960; b.

1945 — The Braves came up with five runs in the 13th inning to beat the Giants, thus snapping a 10-game losing streak.

1954 — Joe Adcock had quite a day. He became the seventh man in major league history to hit four home runs as the Braves slammed Brooklyn, 15–7, extending their winning streak to nine. Adcock hit his blasts off of Newcombe in the 2nd, Palica in the 5th, Wojey in the 7th, and Podres in the 9th. (Combined with his home run from the day before, the total of five in two games tied a major league record.) He added a double to give him the major league record for most total bases in a nine-inning game, breaking Gil Hodges's August 31, 1950, record of 17. (Combined with seven total bases from the day before, the total of 25 in two consecutive games gave him a share of the major league record for that category with Ty Cobb.) He tied the major league record for most long hits in a game: five. (Combined with two from the day before, the total of seven gave him another major legue record.) He established a major league record for most extra bases on long hits in a nine-inning game, 13. (Those, combined with four from the July 30 game, gave him a tie for a major league record.) Eddie Mathews hit two homers as well, and the total of six between the two men gave the infield a major league record for most homers by infielders in one game. To top it all off, Adcock was using a borrowed bat, that of Charlie White.

1955 — On the anniversary of his record-breaking day, Joe Adcock's wrist was broken by a Jim Hearn (Giants) pitch.

1956 — The Braves hit a home run in their 22nd consecutive game (a total of 39 for that stretch) giving them the major league record for most home runs in that number of consecutive games.

1972 — Denny McLain, in his first starting assignment as a Brave, went seven strong innings as the Braves won, 4–3, over the Dodgers.

1978 — Pete Rose hit in his 44th consecutive game. He led off the sixth inning with a seeing-eye single that just eluded the diving Rod Gilbreath. Phil Niekro gave up the single that allowed Rose to tie the *single-season* record for consecutive games with a hit. Wee Willie Keeler still holds the National League record with a 45-game hitting streak strung over the 1896 and 1897 seasons.

AUGUST 1

1897 — Bob Emmerich, 1923; b.

1902 — Howard Freigua, 1928; b.

1903 — Iron Man Joe McGinnity of the Giants, on his way to a 31–20 season, with 434 innings pitched, pitched two complete games, and beat the Braves, 4–1, and 5–2, in New York, yielding only eight hits.

1918 — The Braves tied their own National League record for most hits—extra-inning game, no runs, when they went 21 innings with 15 hits, and lost to the Pirates, 2–0.

1951 — The Braves beat the Cardinals, 2–1, in St. Louis when, in the 7th, Sam Jethroe went from first to third on an infield grounder to Stan Musial, and scored when Musial's throw toward third went wild.

1953 — Richie Ashburn's infield single in the fourth inning spoiled a perfect game for Warren Spahn, as the Braves won, 5–0, over the Phillies in Milwaukee. It was Spahn's second shutout in a row, and his 31st lifetime, tying him with Raffensberger and Leonard, and making him the shutout leader among active NL pitchers.

1954 — On the day after his record-breaking offensive performance, Joe Adcock was beaned by Clem Labine of the Dodgers. The Braves won, however, extending their winning streak to 10, as Gene Conley ran his record to 10–5.

1967 — Henry Aaron broke Eddie Mathews's club record of 8,049 at-bats.

1968 — In a 4–2 win over the Mets, Aaron played in his 2,224th game, breaking Mathews's Braves record.

1970 — The Pirates hit three homers and the Braves hit two in the seventh inning of a 20–10 game, won by the Pirates. The total of five homers in one inning tied the major league record for home runs in one inning by two clubs. Willie Stargell had two homers and three doubles to tie the major league record for total bases in one game. Bill Robinson, Stargell, and José Pagan had successive homers for the Pirates, and Henry Aaron and Rico Carty hit back-to-back shots in the seventh.

1972 — Nate Colbert set a major league record with 13 RBIs in a doubleheader, as the Padres swept the Braves, 9–0, and 11–7, in Atlanta. Colbert hit five home runs off of five different Brave pitchers: in the second inning of the first game off Ron Schueler with two on; a solo shot off of McQueen in the 7th; a slam against Pat Jarvis in the second inning of the second game; a two-run job against Jim Hardin in the seventh, and a two-run blast off of Cecil Upshaw in the 9th. Colbert also set a record with 22 total bases in the doubleheader.

1978 — Pete Rose's 44-game hitting streak came to an end in Atlanta, falling one game short of the National League record of 45 set by Wee Willie Keeler in 1896 and 1897. Rose walked in the first inning, lined to the pitcher in the second, lined to short in the fifth, lined to third in the seventh, and, with Gene Garber on the mound in the ninth, struck out. Larry McWilliams faced him the first three times, and Garber the last two.

1979 — Glenn Hubbard was optioned to Richmond.

August 2

1906 — Bill Posedel, 1939–41; 1946; b.

1959 — Billy Bruton tied a major league record by whacking two bases-loaded triples in an 11–5 win over the Cardinals.

August 3

1886 — Al Kaiser, 1911–12; b.

1889 — Gus Getz, 1909–10; b.

1916 — Johnny Evers and Red Smith of the Reds had a shouting match at the end of the fourth inning. They later met under the stands and thrashed it out. No further details were available.

1956 — Johnny Logan's 451-games-in-a-row streak came to an end because of a deep slump. The streak began on August 7, 1953.

1967 — The Braves tied the National League record for solo homers in a 10–3 win at Wrigley Field as they poled six. The major league record for solo shots in one-game is seven.

1976 — Cito Gaston homered his first two times up against his former mates, the Braves, but the Braves beat the Padres, 7–3, in Atlanta.

August 4

1890 — Adolfo Luque, 1914–15; b.

1914 — Bill Schuster, 1939; b.

1918 — Frank McElyea, 1942; b.

1934 — Catcher Shanty Hogan set a club record with his 121st consecutive errorless game.

1957 — Bob Hazle had a single and a double to help the Braves to a 9–7 win over the Dodgers in Milwaukee. Warren Spahn came on in relief in the ninth to retire Don Zimmer and Junior Gilliam with the bases loaded, to save it for Bob Buhl. The win cut the Cardinal lead to 1½ games.

1968 — Wayne Causey hit his first home run since June 28, 1967, when he was with the Chisox, in a game against the Reds.

1979 — Phil Niekro was wild. In the second game of a doubleheader in Houston (the Braves dropped two: 4–3 and 6–2) Niekro tied Walter Johnson's 1914 major league record of four wild pitches in one inning. He racked up WPs in the sixth and seventh as well to tie the major league record of six in one game set earlier in the year by J. R. Richard.

August 5

1904 — Vic Frazier, 1937; b.

1919 — Buddy Gremp, 1940–42; b.

1921 — Ebba St. Claire, 1951–53; b.

1939 — Tommie Aaron, 1962–63; 1965; 1968–71; b.

1942 — Frank Demaree was unconditionally released.

1946 — The Braves enjoyed their largest crowd since 1932 (41,645), but saw their five-game winning streak come to an end at the hands of the Dodgers, 7–4.

1953 — Ricky Mahler, 1979–   ; b.

1971 — In the longest game ever played in Atlanta, the Braves beat the Mets, 2–1, in 17 innings, Barber over Taylor. Darrell Evans knocked in Sonny Jackson at the 4 hour 23 minute mark in a game in which Felix Millan tied the major league record for double plays by a second baseman: six.

1972 — Sugar Bear Blanks hit his first major league homer off of Jack Billingham in Cincinnati, but the Braves lost, 4–2.

1973 — Phil Niekro threw the first no-hitter by an Atlanta Brave, and the first no-hitter at Atlanta Stadium, against the Padres, 9–0. He walked three.

August 6

1864 — Bobby Wheelock, 1887; b.

1881 — Bud Sharpe, 1905; 1910; b.

1884 — Sherry Magee, 1915–17; b.

Jake Boultes, 1907–09; b.

1892 — Jack Stivetts threw the first no-hitter by a Brave as he blanked the Dodgers in Boston, 11–0. He walked five; three men reached base on errors.

1894 — Jim Bannon hit the first of two grand slams he would hit in consecutive games, a major league record.

1903 — Jim Turner, 1937–39; b.

1914 — Bobby Loane, 1940; b.

Tommy Reis, 1938; b.

1919 — Bobby Sturgeon, 1948; b.

1937 — The Braves became the first team in National League history to lead off a game with back-to-back homers as Johnson and Warstler connected.

1945 — Andy Messersmith, 1976–77; b.

1953 — Warren Spahn lost to the Dodgers for the seventh straight time, dating back to September 25, 1951, this time by a 4–3 score in the first of two in Milwaukee.

1957 — Bob Horner, 1978–   ; b.

1972 — Henry Aaron hit the 660th and 661st homers of his career, breaking Babe Ruth's record for most home runs with one club. Number 661 was the game-winner in the 10th inning of a 4–3 win in Cincinnati.

1973 — Governor Patrick Lucey proclaimed this date to be "Henry Aaron Day" in Wisconsin. The Braves travelled there to play the Brewers in an exhibition game. A crowd of 33,337 watched Aaron, the Atlanta DH, hit a home run in a 7–5 Brewer win.

1974 — Phil Niekro extended the pitching staff's consecutive-scoreless-inning string to 29 before it was broken in the ninth. The Braves won, 5–2, in San Diego. Henry Aaron hit his 14th and 15th homers of the year, Nos. 727 and 728. It was the 62nd time in his career that Aaron had two home runs in one game.

August 7

1871 — Otis Stocksdale, 1895; b.

1876 — Pat Carney, 1901–4,; b.

1886 — Bill McKechnie, 1913; 1930–37; b.

1894 — Jim Bannon hit his second grand slam in as many games, the first man ever to hit two in two games. Only two men have duplicated his feat in the National League.

1899 — Victor Willis threw the first Braves no-hitter from a mound 60'6" away from the plate. It happened in Boston, and the Braves beat Washington by a 7-1 score.

1931 — Ray Crone, 1954-57; b.

1953 — Johnny Logan played in the first of what would be 451 consecutive games. The streak would end on August 3, 1956.

1966 — Wesley Bales became the fourth man in major league history to strike out four times in his first major league game.

1968 — Rookie lefthander George Stone threw his first complete-game win, a six-hitter, at the Cubs, 10-2.

1972 — Luman Harris was fired as manager and was replaced by Eddie Mathews.

1973 — Joe Niekro was purchased from the Detroit Tigers.

August 8

1859 — Hal McClure, 1882; b.

1950 — Bob Elliott's fourth-inning home run gave the team a total of 105 for the season, breaking the 1949 club record. However, it was the only run of the game for the Braves, and they lost, 2-1, to the Giants.

1952 — After being honored by the folks of Pawtucket, R.I., before the game, Max Surkont threw a four-hit shutout over the Giants. Alvin Dark was not one of the Giants who had a hit: His 22-game streak ended.

1953 — Charlie Grimm signed a three-year contract to manage the Braves through the 1956 season.

1963 — Norm Larker was sent to the Giants in a straight cash deal.

1972 — In Eddie Mathews' first appearance as manager of the Braves in front of the home folks, Denny McLain recorded his first complete game in an Atlanta uniform by beating the Astros, 8-4.

August 9

1951 — Catcher Ebba St. Claire participated in three double plays, the last catcher in the National League to do so in a nine-inning game.

1957 — Bob Hazle had three singles, a homer, and two RBIs as the Braves crushed the Cardinals, 13-2.

1966 — A record crowd of 52,270 saw Sandy Koufax give up a leadoff home run to Felipe Alou, and a ninth-inning home run to Eddie Mathews to enable the Braves to beat the Dodgers, 2-1, in Atlanta.

August 10

1914 — The Braves moved into second place for the first time in 1914.

1938 — The Braves obtained Eddie Miller from the Cincinnati Reds for Johnny Babich, Bobby Reis, Gil English, Vince DiMaggio, John Riddle, and cash.

1957 — Bob Hazle went three-for-four as the Braves shut out St. Louis, 9-0.

August 11

1891 — Walter Barbare, 1921-22; b.

1893 — Red Causey, 1919; b.

1907 — Edwin Karger of St. Louis threw seven perfect innings in a rain-shortened game to beat the Braves, 4-0, in the second game of a doubleheader in St. Louis.

1919 — Luis Olmo, 1950-51; b.

1950 — Vern Bickford threw a no-hitter against the Dodgers in Boston, winning, 7-0.

1961 — Warren Spahn won his 300th game, a 2-1 win over the Cubs in Milwaukee. Richie Ashburn of the Cubs was in the lineup as he was for Spahn's 200th, and his 100th.

1964 — Henry Aaron passed Joe DiMaggio on the all-time HR list when he whacked No. 362 in a game against the Cubs at Wrigley Field.

1968 — The Braves signed Satchel Paige to the forty-man roster to enable him to qualify for the major league pension. He was released on October 7.

August 12

1880 — Christy Mathewson, 1923-25; b.

1903 — Joe Stanley and Pat Moran became the first Braves to hit grand slams in the same game.

1921 — Lefty Wallace, 1942; 1945-46; b.

1928 — Bob Buhl, 1953-62; b.

Charlie White, 1954-55; b.

1974 — In the annual Hall of Fame game in Cooperstown, New York, the Braves beat the Chicago White Sox. Henry Aaron, the leadoff hitter, singled in the first inning—his only hit. Vic Correll had two home runs, and Ralph Garr and Paul Casanova had one each.

1975 — Rob Belloir smacked his first major league hit and knocked in his first run as the Braves won, 3-2.

1976 — Frank LaCorte recorded his first major league win after nine straight losses, going back to an 0-3 record in 1975. He lost his first six decisions of 1976 before beating the Phillies, 4-3, in Philadelphia.

August 13

1886 — Lefty George, 1918; b.

1907 — Art Shires, 1932; b.

1917 — Sid Gordon, 1950–53; b.

1933 — Bob Giggie, 1959–60; b.

1940 — Tony Cloninger, 1961–68; b.

1957 — Lou Burdette hit his first two major league homers and beat the Reds, 12–4.

1963 — Warren Spahn became the all-time lefthanded strikeout leader when he whiffed five Dodgers to bring his career total to 2,383, breaking Rube Waddell's record.

August 14

1846 — Harry Schaefer, 1876–78; b.

1899 — Kyle Graham, 1924–26; b.

1901 — Oscar Siemer, 1925–26; b.

1929 — Jim Pisoni, 1959; b.

1971 — The Braves obtained Tony LaRussa from Iowa (American Association).

1972 — Former professional umpire Bernice Gera managed the Braves' wives in a softball game against the husbands.

August 15

1857 — Walter Hackett, 1885; b.

1889 — Braves pitchers allowed the Cleveland club to score in each of their nine innings, the first time that that happened in the National League.

1896 — Bill Sherdel, 1930–32; b.

1906 — Red Perry, 1929; b.

1934 — Joey Jay, 1953–55; 1957–60; 1966; b.

Seth Morehead, 1961; b.

1951 — Warren Spahn won his 100th major league game, a 9–0 shutout of the Phillies.

1954 — The Braves closed to within 3½ games of the top, the closest they would get in 1954, as they beat the Cubs, 2–1, in Milwaukee. Gene Conley (12–5) won his ninth straight.

1955 — Warren Spahn hit a home run off of Mel Wright of the Cardinals, thus giving him the rare distinction of having a circuit clout in every NL park.

1957 — Henry Aaron hit his 100th career homer off Don Gross of the Reds.

1981 — Steve Bedrosian recorded his first major league victory, in relief of Phil Niekro, as the Braves held on to beat the Dodgers 6–4.

August 16

1895 — Fred Bailey, 1916–1918; b.

1900 — Billy Rhiel, 1930; b.

1947 — The Braves beat the Giants, 4–1, in a game shortened by a heavy mist. Giant pilot Mel Ott protested the call in vain for a half hour.

August 17

1874 — Wagon Tongue Keister, 1898; b.

1891 — Kid Nichols threw a no-hitter at the New York Giants.

1892 — Johnny Rawlings, 1917–1920; b.

1920 — Vern Bickford, 1948–53; b.

1971 — Billy Williams of the Cubs rapped his 2,000th base hit in a 5–4 loss to the Braves.

1977 — Jeff Burroughs hit his 31st HR of the year, surpassing his personal high of 30 (with Texas in 1973).

August 18

1857 — Samuel Washington Wise, 1882–88; b.

1874 — Dick Harley, 1905; b.

1876 — Gus Dorner, 1906–9; b.

1893 — Burleigh Grimes, 1930; b.

1898 — Hal Goldsmith, 1926–28; b.

August 19

1880 — The Braves were no-hit victims for the first time. Lawrence Corcoran of the Cubs was the perpetrator, 6–0.

1886 — George Ferguson, 1908–11; b.

1951 — Luis Gomez, 1980–   ; b.

1955 — Terry Harper, 1980–   ; b.

1968 — Felipe Alou's 22-game hitting streak, the longest in Atlanta history at that point, came to an end against Ken Holtzman in Chicago.

1969 — Ken Holtzman of the Cubs threw a no-hitter at the Braves, putting Atlanta 3½ games out, the furthest behind they would be all year (in the year that they won the Western Division title).

August 20

1869 — Frank Bonner, 1903; b.

1908 — Al Lopez, 1936–40; b.

1942 — Johnny McCarthy was purchased from Indianapolis (American Association).

1946 — On "Appreciation Day" a Packard and a Ford were given away to lucky fans before a 16–10 loss to the Pirates in Boston. Lolly Hopkins, a die-hard fan from Providence, R.I., drew the winning ticket stubs.

1952 — The Cardinals' Harvey Haddix, on leave from Fort Dix awaiting his discharge from the Army, made his major league debut against the Braves, throwing a five-hit 7–2 win, in a 7½ inning game shortened by rain.

1969 — The Braves held a team meeting at the urging of Henry Aaron. After the meeting, without the manager and coaches present, the team went 26–10 and into first place—from 3½ games out to 2½ ahead. They reeled off nine in a row right away, and won 16 of their last 19. During the 16–3 streak, Rico Carty hit 405 and drove in 21 runs.

1979 — Terry Harper went onto the disabled list for the sixth time in his five-year minor league career.

1981 — Brett Butler made his Atlanta debut, getting a hit and an RBI as the Braves beat the Mets 6–4.

August 21

1894 — The Braves set a major league record for most runs scored in a doubleheader when they racked up 43 against Cincinnati. No team in baseball has ever topped the total.

1901 — Wes Schulmerich, 1931–33; b.

1908 — Ray Berres, 1940–41; b.

1920 — Ben Cardoni, 1943–45; b.

1939 — Jim Beauchamp, 1965; 1967; b.

1943 — Felix Millan, 1966–72; b.

1948 — Craig Robinson, 1974–77; b.

1948 — On Andy Pafko Night in Milwaukee, Eddie Mathews hit his 39th HR of the year to break Wally Berger's club record. Turk Lown was the Cub pitcher who gave it up.

1961 — Charlie Lau was sold to the Orioles.

1972 — The Braves broke Steve Carlton's 15-game winning streak, 2-1, in 11 innings in Philadelphia.

1979 — Larry Bradford, in relief of Rick Matula, pitched to one Phillie batter to earn his first major league save in a 5-4 win in Philadelphia.

August 22

1919 — Frank LaManna, 1940-42; b.

1927 — Braves' outfielder Ed Brown set a National League record by playing in his 534th consecutive game, thus breaking Fred Luderus's record.

1945 — Nate Andrews was sold to the Reds on waivers.

1948 — The Braves beat the Dodgers, 4-3, in Brooklyn to move ahead of them by two games despite the fact that Brooklyn stole eight bases. That ran their string to 19 of their last 19 against the Braves.

1959 — The 226 busses parked outside of Milwaukee County Stadium broke the 1957 record.

1969 — John Patsy "Tito" Francona was sold to the Athletics.

August 23

1876 — Bob Lawson, 1901; b.

1883 — Lew Richie, 1909-1910; b.

1901 — Guy Bush, 1936-37; b.

1914 — The Braves moved into a first-place tie with New York.

1917 — Jim Prendergast, 1948; b.

1941 — Marty Martinez, 1967-68; b.

1948 — Consecutive doubles in the top of the 14th inning by Phil Masi and Connie Ryan gave the Braves a 3-2 win over the Dodgers in Brooklyn. The Bums dropped to third place, and the Braves moved to a 2½-game lead over the Cardinals. It was the first extra-inning win of the year for the Braves after six losses in overtime.

1963 — After having played the role of a German sergeant in the "Combat" television show earlier in the day, Warren Spahn started his 601st game, one more than the 600 started by Grover Cleveland Alexander, the former NL record-holder.

1968 — Luman Harris was re-hired as manager for the 1969 season.

August 24

1852 — Jim O'Rourke, 1876–78; 1880; b.

1864 — Lew Hardie, 1890; b.

1889 — Hank Gowdy, 1911–17; 1919–23; 1929–30; b.

1894 — Jimmy Cooney, 1928; b.

1897 — Al Bool, 1931; b.

1950 — Max Surkont made his National League debut by beating the Cubs, 11–9, in the first game of a doubleheader sweep.

1954 — Robin Roberts's complete game mastery of the Braves came to an end when he was lifted in the seventh inning of a 5–1 Braves win in Milwaukee. Dating back to August 14, 1951, Roberts compiled 13 consecutive complete games against the Braves, good for a 12–1 record. His only loss was when Jim Wilson threw his June 12, 1954, no-hitter.

1973 — Dusty Baker literally climbed the centerfield fence to rob the Pirates' Richie Hebner of a HR in a 3–2 win in Atlanta (the best catch Eddie Mathews claimed to have ever seen). Baker also homered in the ninth with a man on to win it for the Braves.

1975 — Lou Brock stole his 800th career base in a 6–2 win over the Braves in St. Louis. Carl Morton was on the mound, and Biff Pocoroba behind the plate for the milestone theft.

August 25

1886 — Rube Kroh, 1912; b.

1887 — Dick Rudolph, 1913–1920; 1922–23; 1927; b.

1894 — Johnny Jones, 1920; b.

Tony Boeckel, 1919–23; b.

1921 — Austin McHenry of the Cardinals was the first batter to hit the leftfield fence on the fly at Braves Field in Boston.

1936 — In a game against the St. Louis Cardinals, the Braves pounded seven doubles in the first inning, a major league record.

1957 — Bob Hazle, hitting .526 since being recalled from Wichita, hit two two-run HRs as Warren Spahn beat the Phillies, 7–3. It was Spahn's 219th win, putting him ahead of Earl Whitehill and into 6th place on the all-time list. He also hit his 18th career HR, tying him with Schoolboy Rowe for 6th place on the all-time home run list for pitchers.

August 26

1888 — Frank Allen, 1916–17; b.

August 26 (continued)

1892 — Jesse Barnes, 1915–17; 1923–25; b.

1909 — Gene Moore, 1936–38; 1940–41; b.

1917 — George Barnicle, 1939–41; b.

1956 — Bob Buhl beat the Brooklyn Dodgers for the seventh time in 1956, thus becoming the first pitcher to beat the Dodgers that many times since Bucky Walters did it in 1939. The Braves won, 6–2, as Buhl ran his record to 16–5.

1959 — Del Rice was released and was signed as a coach.

1975 — Braves pitchers Jamie Easterly and Ray Sadecki tied a major league record for most consecutive hits given up, start of game, eight, by yielding seven singles and a triple to the Pirates in Pittsburgh in an 8–2 loss. Easterly gave up the first five, and was relieved by Sadecki, who gave up three more.

1978 — Bob Beall hit his first major league home run as the Cardinals beat the Braves, 9–4, in Atlanta.

August 27

1887 — Mike Kelly had six hits and scored six runs. Ezra Sutton also scored six times to give the Braves a major league record for most players scoring six runs or more in a game. Another Brave scored five times, thus giving them the record for most players with five runs or more, as well.

1892 — Dizzy Nutter, 1919; b.

1894 — The Braves staged a benefit game for catcher Charlie Bennett, who was run over by a Santa Fe Passenger train in January, 1894. In an afternoon game in which boxer James J. Corbett played first base, the Braves beat a local college all-star team, 17–12. Six thousand dollars was raised for Bennett.

1910 — Ewald Pyle, 1945; b.

1915 — Emil Verban, 1950; b.

1966 — Rookie Tom Kelley threw the first shutout and first complete game of his career, a two-hitter (Ron Hunt and Eddie Bressoud were the culprits) over the Mets in Atlanta.

1972 — "Hot Pants Day" at Atlanta Stadium.

August 28

1888 — The Braves obtained Joseph Quinn from Des Moines for $4,000.

1898 — Charlie Grimm, 1952–56; b.

1936 — Tony Gonazalez, 1969–70; b.

1937 — Bob Hartman, 1959; b.

1938 — Billy Cowan, 1965; b.

1951 — The Cubs shut out the Braves, 1–0, in Boston behind Turk Lown's first major league whitewash.

August 29

1888 — Ensign Cottrell, 1914; b.

1898 — Guy Morrison, 1927–28; b.

1930 — Dave Cole, 1950–53; b.

1939 — Dave Nicholson, 1967; b.

1942 — Dan Schneider, 1963–66; b.

1948 — The Braves drop to second place by losing a pair in Pittsburgh, 6–1, and 5–2.

1951 — Johnny Sain wore a Braves uniform for the last time. Later in the day he was traded to the Yankees for Lew Burdette and $50 K, but not before rookie Dick Cole won his first major league game on his 21st birthday, 4–1, over the Cubs.

1954 — Braves pitchers gave up eight runs in the 11th inning to the Dodgers, thus enabling a major league record for most runs given up in an 11th frame. The Braves lost, 12–4, in what was the first game of a doubleheader. They dropped the second, too, 11–4. Their only consolation was the crowd of 45,922: the largest crowd for the Dodgers in Milwaukee in two years; the season's total of 1,841,666 set a new National League attendance record.

1969 — The Braves reeled off their first triple play in Atlanta Stadium. The Cubs' Don Kessinger and Glenn Beckert led off the game with singles against Pat Jarvis. They moved up on a balk. Billy Williams then grounded to Orlando Cepeda at first and while Kessinger held at third, Beckert broke from second and was subsequently nailed in a rundown. While that was happening, Kessinger tried to sneak home, but he was cut down. Rico Carty came in from left field to take a throw to nail Williams trying to get to second base. It was Williams's second triple play in 16 days. Kessinger and Beckert were on base for the first one, too.

1971 — Henry Aaron knocked in his 100th run of the year, thus giving him a National League record of 11 times with 100 or more RBIs.

August 30

1878 — Charlie Starr, 1909; b.

1884 — Andy Sullivan, 1904; b.

1935 — Frank Funk, 1963; b.

1950 — Mike McQueen, 1969–72; b.

1953 — The Braves became the first National League team to hit eight home runs in one game. Jim Pendleton hit three, Eddie Mathews hit two, and Johnny Logan, Del Crandall, and Jack Dittmer had one apiece in the first game of a doubleheader

August 30 (continued)

against the Pirates in Pittsburgh which the Braves won, 19–4. No other NL team has ever hit more homers in a game. In fact, only three other NL teams have hit as many as eight. The Reds did it on August 18, 1956; the Giants did it on April 30, 1961; the Expos did it on July 30, 1978. The amazing thing about all of this is that the Braves were the victims *all three* times. In the second game of the doubleheader on this date, moreover, Mathews, Adcock, Logan, and Gordon added homers to give the Braves another NL record, most home runs in a doubleheader, 12.

1962 — The Giants hit three home runs, the Braves hit two, giving them a National League record for most home runs—game, both clubs, no other runs scored.

1964 — The Braves concession stand was down to $13 in pennies: Prices were slashed to accommodate the shortage. Beer was cut from 31¢ to 30¢; hot dogs from 26¢ to 25¢; hot sandwiches from 62¢ to 60¢.

1978 — Larry McWilliams won his seventh straight game.

August 31

1866 — Dad Clarkson, 1892; b.

1881 — Buster Brown, 1909–1913; b.

1888 — Wally Rehg, 1917–1918; b.

1910 — Ira Hutchinson, 1937–38; 1944–45; b.

1916 — Danny Litwhiler, 1946–48; b.

1940 — Ramon Hernandez, 1967; b.

1950 — Gil Hodges hit four home runs and a single as the Dodgers trounced the Braves, 19–3, in Brooklyn.

1953 — Bill Nahorodny, 1980–   ; b.

1954 — Claudell Washington, 1981–   ; b.

1966 — Paul Richards was named vice-president for baseball operations.

1969 — Morganna, the "Wild One," made her first Atlanta appearance. With Ken Holtzman on the mound for the Cubs and Clete Boyer up for the Braves in the fourth, and with Orlando Cepeda on second base with the first hit off Holtzman in 13 1/3 innings, Morganna, at 44-23-34, vaulted over the third-base railing in what was generously called a mini-dress. Approaching Boyer, she allegedly said, "Clete, you're the greatest," and then kissed him on the cheek. Boyer proceeded to get an RBI single, ending a 1–17 slump. He had two more hits on this date in Braves history and went eight for his next 15.

1974 — Danny Frisella of the Braves made his first start since August 5, 1970, when he was with the New York Mets. After 188 consecutive relief appearances, Frisella started against his old mates in New York; the Mets won, 6–5. Ralph Garr went two-for-five for the Braves, bringing him to the 200 hit mark.

1975 — Connie Ryan's managerial debut: The Braves split a doubleheader in Chicago.

1979 — Jamie Easterly, loaned to the Montreal Expos on June 6, was returned.

SEPTEMBER 1

1894 — Fred Nicholson, 1921–22; b.

1900 — Hub Pruett, 1932; b.

1903 — Foster Edwards, 1925–28; b.

1912 — Claude Wilborn, 1940; b.

1927 — Cloyd Boyer, 1977–   ; b.

1939 — Rico Carty, 1963–72; b.

1945 — Vince DiMaggio hit his fourth grand-slam homer of the year, tying a National League record for slams, as the Phillies beat the Braves, 8–3, in Boston.

1947 — Craig Skok, 1978–80; b.

1964 — Bob Uecker, a .182 hitter coming into the game, hit his first HR of the year, and the second of his three-year career (he had 14, lifetime). This one was a ninth-inning game-winner which beat the Braves, his former mates, 5–4, in St. Louis.

1968 — The Braves announced that Rico Carty, just recently let out of the hospital for treatment of tuberculosis, would spend the remainder of the year with the club.

1972 — Jimmy Freeman made his major league debut memorable by winning a complete game, 11–5 decision over the Phillies in Atlanta.

September 2

1886 — Paul Johnson, 1918; b.

1900 — Joe Heving, 1945; b.

1905 — Bernie James, 1929–30; b.

1945 — On Tommy Holmes Day the Braves split a doubleheader, 6–3 (Holmes hit a HR), losing, 5–4.

1957 — Bob Hazle was four-for-seven with three doubles and two RBIs as the Braves swept the Cubs in Chicago, 23–10, and 4–0. In the first game, Frank Torre scored six runs to tie the major league record.

1959 — Red Schoendienst made his first appearance since recovering from TB, grounding out as a pinch hitter in a game against the Phillies in Milwaukee.

1885 — Ed Konetchy, 1916–18; b.

1898 — Hall of Fame pitcher Kid Nichols played first base for the first time after regular catcher Marty Bergen went AWOL, and George Yeager, the back-up first baseman, was forced into the tools of ignorance. The Braves beat the Giants, despite a patchwork lineup, 6–5.

1913 — Kerby Farrell, 1943; b.

1916 — Eddie Stanky, 1948–49; b.

1926 — Braves pitchers gave up 12 runs in the fifth inning of a game with the Giants, a record for fifth inning runs.

1948 — Jeff Heath's two-run homer in the fourth held up as the Braves beat the Phillies, 3–1, to regain the lead in the NL. The Dodgers dropped two to the Giants.

1951 — Dave Campbell, 1977–78; b.

1953 — The Braves hit two homers, giving them 16 in four games, a National League record which has not been surpassed.

1957 — Warren Spahn set a record for shutouts by a lefthanded pitcher with his 41st, an 8–0 beating of the Cubs at Wrigley.

1966 — Eighteen-year-old Charlie Vaughan beat the Houston Astros, 12–2. Only Joey Jay, a 17-year-old in 1953, was younger among Brave pitchers to win a game. This was to be Vaughan's only major league win; in fact, his only other major league appearance was in relief in 1969.

1972 — A first-inning single by Henry Aaron against Steve Carlton of the Phillies moved Aaron past Stan Musial into first place on the all-time total base list with 6,135. The Phillies won, 8–0.

1973 — Henry Aaron hit home runs Nos. 707 and 708 against the San Diego Padres, tying him with Babe Ruth for the most home runs in one league.

1978 — Willie Stargell of the Pirates got his 2,000th hit as the Braves lost in Pittsburgh, 6–3.

1979 — Gene Garber set a major league record for losses by a relief pitcher as he dropped his 15th of the year, 6–5, to the Reds in Atlanta.

September 4

1869 — Kid Nichols, 1890–1901; b.

1950 — Doyle Alexander, 1980; b.

1966 — Don Schwall got the win, Jay Ritchie got the save; they combined for a six-hit shutout of the Astros in Atlanta to complete a five-game sweep of the Houston club.

1978 — Rookie lefty Larry McWilliams got his first major league loss, 8–4, to San Diego.

1979 — Larry Bradford recorded his first major league save against the Reds, and Mike Lum hit the first of two consecutive pinch-hit HRs.

September 5

1896 — Gil Gallagher, 1922; b.

1900 — Ike Kemp, 1924–25; b.

1908 — Nap Rucker of the Dodgers threw a no-hitter at the Braves, 6–0, in Brooklyn.

1911 — Buddy Hassett, 1939–41; b.

1913 — Boston and Philadelphia combined for one run between them in a doubleheader (Philly won one game 1–0, and the other ended in a 0–0 tie) to enable the two clubs to set a record for fewest runs scored by two clubs in a doubleheader.

1916 — Ernie White, 1946–48; b.

1921 — Vince Shupe, 1945; b.

1954 — Henry Aaron broke his ankle and missed the rest of the season.

1956 — The Braves lost, 12–2, to the Reds, Spahn was pounded, and the Reds moved to within 1½ games of the league-leaders.

1966 — The first grand slam yielded by an Atlanta pitcher was hit by Bill Mazeroski against Phil Niekro in Pittsburgh.

1972 — Frank LaCorte was signed as a free agent.

1973 — The Braves obtained Alan Closter from the Yankees to complete the June 7 deal involving Pat Dobson.

1976 — The Reds beat the Braves, 6–4, to eliminate them from the pennant race. Joe Morgan knocked in his 100th run, thus becoming the first second baseman since Bobby Doerr of the Red Sox in 1950 to accomplish that feat.

1979 — In a game against the Dodgers in Atlanta, Mike Lum hit his second consecutive pinch-hit home run.

September 6

1899 — Del Bissonette, 1945; b.

1903 — Thomas Thevenow, 1937; b.

1910 — Johnny Lanning, 1936–39; 1947; b.

1912 — Vince DiMaggio, 1937–38; b.

September 6 (continued)

1948 — Spahn and Sain began a stretch during which they pitched every other day. (You've heard the Spahn and Sain and a day of rain refrain?) Over a 21-day period, they started 11 of the 16 games played by the Braves: Spahn won four, Sain won five. Each man lost once.

1949 — Mike Thompson, 1974–75; b.

1954 — The Braves became the first team in the National League to draw 2,000,000 fans as a crowd of 43,207 watched them sweep the Cubs, 13–2 and 6–1. Eddie Mathews ran his consecutive hits streak to eight before lining out.

1968 — Rico Carty was released from a Florida hospital after spending 163 days there for treatment of tuberculosis.

September 7

1907 — Bill McAfee, 1931; b.

1929 — Braves pitchers gave up 10 straight hits to the Chicago Cubs in the fourth inning of the first game of a doubleheader, a major league record for consecutive hits given up by one staff.

1980 — Behind two homers by Bob Horner and a game-winner by Dale Murphy, the Braves extended their winning streak to seven, their longest since 1970. The Braves won, 6–5, over the Pirates in Atlanta.

September 8

1886 — Al Demaree, 1919; b.

1896 — Johnny Schulte, 1932; b.

1926 — Lou Sleater, 1956; b.

1932 — Casey Wise, 1958–59; b.

1942 — Steve Hargan, 1977; b.

1949 — The smallest crowd in Boston night baseball history, 5,856, saw the Braves lose to Philadelphia, 3–0, on a one-hitter by Russ Meyer.

1954 — The Braves completed their third 10-game winning streak of the year by winning in Pittsburgh, 5–2. Spahn's 11th win in a row, moving him to a 19-10 record, gave the Braves a four-game lead.

1955 — The Brooklyn Dodgers beat the Braves, 10–2, to achieve the earliest clinching ever of a National League pennant, breaking their September 12, 1953, clinching in Milwaukee. Buhl was the losing pitcher for the Braves on both occasions.

1968 — Ralph Garr stole his first major league base: home.

1969 — Braves farmhand Mickey Rivers and Clint Compton were sent to the California Angels for Hoyt Wilhelm and Bob Priddy.

September 9

1965 — Johnny Blanchard was purchased from the Athletics.

1970 — The Braves split a doubleheader in San Diego, winning 6–3 and losing 7–4. Bob Tillman's 11th-inning HR won the first game for the Braves. In the second game, Earl Wilson recorded his first (and last) National League win; he also whacked his first NL hit, a home run, to knock in the go-ahead runs in the sixth inning.

September 10

1914 — Johnny Evers was thrown out of the game by umpire Mal Eason for swearing. Evers, who subsequently was slapped with a three-day suspension, claimed that he was swearing at the ball, not at the umpire.

1954 — Joe Adcock's HR off of Brooklyn's Billy Loes at Ebbets Field, tied the major league mark of Lou Gehrig and Jimmie Foxx for most HRs in an enemy park in one year. Adcock's ninth HR of the year against the Dodgers was good enough to give him the NL record for that category. Stan Musial and Jim Bottomley held the old record of eight.

1958 — Juan Pizarro notched his first major league shutout, a three-hitter against the Reds.

1968 — Al Santorini made his first start and only appearance ever as a Brave. The Braves lost to the Giants, 4–2; San Francisco got their go-ahead runs when, with one out, Bobby Bolin singled, Bobby Bonds doubled him to third, Santorini bobbled a Ron Hunt dribbler after a force play, and Willie McCovey hit a homer to win it.

1969 — Henry Aaron hit his 40th HR of the year as the Braves won, 8–4. It gave Aaron a tie with Willie Mays for most times—40 or more homers (six) and enabled him to set a major league record for most seasons with 300 or more total bases (14).

1973 — The Braves obtained Dave Cheadle from the New York Yankees to complete the June deal involving Pat Dobson.

1974 — Barry Lerch was sold to the Cardinals.

Mike Thompson was purchased from Tulsa.

September 11

1864 — Con Daily, 1886–87; b.

1868 — Steve Brodie, 1890–91; b.

1947 — Ralph Kiner equalled the major league record for home runs in a doubleheader as he hit four in a 4–3, 10–8 Pirate sweep of the Braves. Kiner had one HR in the first game, and three in the second. He had also hit two the day before: the total of six in three consecutive games tied his own major league record, set in 1947, and set originally by Tony Lazerri in 1936.

1949 — The defending champions were mathematically eliminated as they dropped a doubleheader to the Phillies, 3–1, and 6–3, in Boston.

1955 — Eddie Mathews stole home on the front end of a double-steal in the second game of a doubleheader which the Braves swept from Philadelphia.

1968 — Henry Aaron made his Atlanta debut as a first baseman; he had three hits against Juan Marichal, including his 27th HR of the year which moved him into eighth place on the all-time total-base list ahead of Jimmie Foxx. Pat Jarvis set a club record with his 16th win of the year.

1977 — Gary Matthews, Biff Pocoroba, and Pat Rockett engineered a triple steal in a 7-2 Braves win in Atlanta.

September 12

1925 — Stan Lopata, 1959-60; b.

1940 — Jim Tobin became the last National League pitcher to score four runs in one game.

1947 — Ralph Kiner set a major league record with his eighth HR in four games; he hit two (his 47th and 48th of the year, to take the ML lead) as the Braves lost in Pittsburgh, 4-3.

1956 — The Braves beat the Dodgers, 8-7, in Brooklyn, to break their first place tie. Bob Buhl was the winner in relief, his eighth win of the year against the Dodgers, thus becoming the first Brave ever to win eight games against one opponent in a year. The last National Leaguer to accomplish the feat was Grover Cleveland Alexander in 1916. Billy Bruton had the game-winning RBI in the eighth inning, and Joe Adcock hit his 13th HR of the year against the Dodgers, tying Hank Sauer's and Jimmie Foxx's record for most home runs against one opponent. After the game Bobby Thomson was fined $100 for an unsuccessful, unauthorized, attempted steal of home.

1959 — Enos Slaughter was purchased from the Yankees.

1967 — Rookie Mike Lum's first major league hit produced the game-winning run as the Braves beat the Mets, 4-3, in Atlanta. Jay Ritchie was the winner in relief.

1974 — Darrell Evans and Cesar Geronimo hit grand slam homers in the second inning of the first game of a twilight doubleheader which Cincinnati won, 9-6. It was the last time that two grand slams were hit in one inning by members of different clubs.

September 13

1893 — John Kelleher, 1924; b.

1896 — Pat Collins, 1929; b.

1903 — Rabbit Warstler, 1936-40; b.

1915 — Morris Aderholt, 1945; b.

1952 — Warren Spahn struck out six men in a row, one short of the major league record at the time, as he shut out the Pirates, 8-0, in Boston.

1953 — Eddie Mathews's double broke Tommy Holmes's 1941 club record of 81 extra-base hits in one season.

1956 — The Braves swept a doubleheader from the Phillies, 3–2, in 13 innings, and 4–3 in 12. Henry Aaron had the game-winning RBI in each game. Warren Spahn won the second game, his 200th career win. The sweep allowed the Braves to move two games up on Brooklyn, and three games up on the third-place Reds.

1958 — Spahn won his 20th game of the year by beating St. Louis, 8–2, in Milwaukee. It was the ninth year in which Spahn won 20, surpassing by one year the previous record of eight shared by Ed Plank and Lefty Grove.

1969 — Felix Millan broke up Larry Dierker's (Astros) 8 2/3-inning no-hitter.

September 14

1948 — Johnny Sain won his 20th game of the year (the third year in a row that he won 20) as the Braves won, 10–3, to move five games ahead of Pittsburgh.

1952 — The Braves won their last game in Boston as Max Surkont threw a three-hit shutout at the Cubs. Eddie Mathews hit a ninth-inning HR to win it, 1–0. In the second game the Braves' club record of 37 consecutive shutout innings was broken in the sixth inning with Jim Wilson on the mound.

1971 — Henry Aaron became the National League's all-time RBI leader with 1,953 to pass Stan Musial. Aaron had two HRs and five RBIs in a 5–2 win in Cincinnati.

1976 — Two rookies made their major league debuts and won in Atlanta. In the first game of the doubleheader, Mark Lemongello of the Astros won, 4–3, and in the second Al Autry won, 4–3, for the Braves.

1978 — Jim Bouton recorded his first major league win since 1970 when the Braves won, 4–1, in San Francisco. Bouton started, went six innings, and gave up three hits. Gene Garber and Craig Skok finished up.

September 15

1897 — Hugh McQuillan, 1918–1922; 1927; b.

1907 — Henry Peploski, 1929; b.

1928 — The Braves played their ninth doubleheader in 12 days.

1952 — Don Collins, 1977; b.

1957 — The Braves lost to Philadelphia, 3–2, in 10 innings, their eighth loss in 11 games, cutting their lead to 2½ games.

1977 — Dale Murphy hit his first two major league homers, the second of which was a lead-off job in the top of the tenth which held up as the winning run in an 8–7 decision over the Padres in San Diego.

1978 — With the Braves as opponents, the Dodgers became the first club in history to draw more than 3,000,000 people. They beat the Braves, 5–0.

September 16

1899 — Heinie Mueller, 1928–29; b.

1905 — John McNamara, 1927–28; b.

1949 — Rogelio Moret, 1976; b.

1953 — Eddie Mathews knocked in his 131st run of the year to break Wally Berger's club record set in 1935 when Berger led the league with 130. In the same game, the Pirates' Danny O'Connell, who would be traded to the Braves at the end of the year, extended his hitting streak to 25 games, tying the Pittsburgh record set by Braves manager Charlie Grimm in 1923.

1960 — Warren Spahn threw his first no-hit game, a 4–0 win over the Phillies. This followed, by less than one month, Lew Burdette's August 18 no-hitter against the Phils. The last out of Spahn's came about when Bobby Malkmus hit a grounder off of Spahn's glove which ricocheted to Logan, who threw to Adcock.

September 17

1850 — Ezra Sutton, 1877–88; b.

1920 — Braves pitchers had a tough day. In the fourth inning they gave up 10 consecutive singles, a major league record for most consecutive hits in one inning. On top of that, the inning ended with a hit (a runner was caught in a rundown), and the fifth inning began with two more hits. The 12 straight hits were also a record: most consecutive hits given up by one pitching staff.

1937 — Orlando Cepeda, 1969–72; b.

1965 — The Braves broke the Giants' 14-game winning streak, the longest in the National League since 1951, by belting them, 9–1, in Milwaukee.

1973 — In front of the smallest home crowd in Atlanta history (1,362, including Commissioner Kuhn) Henry Aaron hit his 711th career home run, Carl Morton threw a 10-hit shutout over the Padres, 7–0, and Dave Johnson hit his 42nd HR of the year to tie Rogers Hornsby's record for homers by a second baseman.

1977 — With the Braves as opponents, the Dodgers' crowd of 52,527 put them at a total of 2,756,464, a new major league record.

September 18

1928 — The Braves and Cubs grounded into eight double plays between them to set a National League record for DPs in one game.

1941 — Dick Dietz, 1973; b.

1956 — The Braves beat Pittsburgh, 6–4, to pull within .001 of Brooklyn. Warren Spahn got credit for a save in the ninth inning in a game which featured a spectacular catch by Billy Bruton with two men on.

1973 — Eddie Mathews was rehired as manager for the 1974 season.

September 19

1860 — Ed Glenn, 1888; b.

1872 — Henry Lampe, 1894; b.

1890 — Stuffy McInnis, 1923–24; b.

1892 — Charles Nichols set a National League record for most runs batted in two consecutive innings when he had a grand-slam homer and a bases-loaded triple. The record of seven still stands.

1913 — Red Barkley, 1939; b.

1926 — Murray Wall, 1950; b.

1929 — Ray Shearer, 1957; b.

1939 — Dick Coffman was signed as a free agent.

1955 — Flagpole-sitter Bill Sherwood, perched since June 23, decided to come down after the Braves lost their chance to win seven straight. Sherwood, after 89 days, failed in his pledge to sit until the Braves won seven in a row. During his "streak" the Braves won six in a row three times.

1973 — Dave Johnson set a major league record for home runs by a second baseman by hitting his 43rd.

September 20

1898 — Chuck Dressen, 1960–61; b.

1946 — Roric Harrison, 1973–75; b.

1953 — The Braves set a new National League attendance record in their first year in Milwaukee—1,826,397—as they split a doubleheader with the Reds. In the first game, Del Crandall hit a home run in a losing cause, but it was the club's 148th, a new record for the franchise. In the second game, bonus rookie Joey Jay made his first start and received credit for a 3–0, 3-hit victory in a game called after 6½ innings because of darkness.

1954 — Warren Spahn won his 20th game of the year, the sixth time he reached that magic number, a new NL record for lefthanders.

1965 — Henry Aaron hit the last HR by a Milwaukee Brave. Ray Culp of the Phillies served it up.

1972 — Johnnie B. Baker tied the major league record for most times facing a pitcher in one inning: three (as well as most at-bats: three) as the Braves scored 13 runs in the second inning of the second game of a doubleheader with the Astros. This tied the major league record for most runs in a second inning, tied the club record for runs in any inning, and the 12 hits was a new record for the Braves. In the 13–6 win, Felix Millan knocked in five runs, in an inning that lasted 38 minutes in the Braves' half.

September 21

1860 — Tom Brown, 1888–89; b.

1868 — Joe Daly, 1892; b.

1869 — Jim Garry, 1893; b.

1889 — Bristol Lord, 1913; b.

1909 — Al Blanche, 1935–36; b.

1947 — Warren Spahn became the first Braves lefthanded pitcher to win 20 games since Irving Young of the 1905 club did it. Spahn threw a 4–0 shutout at the Dodgers thus delaying their clinching of the 1947 pennant.

1952 — The last game at Braves Field, Boston, Massachusetts. Brooklyn 8, Boston 2, in front of 8,822 (the second largest crowd of the year). With the win, the Dodgers clinched at least a tie for the NL pennant. In his first major league start, Joe Black threw a three-hitter. It was his 55th appearance, breaking Les Webber's 1943 record for most appearances by a Dodger pitcher. Black, thus, was the last man to win at Braves Field, Jim Wilson was the last loser, Roy Campanella hit the last home run (off of Wilson), Warren Spahn was the last pinch-hit hitter grounding out for Virgil Jester in the eighth inning. Carl Furillo had the last error. Sob.

1958 — The Braves clinched their second straight pennant by beating Cincinnati, 6–5. Henry Aaron hit his 30th home run, a double, and knocked in four. Warren Spahn won his 21st game of the year.

1975 — Fan Appreciation Night drew 6,858 people in Atlanta.

September 22

1875 — Doc Marshall, 1904; b.

1931 — Ken Aspromonte, 1962; b.

1934 — Sweet Lou Johnson, 1962; b.

1946 — Johnny Sain became the first Brave since 1937 to win 20 games as he beat the Dodgers, 4–2.

1951 — Sal Maglie became the first New York Giant pitcher to win 22 games since Carl Hubbell did it in 1937 as he beat the Braves and Max Surkont, 4–1, in NY.

1954 — The Braves were apparent 3–1 winners over the Reds in Milwaukee as a ninth inning rally by Cincinnati fell short on an unusual double play. With Gus Bell on second and Wally Post on first with one out, the Reds' Bob Borkowski swung at and missed a wild-pitch third strike. When Braves catcher Crandall retrieved the ball, he fired to third baseman Mathews; meanwhile Borkowski took off for first and Mathews, seeing him, threw there to try to get him, but the ball hit him and bounded into right field. Bell and Post scored. But, the umpires ruled a double-play: Borkowski out on the strikeout and Bell out at the plate because Borkowski illegally drew a throw. Manager Tebbetts of the Reds filed a protest.

102

President Giles upheld the protest, saying that the game should be resumed on September 24 with two outs, and runners on second and third. See September 24 for the outcome.

1957 — Bob Hazle went four-for-five against the Cubs, including a game-winning HR in the 10th inning.

1965 — The last game at Milwaukee County Stadium for the Braves. The Dodgers, the same team which closed Braves Field, beat the Braves, 7-6, in 11 innings. A crowd of 12,577 watched as Chi Chi Olivo got the loss, Frank Bolling hit a grand slam off of Sandy Koufax, Gene Oliver hit the last home run, and Sweet Lou Johnson had the last hit and the last RBI.

1970 — Hoyt Wilhelm was claimed by the Cubs from the Braves on waivers.

1978 — Cito Gaston was sold to the Pirates.

September 23

1889 — Joe Kelley, 1917-19; b.

1893 — Elton "Ice Box" Chamberlain of the Reds threw a seven-inning perfect game against the Braves in Cincinnati in the second game of a doubleheader.

1942 — Woody Woodward, 1963-68; b.

1950 — Johnny Sain, trying to win his 20th of the year, failed to do that but hit his first major league HR in a 4-3 loss to the Giants.

1953 — Brian Asselstine, 1976-   ; b.

1956 — Billy Bruton hit his first major league grand slam as the Braves beat the Cubs, 7-6, in Milwaukee behind Bob Buhl.

1957 — The Braves clinched their first pennant since 1948 by beating the Cardinals, 4-2. Henry Aaron hit an 11th inning HR with Johnny Logan on base to give Gene Conley the win, and Billy Muffett the loss. The Braves had knocked out Vinegar Bend Mizell in the second inning: Aaron and Joe Adcock singled, Andy Pafko beat out a bunt. Wally Moon dropped Wes Covington's sacrifice fly. Larry Jackson replaced Mizell for the Cardinals and got two force plays at the plate and a line out. St. Louis got two in the top of the sixth when Moon singled, Musial doubled, and Dark singled. Eddie Mathews doubled Red Schoendienst home in the seventh to tie it up at two. In the 11th, Logan singled with two outs and Aaron hit Muffett's first pitch over the center field fence, his 43rd HR of the year.

1969 — The Braves moved into first place to stay by beating Houston, 10-2, at the Dome. George Stone beat Jim Bouton.

1977 — George Foster of the Reds became only the fifth man in NL history to hit at least 50 home runs in a year when he hit No. 50 off of the Braves Buzz Capra in the ninth inning of a 5-1 Cincinnati win in Atlanta. Foster joined Hack Wilson, Ralph Kiner, Johnny Mize, and Willie Mays on the select list.

1978 — Glenn Hubbard hit his first major league home run off of Manny Sarmiento of the Reds as the Braves won, 8-1, in Atlanta.

September 24

1890 — Miguel Gonzalez, 1912; b.

1931 — Mike Krsnich, 1960; 1962; b.

1952 — Rod Gilbreath, 1972–80; b.

1954 — In the completion of the September 22 game ordered replayed from the ninth inning (See September 22), the Braves hung on to win, 4–3. The replay began with Gus Bell on third, Escalera running for Post at second, and two outs, and a 3–1 score in the ninth inning. Jolley was in for the Braves, replacing Spahn. Johnny Temple singled for the Reds to score Bell, and when Bruton misplayed the ball, Escalera scored, too, to tie it at three. But the Braves scored in their half of the ninth to win it, 4–3. In the regularly scheduled game, the Braves beat the Cardinals, 4–2, as Spahn won No. 21.

1955 — Eddie Mathews hit his 153rd career home run, tying him with Mel Ott for hitting more home runs at age 23 than any other player in history.

1957 — Henry Aaron hit his first career grand slam in a 6–1 win over St. Louis.

1961 — Warren Spahn won No. 20 for the twelfth time in his career by two-hitting the Cubs, 8–0.

1980 — Rick Camp made his 74th appearance, breaking Clay Carroll's 1966 club record, and picked up his 20th save of the year in a 4–2 win over the Astros in Atlanta.

September 25

1917 — Johnny Sain, 1942; 1946–51; b.

1942 — Hank Majeski was sold to the Yankees.

1955 — For the second year in a row, Wally Moon hit a home run in his last at-bat of the year against the Braves. This year's blast came against Chet Nichols in an 8–5 Braves loss in St. Louis. Moon's HR was the 1,263rd in the National League in 1955, a new record.

1957 — Glenn Hubbard, 1978–   ; b.

1966 — Henry Aaron hit the club's 200th HR of the year, a new record.

1969 — The Braves sign free-agent Taylor Phillips so that he could qualify for the major league pension.

1970 — The Braves leave 18 men on base in a 12 inning, 7–4 loss to Houston.

September 26

1876 — Tom Asmussen, 1907; b.

1877 — Outfielder Harry Schafer became the first of only eight men to have four assists in a nine-inning game. The last man in either league to do it was the Braves Wally Berger on April 27, 1931.

1895 — Bernie Neis, 1925–26; b.

1910 — Joe Sullivan, 1939–41; b.

1942 — Warren Spahn's first major league complete game ended after seven innings, leaving him with no decision, and leaving the Braves with a forfeit loss. Youngsters, who had been admitted for free upon presenting 10 pounds of scrap metal for the war effort, walked onto the field and refused to leave. Umpire Ziggy Sears forfeited the game to the Giants, who were trailing at the time, 5–2.

1948 — The Braves clinched their first pennant since the miracle year, 1914. They beat the Giants, 3–2, in Boston on a combined five-hitter by pitchers Bickford and Potter. Bob Elliott hit a three-run HR in the first inning.

1950 — Jim Konstanty of the Phillies set a major league record for appearances with his 71st, as the Phils beat the Braves, 8–7, in Boston in front of 1,987.

1952 — The Boston Braves suffered their last loss. Carl Erskine and rookie Ken Lehman combined to beat them, 8–4, in Brooklyn. It was Lehman's first big league victory. Billy Cox had a HR for the Dodgers. Jim Wilson took Boston's last loss.

1954 — Rookie Wally Moon, who homered in his first major league at-bat in April, hit a home run in his last at-bat of the season, an 11th-inning game-winner against the Braves in Milwaukee. The Cardinals won, 2–0.

1958 — Lew Burdette won 20 games for the first time by beating the Reds, 2–1, in Milwaukee.

1959 — On the next-to-last day of the regular season, the Braves beat the Phillies, 3–2, in Milwaukee, and the Dodgers lost, 12–2, in Chicago to create a first place tie between the Braves and Dodgers. In the Braves game, Warren Spahn threw a five-hitter for his 21st win of the year, making him the winningest lefthanded pitcher in National League history, passing Eppa Rixey. Spahn struck out seven, and gave up solo homers to Gene Freese and Wally Post. In the eighth inning, with the score tied, 2–2, Mathews and Aaron singled, Joe Adcock sacrificed, Lee Maye was intentionally walked, and Bobby Avila hit a slow roller to shortstop Joe Koppe who could get only a forceout at second as the go-ahead run scored. In the Dodger loss, Alvin Dark hit a three-run homer to pace an 18-hit attack, as Johnny Podres was bombed. Dave Hillman got the win for the Cubs.

1979 — Phil Niekro recorded his 20th win of the year, thus becoming the first NL pitcher since Irv Young in 1905 to both win and lose 20 in a year. He and brother Joe also became the first brothers to win 20 games in the same season.

September 27

1876 — Harry Steinfeldt, 1911; b.

1883 — The Braves clinched their first pennant in five years by beating Cleveland, 4–1.

1890 — Frank Gibson, 1921–27; b.

1898 — Bill Clarkson, 1928–29; b.

1952 — Rookie Eddie Mathews hit three HRs as the Braves beat the Dodgers, 11–3, in Brooklyn, the last win for the Boston franchise. Virgil Jester got credit for the win (his last in the majors), as the Braves stopped a ten-game losing streak.

1959 — On the last day of the regular season, with the Braves and Dodgers tied for first place, both clubs won. The Dodgers beat the Cubs, 7–1, and the Braves beat the Phillies, 5–2. The Giants, who could have made it a three-way tie for first, dropped two to the Cardinals. All of the Braves runs were unearned. Bob Buhl and Don McMahon held off the Phillies. In the seventh inning, with the score tied at one, Del Crandall singled to lead off. Jim Owens was replaced by Humberto Robinson for Philadelphia. Logan sacrificed Crandall to second. Enos Slaughter pinch-hit for Buhl and walked. John Demerit ran for Slaughter. Billy Bruton hit a grounder to Ed Bouchee at first, but shortstop Joe Koppe dropped two to the Cardinals. All of the Braves runs were unearned. Bob Buhl and Don McMahon held off the Phillies. In the seventh inning, with the score passed ball by Carl Sawatski moved Mathews to second, Demerit holding at third. Robinson, forgetting that Mathews moved up on a passed ball, threw to first, balking, and Demerit scored. Aaron singled to score Mathews. That was enough for the Braves to win.

September 28

1876 — Shad Barry, 1900–01; b.

Red Long, 1902; b.

1885 — Wilbur Good, 1910–11; b.

1889 — Pete Compton, 1915–16; b.

1892 — Jack Fournier, 1927; b.

1893 — Mike Massey, 1917; b.

1906 — Dick Barrett, 1934; b.

1912 — Mike Gonzalez became the first Latin ever to wear a Boston baseball uniform in a regular season game.

1917 — Mike Ulisney, 1945; b.

1928 — Braves pitchers gave up seven runs to St. Louis in the 15th inning to establish the major league record for most runs given up in a 15th inning.

1947 — Coach Ernie White, after receiving a special exemption from the office of President Frick, was allowed to pitch in a regular season game. He pitched four scoreless innings, giving up a hit, a walk, and striking out one. Johnny Sain came on in relief and chalked up his 21st win.

1952 — The Braves' last game as a Boston franchise ended in a 12-inning 5–5 tie in Brooklyn. Eddie Mathews had the last Boston hit, a double, and the last RBI. Johnny Logan scored the last run. The Dodgers set a league strikeout record when Jim Hughes fanned Sid Gordon in the 12th.

1953 — Atlanta farmhand Gene Mauch was sold to the Cubs' Los Angeles farm team.

1957 — Bob Hazle had the only hit, an eighth-inning single, off of Johnny Klippstein as the Braves lost to the Reds, 6–0.

1959 — In the first game of the best-of-three playoffs for the National League pennant, the Braves lost, 3–2, to the Dodgers in Milwaukee. A crowd of 18,297 sat in a cold drizzle and watched Johnny Roseboro homer off of Carlton Willey in the top of the sixth with the score tied, 2–2. Danny McDevitt, the surprise starter for LA, lasted only 1 1/3 innings, giving up two runs on two hits. Rookie Larry Sherry came on in relief and went 7 2/3 scoreless innings to get the win.

1969 — Henry Aaron scored his 100th run of the year, the fourteenth time he did that—a major league record.

1971 — Tom House recorded his first major league win, and Jimmy Breazeale hit his first major league home run as the Braves won, 6–2, in Atlanta.

1976 — Rafael Ramirez was signed as a free agent.

1977 — Pat Rockett hit his first major league homer but the Braves lost, 2–1, to the Astros in Atlanta.

September 29

1899 — Jim Matthews, 1922; b.

1905 — Bruce Cunningham, 1929–32; b.

1913 — Dan McGee, 1934; b.

1935 — Howie Bedell, 1962; b.

1957 — The Braves won their 95th game of the year, a new club record, breaking the 1914 mark of 94.

1959 — In the second game of the best-of-three series to determine the National League pennant winner, the Braves were defeated by the Los Angeles Dodgers, 6–5, in 12 innings in Los Angeles. In the bottom of the ninth inning, with the Braves ahead, 5–2, Los Angeles rallied for three runs to tie it. Wally Moon singled to lead off. Duke Snider and Gil Hodges also singled to load the bases. Don McMahon replaced Lew Burdette, the starter, and gave up a two-run single to Norm Larker. Spahn replaced McMahon. Carl Furillo, batting for Roseboro, hit a sacrifice fly to score Hodges with the tying run.

In the bottom of the twelfth inning, with Bob Rush on the mound (he came on with the bases loaded and two out in the 11th), Hodges walked, Joe Pignatano singled, and Carl Furillo came to the plate. He hit a grounder over the second base bag which Felix Mantilla (playing shortstop) fielded, but Mantilla threw wildly past first baseman Frank Torre, and Hodges scored the winning run.

1962 — With a 4–3 win over the Pirates in Milwaukee, Warren Spahn became the winningest lefthanded pitcher in baseball history. It was Spahn's 327th win.

1963 — Henry Aaron, on the last day of the season, hit his 44th home run to tie Willie McCovey for the league lead.

1970 — Mike McQueen recorded his first major league win by beating the Reds, 2-1.

1971 — Luman Harris was hired to manage the 1972 club.

1973 — Henry Aaron's 40th HR of the year, off Jerry Reuss, gave the Braves three men with 40 homers (Darrell Evans and Dave Johnson were the others). The Braves thus became the only team ever to have three men with 40 or more HRs.

1976 — John Montefusco of the Giants threw a 9-0 no-hitter at the Braves in Atlanta.

September 30

1882 — Gabby Street, 1905; b.

1883 — Forrest More, 1909; b.

1913 — Nate Andrews, 1943-45; b.

1916 — For the second game in a row, the Braves accounted for just one hit in a nine-inning game. No team has ever had fewer hits in two consecutive games.

1924 — Bennie Taylor, 1955; b.

1946 — The Braves obtained Bob Elliott and Hank Camelli from the Pirates in exchange for Billy Herman, Elmer Singleton, Billy Wietelmann, and Stan Wentzel.

1968 — Satchel Paige, signed earlier in the year to allow him to qualify for the major league pension, was given his unconditional release, and was signed as a coach for the 1969 season.

1969 — The Braves clinched their first Western Division title by winning their tenth game in a row, 3-2, over the Reds in Atlanta. Trailing 2-1 in the seventh inning, the Braves went ahead when Mike Lum singled, and Ralph Garr walked; Wayne Granger relieved Gary Nolan for the Reds. Felix Millan forced Lum at third, Orlando Gonzalez singled (his fourth straight hit) to score Garr, Henry Aaron walked, and Rico Carty hit a sacrifice fly to score the winning run. Hoyt Wilhelm saved it for Phil Niekro (23-13) by retiring the last six men he faced, three of them on strikeouts.

1974 — Clyde King became the first man to receive a multiyear contract to manage the Atlanta club as he signed on to manage through the 1976 season.

OCTOBER 1

1918 — Jim Russell, 1948-49; b.

1926 — Bob Boyd, 1961; b.

1946 — Angel Hermoso, 1967; b.

1947 — Buzz Capra, 1974-77; b.

1949 — The Braves obtained Sam Jethroe from the Dodgers' Montreal farm club.

1958 — In the first World Series game with the American League pennant-winning New York Yankees, the Braves won, 4–3, in 10 innings in Milwaukee. The Yankees were ahead in the eighth inning on the strength of a solo home run by Bill Skowron in the fourth, and a two-run shot by Hank Bauer in the fifth, both off of starter Warren Spahn. But Milwaukee tied it up as Mathews walked, Aaron doubled; Ryne Duren replaced Whitey Ford and fanned Joe Adcock, only to have Wes Covington drive in Mathews with a sacrifice fly. In the tenth, Adcock and Del Crandall singled, and Billy Bruton drove home the winning run with a long single.

October 2

1874 — Ernie Diehl, 1906; 1909; b.

1896 — Sid Womack, 1926; b.

1939 — Mike de la Hoz, 1964–67; b.

Paul Doyle, 1969; b.

1957 — In the first World Series game with the New York Yankees, the Braves lost, 3–1, in New York. Spahn was knocked out in the sixth when Andy Carey singled home a run, and Jerry Coleman squeezed an insurance run home. The Braves' only run came in the seventh when Wes Covington doubled and Red Schoendienst singled him home.

1958 — The Braves exploded for seven runs in the first inning against Bob Turley and Duke Maas to coast to a 13–5 win in game No. 2 of the World Series. The seven runs is a record for most runs in a first inning of a World Series game. A crowd of 46,367 Milwaukee fans watched the Yankees load the bases in the first inning; however, they scored only one run, enough to stop Lew Burdette's scoreless inning streak in World Series competition at 24.

1974 — Henry Aaron, who had hit a home run in the first game of 1974, hit a home run in his last game as a Brave, and in his last at-bat to boot. Rawley Eastwick was the victim of HR No. 733 and hit No. 3,600.

1976 — Phil Niekro threw a one-hitter at the Cincinnati Reds, winning, 3–0.

1977 — In his first two major league at-bats, Mickey Mahler had two hits (one right-handed, and one lefthanded), in a game against the Reds.

October 3

1862 — Bill Higgins, 1888; b.

1874 — Al Shaw, 1909; b.

1895 — The oldest Brave, Harry Wright, died in Atlantic City, New Jersey.

1905 — Johnny Riddle, 1937–38; b.

1906 — George and John Dovey of South Carolina purchased the Braves from Arthur Soden and company for $75,000, including the grounds. The Braves became known as the Doves. Manager Fred Tenney negotiated the sale and even kept

October 3 (continued)

his stock after he was traded to the Giants, a practice which was later ended by the Commissioner's office.

1949 — Jim Breazeale, 1969; 1971–72; b.

1957 — The Braves tied the World Series at one game apiece by beating the Yankees, 4–2, in New York. The Braves broke a two-all deadlock in the fourth when Joe Adcock and Andy Pafko singled. Wes Covington, after fouling off a couple of bunt attempts, singled to left, and Tony Kubek dropped a relay throw.

1972 — Gary Nolan of the Reds beat the Braves, 6–1. Nolan pitched in only two games in 1973, going 0–1. He then sat out the 1974 season with an injury. His first game back was in 1975, and he beat the Braves by the same score on May 3.

1976 — In his last major league at-bat, Henry Aaron of the Brewers singled, his 3,771st hit, against the Tigers in Milwaukee.

October 4

1878 — Bob Dresser, 1902; b.

1939 — Ted Davidson, 1968; b.

1944 — Tony LaRussa, 1971; b.

1957 — The Yankees won game No. 3 of the World Series by beating the Braves, 12–3. Tony Kubek made his home-town debut by whacking two homers and knocking in five runs. The Braves tied two Series records by leaving 14 men on base and walking 11 Yankees. The Yankee pitchers walked eight of their own, and the combined total of 19 was a new Series record. Bob Buhl, who went only two-thirds of an inning, took the loss.

1958 — In game No. 3 of the World Series with the Yankees, the Braves were the victims of a six-hit combined shutout by Don Larsen and Ryne Duren. Hank Bauer got all of the Yankee RBIs on a bases-loaded single and a two-run HR. Bob Rush took the loss.

1969 — In the first game of the National League Championship Series with the New York Mets in Atlanta, the Braves lost, 9–5. Henry Aaron hit a home run against Tom Seaver in the seventh to give the Braves a 5–4 lead; however, in the eighth inning the Mets scored five runs off of Phil Niekro—a championship series record for runs given up by one pitcher. The total of nine was also a series record at the time.

October 5

1859 — Gurdon Whitely, 1885; b.

1873 — Claude Ritchey, 1907–09; b.

1906 — Si Johnson, 1946–47; b.

1953 — Donald Davidson was named Director of Public Relations.

1958 — In the fourth game of the World Series with the Yankees, Warren Spahn pitched a two-hit shutout as the Braves won, 3–0. Hank Bauer's 17-game World Series hitting streak came to an end. Norm Siebern lost a couple of balls in the sun helping the Braves to get some unearned runs. While Siebern wasn't charged with any errors, Tony Kubek chipped in with one after Norm lost a Red Schoendienst fly ball in the sun. It was the Braves' last win of the 1958 World Series.

1969 — In game No. 2 of the Championship Series with the Mets, New York built up an 8–0 lead after four innings, and coasted to an 11–6 win. Tommy Agee, Ken Boswell, and Cleon Jones hit two-run homers for the Mets, and Henry Aaron hit a three-run job for the Braves. Ron Reed took the loss, and Ron Taylor (W) and Tug McGraw (SV) stymied the Braves.

October 6

1854 — Pop Snyder, 1878–79; 1881; b.

1946 — Gary Gentry, 1973–75; b.

1947 — Steve Kline, 1977; b.

Charlie Vaughan, 1966; 1969; b.

1948 — In the first game of the World Series with the Cleveland Indians (who had won the American League pennant by beating the Red Sox in a playoff game), the Braves beat Bob Feller, 1–0, despite having only two hits. In the eighth inning, Bill Salkeld walked to lead off and Phil Masi ran for him. Mike McCormick sacrificed him to second, Eddie Stanky was intentionally walked, and Feller then made what seemed to him and to Lou Boudreau, who took it, a perfect throw to pick off Masi at second. Umpire Bill Stewart said no, however, and after Sain flied out, Tommy Holmes singled Masi home. Sain gave up only four hits for the Braves.

1957 — In game 4 of the World Series, the Braves evened it up at two games apiece by winning, 7–5, in Milwaukee. After the Yanks got a run in the first, the Braves tallied four times in the fourth as Aaron hit a three-run homer, and Frank Torre added a solo shot against Tom Sturdivant. Spahn went into the ninth with the 4–1 lead and had two outs with two on and a count of three-and-two on Elston Howard, only to yield a game-tying home run to left. Spahn stayed in the game, however, and in the tenth inning, Tony Kubek beat out an infield hit and scored on Hank Bauer's triple. In the bottom of the inning, Nippy Jones, batting for Spahn, was hit on the foot by Yankee pitcher Tommy Byrne (an event which at first eluded umpire Augie Donatelli). Jones retrieved the ball and showed it, specked with his shoe polish, to Donatelli, who then ordered him to first base. Felix Mantilla ran for Jones and Bob Grim relieved Byrne. Johnny Logan promptly tied it by doubling Mantilla home, and Eddie Mathews won it by hitting a home run.

1958 — In game 5 of the World Series, Bob Turley of the Yankees pitched a five-hit shutout and his mates scored seven runs as the Braves saw their three-to-one edge drop to three-to-two in the Series.

1967 — The Braves released Bob Uecker as a player, but signed him on as a coach.

1969 — The Braves lost their third straight game in the Championship Series with the

October 6 (continued)

Mets, 7–4, at Shea Stadium. After Henry Aaron homered in the first, and Orlando Cepeda's fifth inning HR put them ahead, 4–3, the Braves did very little against Nolan Ryan (in relief of Gary Gentry). Agee, Boswell, and Wayne Garrett homered for the Mets. Pat Jarvis took the loss for the Braves.

October 7

1885 — Fred Liese, 1910; b.

1948 — In game 2 of the World Series with the Cleveland Indians, the Braves lost, 4–1, in Boston. Bob Lemon scattered eight hits for the Indians, and Warren Spahn took the loss for the Braves.

1957 — The Braves took a three-to-two advantage in World Series games with the Yankees by beating them, 1–0, in Milwaukee. The only run of the game came about in the sixth inning when Eddie Mathews beat out an infield hit with two outs, and Aaron and Adcock singled. Lew Burdette threw the seven-hit shutout.

October 8

1857 — John Bergh, 1880; b.

1887 — Doc Crandall, 1918; b.

1916 — Joe Callahan, 1939–40; b.

1917 — Danny Murtaugh, 1947; b.

1921 — George Metkovich, 1954; b.

1949 — Gene Bearden of the Cleveland Indians threw a five-hit shutout in game 3 of the World Series against the Braves in Cleveland. Bearden also doubled in the third inning, and then scored on Alvin Dark's error.

1958 — The Yankees tied the Series at three games apiece by winning, 4–3, in 10 innings. Bauer homered in the top of the first, and the Braves tied it up against Whitey Ford in their half. In the second inning, Wes Covington, Andy Pafko, and Warren Spahn singled, and the Braves led, 2–1. Red Schoendienst walked and Art Ditmar relieved Ford. Johnny Logan hit a short fly ball to Elston Howard in left, and Pafko was nailed at the plate trying to score. The Yankees tied the score in the sixth. In the top of the tenth, Gil McDougald homered, and with two outs Howard and Yogi Berra singled, prompting Manager Haney to bring on Don McMahon in relief of Spahn. Moose Skowron smacked a single to score what proved to be the winning run. In the Braves half of the tenth, Logan walked, Aaron singled, and Adcock singled home a run. But Bob Turley came on for the Yankees and retired Frank Torre on a lineout to second base.

1967 — Denis Menke and Denny LeMaster were traded to Houston for Sonny Jackson and Chuck Harrison.

October 9

1889 — Rube Marquard, 1922–25; b.

1890 — Ray Massey, 1918; b.

1902 — Jimmy Welsh, 1925–27; 1929–30; b.

1912 — Mickey Haefner, 1950; b.

1914 — The Miracle Braves opened the first game of the World Series with a 7–1 bombing of Connie Mack's Philadelphia Athletics in Philadelphia. Hank Gowdy, who would hit .545 in the four-game Series (the first sweep in Series history), had a single, double, and triple on this date in Braves history as he and his mates knocked Chief Bender out of the pitching box for the first time in World Series competition. Bender had had two complete games in 1905 and 1910, three in 1911, and two more in the 1913 Series. Dick Rudolph threw his first of two complete game victories for the Braves.

1940 — Joe Pepitone, 1973; b.

1948 — The Braves dropped their third straight World Series game to the Cleveland Indians after having won the first game of the 1948 "Fall Classic." This time Steve Gromek stymied them, except for Rickert's seventh-inning home run. Larry Doby's home run in the third proved to be the decisive run for the Indians, and the downfall of the Braves and Johnny Sain, who went all the way.

1957 — The Yankees won the sixth game of the World Series, tying it at three games apiece. Hank Bauer homered in the bottom of the seventh to make the score 3–2, the final, as it were. Ernie Johnson took the loss in relief of Bob Buhl. Bob Turley went all the way for the Yankees.

1958 — The Yankees won the seventh game of the World Series, 6–2, in Milwaukee. They thus became the first club since 1925 to win the Series after being down three-games-to-one. The Braves loaded the bases in the first inning against Don Larsen but came up with only one run. In the second inning, after Yogi Berra walked, Frank Torre was charged with two consecutive throwing errors; the first on a bunt attempt by Elston Howard, and the second on a groundball by Jerry Lumpe. Two runs ultimately scored. In the eighth, with the score tied, 2–2, and with two outs, Berra doubled, and Howard singled him home for what proved to be the winning run. Andy Carey singled, and Skowron followed with a home run, and it was wait 'til next year.

October 10

1905 — Wally Berger, 1930–37; b.

1914 — In game 2 of the World Series with the Athletics, the Braves and Bill James won, 1–0. James pitched a masterful two-hitter, and the Braves got a run in the top of the ninth when outfielder Amos Strunk misjudged Charlie Deal's fly ball. Deal ended up on second and was quickly singled home by Les Mann.

1929 — Bob Tiefenauer, 1963–65; b.

1940 — Larry Maxie, 1969; b.

1942 — Warren Spahn joined the U.S. Army.

1948 — The Braves won their second, and last, game of the 1948 World Series with the Cleveland Indians. Bob Elliott hit two home runs and drove in four by the third

113

inning. In the seventh inning, the Braves broke a 5–5 tie with five singles off of four Indian pitchers. Bob Feller took the loss, and Warren Spahn, in relief of Nelson Potter, got the win.

1957 — The Braves were World Champions for the first time since the 1914 Miracle as Lew Burdette, with only two days rest, pitched his third complete game win, a seven-hit shutout of the New York Yankees. Tony Kubek's third-inning error opened the gates for four runs. No pitcher since Stan Coveleski in 1920 had won three complete games in a World Series. The Braves won despite having a .209 batting average for the seven games (the lowest in Series history for a seven-game series).

1967 — Deron Johnson was obtained from the Reds for Mack Jones, Jay Ritchie, and Jim Beauchamp.

1975 — Dave Bristol was named manager for the 1976 season.

October 11

1854 — Will White, 1877; b.

1912 — Wayne Osborne, 1936; b.

1918 — Bob Chipman, 1950–52; b.

1948 — In the sixth game of the World Series against the Indians, the Braves lost the game, 4–3, and the Series, 4–2. Bob Lemon coasted with a 4–1 lead into the eighth, but with one out, the Braves loaded the bases. Clint Conaster hit a fly ball for one run, and pinchhitter Phil Masi doubled another run home. Mike McCormick lined to Bearden, however, and the inning was over. He retired the side in order in the ninth and the Braves were World Series losers.

October 12

1856 — Charles Smith, 1889–1890; b.

1869 — Malachi Kittredge, 1901–03; b.

1903 — Dutch Holland, 1932–33; b.

1912 — Ed Moriarty, 1935–36; b.

1914 — The Braves won their third in as many World Series games against Philadelphia. Joe Bush's wild throw in the 12th inning allowed the winning run to score. The Braves nearly lost in the 10th inning when Johnny Evers kicked a groundball and then held onto it as two runs scored. Hank Gowdy had two doubles and a homer, and Bill James pitched two innings of scoreless relief as the Braves won, 5–4.

1916 — Sam Gentile, 1943; b.

October 13

1858 — Fred Lewis, 1881; b.

1914 — The Braves completed their Miracle Year by completing a sweep of the heavily-favored Philadelphia Athletics, the first four-game sweep in World Series history. Johnny Evers's two-run single in the fifth inning proved to be enough. Dick Rudolph recorded his second win of the Series.

1931 — Eddie Mathews, 1952–66; b.

1951 — Bob Addis was shipped to the Cubs for Jack Cusick.

1952 — Frank LaCorte, 1975–79; b.

1959 — Mickey Vernon and Enos Slaughter were released.

1966 — Lee Bales, Dan Schneider, and Tom Dukes were traded to the Astros for Ed Pacheco, John Hoffman, and Gene Ratliff.

October 14

1857 — Tom Poorman, 1885–86; b.

1861 — Paul Radford, 1883; b.

1897 — Dinty Gearin, 1924; b.

1915 — Max Macon, 1944; 1947; b.

1924 — Dave Jolly, 1953–57; b.

1960 — Red Schoendienst and Stan Lopata were released.

1971 — Lew Burdette was named pitching coach.

October 15

1860 — Edgar Smith, 1883; b.

1889 — Chick Evans, 1909–1910; b.

1892 — Jack Stivetts of the Braves threw a five-inning perfect game at Washington, winning, 6–0. It was the second game of a doubleheader, called because of darkness.

1893 — Gil Whitehouse, 1912; b.

1896 — Mule Watson, 1920–23; b.

1904 — Bill Lewis, 1935–36; b.

1939 — Lou Klimchock, 1962–65; b.

1957 — Dave Jolly was sold to the Giants.

1959 — The Braves obtained Charlie Lau and Don Lee from the Tigers for Don Kaiser, Mike Roarke, and Casey Wise.

October 16

1866 — Fred Lake, 1891; 1897; 1910; b.

1879 — Art Devlin, 1912–13; b.

1902 — Grapefruit Yeargin, 1922; 1924; b.

1909 — John Hill, 1939; b.

1979 — Darrell Chaney was released.

October 17

1915 — Mike Sandlock, 1942; 1944; b.

1919 — Charlie Cozart, 1945; b.

1979 — Jamie Easterly was traded to the Expos for a player to be named later.

October 18

1859 — Cliff Carroll, 1893; b.

1868 — Boileryard Clark, 1899–1900; b.

1952 — Jerry Royster, 1976–   ; b.

1963 — Amado Samuel was sold to the Mets.

October 19

1869 — Ralph McLeod, 1938; b.

1874 — Tom McCreery, 1903; b.

1887 — Fred Snodgrass, 1915–16; b.

1893 — Lloyd Christenbury, 1919–22; b.

1930 — Joe Koppe, 1958; b.

1943 — Sandy Alomar, 1964–66; b.

1950 — Ground was broken for Milwaukee County Stadium.

October 20

1862 — Marty Sullivan, 1890–91; b.

1972 — Tony LaRussa was traded to the Cubs for Tom Phoebus.

October 21

1863 — George Rooks, 1891; b.

1909 — Bill Lee, 1945–46; b.

1916 — Eddie Carnett, 1941; b.

1964 — The Braves Board of Directors formally requested the National League to approve the transfer of the franchise to Atlanta.

1969 — The Braves obtained Dave Wickersham from the Athletics for Ron Tompkins.

October 22

1856 — Dan O'Leary, 1880; b.

1857 — Ed Rowen, 1882; b.

1866 — Michael Madden, 1887–89; b.

1900 — Jumbo Elliott, 1934; b.

1920 — Jim Hickey, 1942; 1944; b.

1942 — Cecil Upshaw, 1966–69; 1971–73; b.

October 23

1866 — Mike Sullivan, 1898–99; b.

1886 — Lena Blackburne, 1919; b.

1974 — Norm Miller and Sonny Jackson were released.

October 24

1895 — Al Pierotti, 1920–21; b.

October 25

1868 — Dan Burke, 1892; b.

1871 — Marty Bergen, 1896–99; b.

1887 — Oscar Dugey, 1913–14; 1920; b.

1918 — Nanny Fernandez, 1942; 1946–47; b.

1923 — Bobby Thomson, 1954–57; b.

1925 — Roy Hartsfield, 1950–52; b.

1937 — Casey Stengel agreed to terms to manage the 1938 club.

1944 — Skip Guinn, 1968; b.

1952 — Rowland Office, 1972; 1974–79; b.

1955 — Tommy Boggs, 1978–   ; b.

October 26

1859 — Frank Selee, 1890–1901; b.

1866 — Pete Sommers, 1888; b.

1884 — Chet Chadbourne, 1918; b.

1889 — Tommy Griffith, 1913–14; b.

1959 — Stan Lopata and Andy Pafko were released.

October 27

1922 — Del Rice, 1955–59; b.

1945 — Mike Lum, 1967–75; 1979–   ; b.

1953 — Barry Bonnell, 1977–79; b.

1961 — Sammy White was released.

1972 — Rico Carty was traded to the Texas Rangers for Jim Panther.

1977 — Junior Moore was granted free agency.

October 28

1863 — Tommy Tucker, 1890–97; b.

1877 — Vive Lindaman, 1906–09; b.

1886 — Ed McDonald, 1911–12; b.

1899 — Percy Jones, 1929; b.

1900 — Johnny Neun, 1930–31; b.

1925 — Luis Marquez, 1951; b.

1970 — Jimmie Hall was released.

October 29

1944 — Gary Niebauer, 1969–73; b.

October 30

1871 — Buck Freeman, 1900; b.

1874 — Sam Curran, 1902; b.

1891 — Charlie Deal, 1913–14; b.

1917 — Bobby Bragan, 1963–66; b.

1927 — Joe Adcock, 1953–62; b.

1975 — After receiving negative fan reaction from across the country, the Braves fired a chimpanzee they had hired to sweep the bases after the fifth inning of each game.

October 31

1874 — Harry Smith, 1908–1910; b.

1904 — Allyn Stout, 1943; b.

1910 — Mickey Haslin, 1936; b.

1913 — Warren Huston, 1944; b.

NOVEMBER 1

1892 — Earl Blackburn, 1915–16; b.

1979 — Rowland Office was granted free agency.

November 2

1924 — George Estock, 1951; b.

1927 — Jack Slattery was named manager for the 1928 season.

1942 — Ron Reed, 1966–75; b.

1943 — Max Macon was drafted from the Brooklyn farm system.

1946 — Tom Paciorek, 1976–78; b.

1951 — Chico Ruiz, 1978; b.

1957 — Bill Herman signed on as a third-base coach.

1974 — Henry Aaron was traded to the Milwaukee Brewers for Dave May and a player to be named later (Roger Alexander was sent to the Braves on December 2). In a home run contest at Korakuen Stadium in Tokyo, Aaron beat Sadaharu Oh, 10–9.

November 3

1866 — Harry Staley, 1891–94; b.

1875 — Phil Geier, 1904; b.

1890 — Larry Kopf, 1922–23; b.

1946 — Garry Hill, 1969; b.

November 4

1927 — Carl Sawatski, 1957–58; b.

1933 — Tito Francona, 1967–69; b.

November 5

Nothing of importance happened on this date.

November 6

1891 — Red Torphy, 1920; b.

1893 — Dana Fillingim, 1918–1923; b.

1907 — Earl Clark, 1927–33; b.

1911 — Frank Gabler, 1937–38; b.

1920 — George Stallings, whose winning percentage went down every year after 1914, resigned.

1922 — Buddy Kerr, 1950–51; b.

1925 — Bob Addis, 1950–51; b.

1938 — Mack Jones, 1961–63; 1965–67; b.

1945 — Billy Southworth signed to manage the 1946 club.

1973 — Herm Starette was named pitching coach.

November 7

1872 — Billy Ging, 1899; b.

1910 — Bill Brubaker, 1943; b.

1919 — Tommy Neill, 1946–47; b.

1944 — Joe Niekro, 1973–74; b.

November 8

1901 — Frank McGowan, 1937; b.

1907 — Tony Cuccinello, 1936–40; 1942–43; b.

1922 — Bob Brady, 1946–47; b.

1974 — Danny Frisella was traded to the Padres for Cito Gaston.

November 9

1916 — Walt Lanfranconi, 1947; b.

November 10

1873 — Billy Lush, 1901–02; b.

1886 — Jimmy Riley, 1910; b.

1890 — Eddie Eayrs, 1920–21; b.

1912 — Birdie Tebbetts, 1961–62; b.

1930 — Gene Conley, 1952; 1954–58; b.

November 11

1859 — Mert Hackett, 1883–85; b.

1891 — Rabbit Maranville, 1912–20; 1929–33; 1935; b.

1899 — Bill Vargus, 1925–26; b.

1912 — Al Wright, 1933; b.

1919 — Glenn Elliott, 1947–49; b.

November 12

1868 — John Ryan, 1894–96; b.

1875 — Fred Raymer, 1904–5; b.

1922 — Bill Reed, 1952; b.

1923 — The Braves obtained Casey Stengel, Bill Cunningham, and Dave Bancroft in a trade with the Yankees.

1927 — Harry Hanebrink, 1953; 1957–58; b.

1936 — Joe Hoerner, 1972–73; b.

November 13

1878 — Otto Hess, 1912–15; b.

1887 — Josh Devore, 1914; b.

1905 — Milt Shoffner, 1937–39; b.

1945 — Gene Garber, 1978–   ; b.

1957 — Henry Aaron was named National League MVP over Stan Musial.

1980 — In the free-agent re-entry draft, the Braves selected Stan Bahnsen, Gaylord Perry, Dave Roberts, Don Sutton, Claudell Washington, and Dave Winfield.

November 14

1890 — Gene Cocreham, 1913–15; b.

1980 — Claudell Washington, selected in the free-agent draft the day before, signed a five-year contract.

November 15

1881 — Jack Schulte, 1906; b.

1888 — Pat Ragan, 1915–19; b.

1901 — Bunny Roser, 1922; b.

1913 — Swede Larson, 1936; b.

1914 — Mickey Livingston, 1949; b.

1928 — Gus Bell, 1962–64; b.

 Norm Roy, 1950; b.

1935 — Jack Smith, 1964; b.

November 16

1905 — Ab Wright, 1944; b.

1931 — Frank Bolling, 1961–66; b.

1957 — Casey Wise was obtained from the Cubs for minor leaguers Chick King, Len Williams, and Ben Johnson.

November 17

1857 — Pat Deasley, 1881–82; b.

1867 — George Stallings, 1912–1920; b.

1886 — Fred Beck, 1909–1910; b.

1901 — Eddie Taylor, 1926; b.

1933 — Dan Osinski, 1965; b.

1938 — Aubrey Gatewood, 1970; b.

1975 — The Braves obtained Jim Wynn and Tom Paciorek, as well as Lee Lacy and Jerry Royster from the Dodgers, for Dusty Baker and Ed Goodson.

1976 — Gary Matthews signed as a free agent.

November 18

1893 — Les Mann, 1913-14; 1919-20; 1924-27; b.

1909 — Joe Coscarart, 1935-36; b.

1925 — Gene Mauch, 1950-51; b.

1947 — Johnny Hopp and Danny Murtaugh were traded to the Pirates for Jim Russell, Bill Salkeld, and Al Lyons.

November 19

1926 — Bob Thorpe, 1951-53; b.

1930 — Joe Morgan, 1959; b.

1938 — Ted Turner (owner); b.

November 20

1888 — Ray Powell, 1917-24; b.

1897 — Larry Benton, 1923-27; 1935; b.

1898 — Tim McNamara, 1922-25; b.

1906 — Joe Ogrodowski, 1925; b.

1951 — Scout Ed Scott signed Henry Aaron to an Indianapolis Clowns contract.

1953 — Duane Theiss, 1977-78; b.

1979 — Al Hrabosky signed as a free agent.

November 21

1851 — Bobby Mathews, 1881-82; b.

1854 — Charlie Bennett, 1889-93; b.

1897 — Andy High, 1925-27; b.

1905 — Les Mallin, 1934-35; b.

November 22

1926 — Lew Burdette, 1951-63; b.

1943 — Wade Blasingame, 1963-67; b.

1953 — Rick Matula, 1979–   ; b.

1977 — Bobby Cox became the Atlanta Braves' seventh full-time manager.

November 23

1897 — Fred Leach, 1932; b.

1913 — Les Scarsella, 1940; b.

1914 — Mel Preibisch, 1940–41; b.

1915 — Bob Kahle, 1938; b.

1940 — Luis Tiant (Richmond farmhand, 1971); b.

1947 — Frank Tepedino, 1973–75; b.

1959 — Brook Jacoby, 1981–   ; b.

1964 — The Mets purchased Warren Spahn.

November 24

1853 — Bill Hawes, 1879; b.

1876 — Harvey Bailey, 1899–1900; b.

1911 — Joe Medwick, 1945; b.

November 25

1848 — Sam Wright, 1876; 1881; b.

1893 — Gene Bailey, 1919–20; b.

1946 — Wenty Ford, 1973; b.

November 26

1866 — Hugh Duffy, 1892–1900; b.

1871 — Fred Tenney, 1894–1911; b.

1916 — Bob Elliott, 1947–51; b.

Eddie Miller, 1939–42; b.

1956 — Bob Walf, 1981–   ; b.

November 27

1918 — Pat Capri, 1944; b.

1962 — Joe Adcock and Jack Curtis were traded to the Cleveland Indians for Don Dillard, Frank Funk, and a player to be named later.

1967 — Charlie Lau was released.

November 28

1891 — Frank O'Rourke, 1912; b.

1916 — Max West 1938–1942; 1946; b.

1928 — Doc Queen, 1954; b.

1960 — Dick Brown was purchased from the White Sox.

1961 — Frank Thomas was traded to the Mets for cash and a player to be named.

November 29

1864 — Bill Sowders, 1888–89; b.

1966 — The Braves traded ChiChi Olivo and Bill Robinson to the Yankees for Clete Boyer and a player to be named.

1977 — Bobby Cox named Cloyd Boyer, Pete Ward, and Tom Burgess as coaches.

November 30

1870 — Frank Killen, 1899; b.

1883 — Ben Houser, 1911–12; b.

1901 — Sid Graves, 1927; b.

1972 — Earl Williams and Taylor Duncan were traded to Baltimore for Johnny Oates, Pat Dobson, Roric Harrison, and Dave Johnson.

DECEMBER 1

1882 — Ed Reulbach, 1916–17; b.

1914 — Braves President James Gaffney announced the purchase of the Allston Golf Club property near Boston University, the future site of Braves Field.

1962 — Ken Aspromonte was traded to the Mets for Jim McKnight.

December 2

1891 — Larry Gilbert, 1914–15; b.

1951 — Adrian Devine, 1973; 1975–76; 1978–80; b.

1968 — The Braves drafted Darrell Evans from Vancouver (Oakland A's farm team).

1971 — Bob Tillman was traded to the Brewers for Hank Allen, Paul Click, and John Ryan.

December 2 (continued)

1971 — Hal King was traded to Texas for Paul Casanova.

1974 — The Braves obtained Roger Alexander from the Brewers to complete the November 2 deal involving Henry Aaron and Dave May.

December 3

1872 — Cozy Dolan, 1895–96; 1905–6; b.

1895 — Bill Anderson, 1925; b.

1902 — Al Spohrer, 1928–1935; b.

1936 — Dave Eilers, 1964–65; b.

1960 — The Braves bought Billy Martin from the Reds.

1963 — The Braves obtained Felipe Alou, Billy Hoeft, Ed Bailey, and a player to be named, from the Giants, for Bob Hendley, Bob Shaw, and Del Crandall.

1968 — Deron Johnson was sold to the Phillies.

1969 — Felipe Alou was traded to the A's for Jumbo Jim Nash.

1973 — Ron Schueler was sent to the Phillies for Craig Robinson and Barry Lerch.

1974 — The Braves obtained Dick Allen from the White Sox for a player to be named.

1979 — The Braves obtained Bill Nahorodny from the White Sox for Rick Wieters.

December 4

1916 — Ray Sanders, 1946; 1948–49; b.

1942 — Eddie Miller was sent to the Reds for Eddie Joost and Nate Andrews.

1944 — Lee Bales, 1966; b.

December 5

1868 — Frank Bowerman, 1908–9; b.

1871 — Tom Smith, 1894; b.

1873 — Mike Mahoney, 1897; b.

1901 — Ray Moss, 1931; b.

1911 — Don Padgett, 1946; b.

1957 — Taylor Phillips and Sammy Taylor sent to the Cubs for Bob Rush, Don Kaiser, and Ed Haas.

1979 — Pat Rockett, Barry Bonnell, and Joey McLaughlin sent to the Blue Jays for Chris Chambliss and Luis Gomez.

December 6

1873 — Harry Wolverton, 1905; b.

1938 — Amado Samuel, 1962–63; b.

Federico Velazquez, 1973; b.

1939 — The Braves obtained Jim Tobin from the Pirates for John Lanning.

Jim Turner was sent to Cincinnati for Les Scarsella.

1942 — Arnie Umbach, 1964, 1966; b.

1959 — Steve Bedrosian, 1981–   ; b.

1979 — Adrian Devine, Pepe Frias, and a player to be named were sent to the Rangers for Doyle Alexander and Sugar Bear Blanks.

December 7

1847 — Deacon White, 1877; b.

1863 — Tom Lovett, 1894; b.

1927 — Dick Donovan, 1950–52; b.

1935 — Don Cardwell, 1970; b.

1953 — George Metkovich was purchased from the Cubs.

1960 — Billy Bruton, Chuck Cottier, Terry Fox, and Dick Brown were shipped to the Tigers for Frank Bolling and Neil Chrisley.

1967 — Bobby Cox was traded to the Yankees for Bob Tillman and Dale Roberts.

December 8

1874 — Joe Connor, 1900; b.

1939 — Dan MacFayden was sent to the Pirates for Bill Swift.

1977 — Andy Messersmith was sold to the Yankees.

Willie Montanez was traded to the Rangers for Adrian Devine, Tommy Boggs, and Eddie Miller. The Rangers then traded Montanez, Tom Grieve, and a player to be named to the Mets for John Milner and Jon Matlack. (Ken Henderson was later sent to the Rangers to complete the deal.) Texas then sent Milner and Bert Blyleven to the Pirates for Al Oliver and Nelson Norman.

December 9

1871 — Joe Kelley, 1891; 1908; b.

1872 — Cy Seymour, 1913; b.

December 9 (continued)

1889 — Ed Fitzpatrick, 1915–17; b.

1914 — Hank Camelli, 1947; b.

1917 — George Woodwend, 1944; b.

1928 — Billy Klaus, 1952–53; b.

1930 — Bob Hazle, 1957–58; b.

1946 — Red Barrett was purchased from St. Louis.

1976 — The Braves obtained Jeff Burroughs from the Rangers for Ken Henderson, Dave May, Carl Morton, Rogelio Moret, Adrian Devine, and $250,000.

December 10

1889 — Jimmy Johnston, 1926; b.

1897 — Art Conlon, 1923; b.

1931 — Bob Roselli, 1955–56; 1958; b.

1939 — Bob Priddy, 1969–1971; b.

1973 — Bob Beall obtained from the Phillies for Gil Garrido.

December 11

1854 — Old Hoss Radbourn, 1886–89; b.

1885 — Art Wilson, 1918–20; b.

1886 — Joe Riggert, 1919; b.

1896 — Cy Morgan, 1921–22; b.

1905 — Al Weston, 1929; b.

1925 — Dick Hoover, 1952; b.

1930 — Johnny O'Brien, 1959; b.

1934 — Lee Maye, 1959–65; b.

1970 — Rico Carty broke a leg in a collision with Matty Alou during a Dominican League game. Carty missed the 1971 season because of it.

December 12

1876 — Joe Rickert, 1901; b.

1904 — Ray Boggs, 1928; b.

1917 — Clyde Kluttz, 1942–45; b.

1935 — Ed Brandt and Randolph Moore were sent to the Dodgers for Al Lopez, Ray Berge, Tony Cuccinello, and Bobby Reis.

1945 — Ralph Garr, 1968–1975; b.

1975 — Tom House was sent to the Red Sox for Rogelio Moret.

Mike Lum was sent to the Reds for Darrell Chaney.

Ralph Garr and Larvell Blanks were sent to the White Sox for Ken Henderson, Dick Ruthven, and Danny Osborne.

1980 — The Braves obtained John Montefusco and Craig Landis from the Giants for Doyle Alexander.

December 13

1882 — Gene Good, 1906; b.

1887 — Frank Hershey, 1905; b.

1916 — Hank Majeski, 1939–41; b.

1931 — Bubba Morton, 1963; b.

1938 — Eugene Moore and Ira Hutchinson were traded to the Dodgers for Jimmy Outlaw and Buddy Hassett.

1976 — Steve Kline was purchased from the Indians.

1977 — Steve Hargan was released.

December 14

1889 — Lefty Tyler, 1910–1917; b.

1901 — Les Bell, 1928–29; b.

1929 — Pete Whisenant, 1952; b.

1949 — Bill Voiselle was traded to the Cubs for Gene Mauch.

December 15

1863 — Bill Van Dyke, 1893; b.

1906 — Tom Kane, 1938; b.

1948 — Mike McCormick was traded to the Dodgers for Pete Reiser.

1960 — Juan Pizarro and Joey Jay were traded to the Reds for Roy McMillan and a player to be named.

1961 — Joe Azcue, Ed Charles, and Manny Jimenez were traded to the Athletics for Bob Shaw and Lou Klimchock.

1965 — Dan Osinski and Bob Sadowski were traded to the Red Sox for Lee Thomas and Arnold Earley.

1966 — Free-agent Pablo Torrealba signed.

December 16

1856 — Pete Hotaling, 1882; b.

1876 — Fred Crolius, 1901; b.

1891 — Fred Tyler, 1914; b.

1898 — Dee Cousineau, 1923–25; b.

1931 — Neil Chrisley, 1961; b.

1938 — Ray Mueller was traded to the Pirates for Al Todt and Johnny Dickshot.

1974 — Lew Krausse was released.

December 17

1892 — Tex Covington, 1917–18; b.

December 18

1897 — Lancelot Richbourg, 1927–31; b.

1906 — Dick Coffman, 1940; b.

1915 — Johnny Barrett, 1946; b.

1929 — Gino Cimoli, 1961; b.

1939 — Zoilo Versalles, 1971; b.

1970 — The Braves announced that Savannah would be the new AA club.

December 19

1875 — Kid O'Hara, 1904; b.

1887 — Art Butler, 1911; b.

1893 — Paul Strand, 1913–15; b.

1936 — Eddie Mayo was purchased from the Giants.

December 20

1853 — Jack Manning, 1876; 1878; b.

1856 — Harry Stovey, 1891–92; b.

1891 — Joe Wilhoit, 1916–17; b.

1972 — Jim Breazeale and Mike McQueen were injured in a car accident in Uvalde, Texas.

December 21

1869 — Joe Harrington, 1895–96; b.

1882 — Charlie Weeden, 1911; b.

1884 — Steve White, 1912; b.

1897 — Hal Haid, 1931; b.

1913 — Heinie Heltzel, 1943; b.

1925 — Bob Rush, 1958–60; b.

1927 — Jack "Sour Mash" Daniels, 1952; b.

1951 — Larry Bradford, 1977; 1979-   ; b.

December 22

1861 — Edward Tate, 1885–88; b.

1908 — Ed Fallenstin, 1933; b.

1910 — Stan Klopp, 1944; b.

1923 — Bob Hall, 1949–50; b.

1929 — Billy Bruton, 1953–60; b.

1970 — Don Cardwell was released.

December 23

1883 — San Frock, 1907; 1910–11; b.

1901 — Ox Eckhardt, 1932; b.

1943 — Dave May, 1975–76; b.

December 24

1869 — Zeke Wilson, 1895; b.

December 24 (continued)

1877 — Del Howard, 1906–7; b.

1913 — George Jeffcoat, 1943; b.

1959 — Rico Carty signed as a free agent.

December 25

1864 — Joe Quinn, 1888–89; 1891–92; b.

1871 — Mike Hickey, 1899; b.

1872 — Ted Lewis, 1896–1900; b.

1892 — Walter Holke, 1919–1922; b.

1899 — Gene Robertson, 1929–1930; b.

1901 — Buster Chatham, 1930–31; b.

1904 — Bill Akers, 1932; b.

December 26

1895 — Bonnie Hollingsworth, 1928; b.

1901 — Doc Farrell, 1927–29; b.

1902 — Bill Cronin, 1928–31; b.

1927 — Stu Miller, 1968; b.

1936 — Wayne Causey, 1968; b.

1939 — John Brown, 1964; b.

1940 — Ray Sadecki, 1975; b.

1940 — Earl Torgeson was purchased from Seattle (PCL).

1948 — Chris Chambliss, 1980–   ; b.

1953 — Max Surkont, Larry LaSalle, Fred Waters, Sid Gordon, Sam Jethroe, and $70K were sent to the Pirates for Danny O'Connell.

December 27

1885 — Jiggs Parsons, 1910–1911; b.

1912 — Jim Tobin, 1940–45; b.

1930 — Norm Larker, 1963; b.

1941 — Chief Nokahoma (mascot); b.

December 28

1888 — John Henry, 1918; b.

1923 — Don Thompson, 1949; b.

1924 — Steve Kuczek, 1949; b.

December 29

Nothing of importance happened on this date.

December 30

1931 — Frank Torre, 1956-60; b.

December 31

1857 — King Kelly, 1887-89; 1891-92; b.

1918 — Al Lakeman, 1949; b.

1925 — Dick Manville, 1950; b.

1941 — Paul Casanova, 1972-74; b.

1966 — Arnold Umbach and Eddie Mathews were traded to the Astros for Dave Nicholson and Bob Bruce.

BOSTON BRAVES ALL-TIME ROSTER, 1876–1952

Ed Abbaticchio, 1903–5, 1910, 2B/SS
Bob Addis, 1950–51, OF
Morrie Aderholt, 1945, P
Bill Akers, 1932, 3B
Bob Allen, 1897, SS
Frank Allen, 1916–17, P
Myron Allen, 1886, 2B
Bill Anderson, 1925, P
Nate Andrews, 1943–45, P
Stan Andrews, 1939–40, C
Bill Annis, 1884, OF
Johnny Antonelli, 1948–50, P*
Tom Asmussen, 1907, C
Harvey Aubrey, 1903, SS
Chick Autry, 1909, OF
Earl Averill, 1941, OF
Johnny Babich, 1936, P
Bill Bagwell, 1923, OF
Fred Bailey, 1916–18, OF
Gene Bailey, 1919–1920, OF
Harvey Bailey, 1899–1900, P
Mike Balas, 1938, P
Jim Ball, 1907–08, C
Dave Bancroft, 1924–27, SS
Bill Banks, 1895–96, P
Jimmy Bannon, 1894–96, OF
Walter Barbare, 1921–22, IF
Frank Barberich, 1907, P
George Barclay, 1904–5, OF
Red Barkley, 1939, IF
Jesse Barnes, 1915–17, 1923–25, P
Ross Barnes, 1881, SS
Virgil Barnes, 1928, P
George Barnicle, 1939–41, P
Dick Barrett, 1934, P
Frank Barrett, 1946, P
Johnny Barrett, 1946, OF
Marty Barrett, 1884, C
Red Barrett, 1943–45, 1947–49, P
Red Barron, 1929, OF
Shad Barry, 1900–1, UT
Doc Bass, 1918, PH
Joe Batchelder, 1923–25, P
Johnny Bates, 1906–9, OF
Ginger Beaumont, 1907–9, OF
Johnny Beazley, 1947–49, P
Fred Beck, 1909–10, OF/1B
Beals Becker, 1908–9, OF
Les Bell, 1928–29, 3B
Ray Benge, 1936, P

Charlie Bennett, 1889–93, C
Larry Benton, 1923–27, 1935, P
Marty Bergen, 1896–99, C
Wally Berger, 1930–37, OF
John Bergh, 1880, C
Ray Berres, 1940–41, C
Huck Betts, 1932–35, P
Vern Bickford, 1948–52, P*
Earl Blackburn, 1915–16, C
Lena Blackburne, 1919, 3B
Al Blanche, 1935–36, P
Tony Boeckel, 1919–23, 3B
Ray Boggs, 1928, P
Tommy Bond, 1877–81, P/OF
Frank Bonner, 1903, IF
Al Bool, 1931, C
Joe Bordon, 1876, P
Jake Boultes, 1907–9, P
Frank Bowerman, 1908–9, C/1B
Buzz Boyle, 1929–30, OF
Foghorn Bradley, 1876, P
Bill Brady, 1912, P
Bob Brady, 1946–47, C/PH
King Brady, 1912, P
Dave Brain, 1906–7, 3B
Ed Brandt, 1928–35, P
Kitty Bransfield, 1898, C/1B
Garland Braxton, 1921–22, P
Buster Bray, 1941, OF
Al Bridwell, 1906–7, 1911–12, SS
Steve Brodie, 1890–91, OF
Siggy Broskie, 1940, C
Dan Brouthers, 1889, 1B
Bob Brown, 1930–36, P
Buster Brown, 1909–13, P
Drummond Brown, 1913, C
Eddie Brown, 1926–28, OF
Fred Brown, 1901–2, OF
Lew Brown, 1876–77, 1883, C
Sam Brown, 1906–7, UT
Tom Brown, 1888–89, OF
George Browne, 1908, OF
Bill Brubaker, 1943, IF
Bob Brush, 1907, 1B
Charlie Brynan, 1891, P
Art Bues, 1913, IF
Charlie Buffinton, 1882–86, P/OF
Lew Burdette, 1951–52, P*
Jack Burdock, 1878–88, 2B
Pete Burg, 1910, 3B

---

*Indicates that man played for Braves in another city as well.

Billy Burke, 1910–11, P
Dan Burke, 1892, C
Frank Burke, 1907, OF
Joe Burns, 1943, 3B
Paul Burris, 1948, 1950, 1952, C*
Dick Burrus, 1925–28, 1B
Guy Bush, 1936–37, P
Art Butler, 1911, IF
Bill Calhoun, 1913, 1B
Joe Callahan, 1939–40, P
Hank Camelli, 1947, C
John Cameron, 1906, OF/P
Vin Campbell, 1912, OF
Hugh Canaban, 1918, P
Rip Cannell, 1904–5, OF
Ben Cantwell, 1928–36, P
Pat Capri, 1944, 2B
Ben Cardoni, 1943–45, P
Eddie Carnett, 1941, P
Pat Carney, 1901–4, OF/P
Cliff Carroll, 1893, OF
Dixie Carroll, 1919, OF
Ted Cather, 1914–15, OF
Red Causey, 1919, P
Chet Chadbourne, 1918, OF
Rome Chambers, 1900, P
Tiny Chaplin, 1936, P
Larry Chappell, 1916–17, OF
Bill Chappelle, 1908–9, P
Buster Chatham, 1930–31, IF
Larry Cheney, 1919, P
Bob Chipman, 1950–52, P
Lloyd Christenbury, 1919–22, UT
Earl Clark, 1927–33, OF
Boileryard Clarke, 1899–1900, C
Josh Clarke, 1911, OF
Bill Clarkson, 1928–29, P
Buzz Clarkson, 1952, IF
Dad Clarkson, 1892, P
John Clarkson, 1888–92, P/OF
Chet Clemens, 1939, OF
Jack Clements, 1900, C
Otis Clymer, 1913, OF
Gene Cocreham, 1913–15, P
Jack Coffey, 1909, SS
Dick Coffman, 1940, P
Ed Cogswell, 1879, 1B
Dave Cole, 1950–52, P*
Bill Coliver, 1885, OF
Bill Collins, 1910–11, OF
Cyril Collins, 1913–14, OF
Jimmy Collins, 1895–1900, 3B
Pat Collins, 1929, C

Zip Collins, 1915–17, OF
Pete Compton, 1915–16, OF
Clint Conaster, 1948–49, OF
Gene Conley, 1952, P*
Art Conlon, 1923, IF
Frank Connaughton, 1894, 1906, UT
Joe Connolly, 1913–16, OF
Joe Connor, 1900, C
John Connor, 1884, P
Dick Conway, 1887–88, P
Rip Conway, 1918, IF
Duff Cooley, 1901–4, OF/1B
Bill Cooney, 1909–10, P/UT
Jimmy Cooney, 1928, IF
Johnny Cooney, 1921–30, 1938–42, P/OF/1B
Mort Cooper, 1945–47, P
Walker Cooper, 1950–52, C*
Joe Coscarart, 1935–36, UT
Ensign Cottrell, 1914, P
Ernie Courtney, 1902, OF
Dee Cousineau, 1923–25, C
Tex Covington, 1917–18, 1B/PH
Bill Coyle, 1893, P
Charlie Cozart, 1945, P
Del Crandall, 1949–50, C*
Doc Crandall, 1918, P/OF
Connie Creedon, 1943, PH
Fred Crolius, 1901, OF
Bill Cronin, 1928–31, C
George Crowe, 1952, 1B*
Bill Crowley, 1881, OF
Walton Cruise, 1919–24, OF
Cal Crum, 1917–18, P
Dick Crutcher, 1914–15, P
Tony Ciccinello, 1936–40, 1942–43; IF
Dick Culler, 1944–47, SS
Jack Cummings, 1929, C
Bill Cunningham, 1924, OF
Bruce Cunningham, 1929–32, P
Nig Cuppy, 1900, P
Sam Curran, 1902, P
Cliff Curtis, 1909–11, P
Jack Cusick, 1952, IF
John Dagenhard, 1943, P
Bill Dahlen, 1908–9, IF
Babe Dahlgren, 1941, 1B
Con Daily, 1886–87, C
Bill Daly, 1889, P
Joe Daly, 1892, C
Bill Dam, 1909, OF
Jack Daniels, 1952, OF
Alvin Dark, 1946, 1948–49, SS*

Daisy Davis, 1884–85, P
George Davis, 1913–15, P
Charlie Deal, 1913–14, 3B
Pat Dealey, 1885–86, UT
Pat Deasley, 1881-82, P
Jim Delahanty, 1904–5, UT
Art Delaney, 1928–29, P
Al Demaree, 1919, P
Frank Demaree, 1941–42, OF
Gene DeMontreville, 1901–2, IF
Rube Dessau, 1907, P
Ducky Detweiler, 1942, 3B/PH
Art Devlin, 1912–13, UT
Rex DeVogt, 1913, C
Josh Devore, 1914, OF
Charlie Dexter, 1902–3, UT
Walt Dickson, 1912–13, P
Ernie Diehl, 1906, OF
George Diehl, 1942–43, P
Steve Dignan, 1880, OF
Vince DiMaggio, 1937–38, OF
Bill Dinneen, 1900–1, P
Jack Dittmer, 1952, 2B*
Cozy Dolan, 1895–96, 1905–6, UT
Art Doll, 1935–36, 1938, P
Mike Donlin, 1911, OF
Blix Donnelly, 1951, P
Ed Donnelly, 1911–12, P
Bill Donovan, 1942–43, P
Dick Donovan, 1950–52, P
Patsy Donovan, 1890, OF
Gus Dorner, 1906–9, P
Bill Dreesen, 1931, 3B
Bob Dresser, 1902, P
Frank Drews, 1944–45, 2B
John Dudra, 1941, UT
Hugh Duffy, 1892–1900, OF
Joe Dugan, 1929, UT
Oscar Dugey, 1913–14, 1920, UT
Bill Dunlap, 1929–30, OF
Tom Earley, 1938–42, 1945, P
Mal Eason, 1902, P
Eddie Eayrs, 1920–21, OF/P
Ox Eckhardt, 1932, PH
Foster Edwards, 1925–28, P
Dick Egan, 1915–16, UT
Bob Elliott, 1947–51, 3B
Glenn Elliot, 1947–49, P
Jumbo Elliott, 1934, P
Rowdy Elliott, 1910, C
Bob Emmerich, 1923, OF
Gil English, 1937–38, UT
Dick Errickson, 1938–42, P

George Estock, 1951, P
Buck Etchison, 1943–44, 1B
Chick Evans, 1909–10, P
Johnny Evers, 1914–17, 1929, 2B
Ed Fallenstin, 1933, P
Doc Farrell, 1927–29, IF
Kerby Farrell, 1943, 1B/P
Gus Felix, 1923–25, OF
George Ferguson, 1908–11, P
Nanny Fernandez, 1942, 1946–47, UT
Wes Farrell, 1941, P
Lou Fette, 1937–40, 1945, P
Dana Fillingim, 1918–23, P
Tom Fisher, 1904, P
Charlie Fitzberger, 1928, PH
Ed Fitzpatrick, 1915–17, UT
Patsy Flaherty, 1907–8, 1911, P/OF
Elbie Fletcher, 1934–35, 1937–39, 1949,
  1B
Curry Foley, 1879–80, P/OF/1B
Gene Ford, 1936, P
Hod Ford, 1919–23, 1932–33, IF
Jack Fournier, 1927, 1B
John Fox, 1881, P
Fred Frankhouse, 1930–35, 1939, P
Chick Fraser, 1905, P
Vic Frazier, 1937, P
Buck Freeman, 1900, OF/1B
Howard Freigau, 1928, IF
Hon Fricken, 1890, P
Charlie Frisbee, 1899, OF
Sam Frock, 1907, 1910–11, P
Frank Gabler, 1937–38, P
Gil Gallagher, 1922, SS
Daff Gammons, 1901, UT
Charlie Ganzel, 1889–97, C/UT
Debs Garms, 1937–39, UT
Jim Garry, 1893, P
Hank Gastright, 1893, P
Doc Gautreau, 1925–28, 2B
Dinty Gearin, 1924, P
Phil Geier, 1904, UT
Joe Genewich, 1922–28, P
Sam Gentile, 1943, PH
Lefty George, 1918, P
Ben Geraghty, 1943–44, UT
Lefty Gervais, 1913, P
Gus Getz, 1909–10, UT
Charlie Getzein, 1890–91, P
Frank Gibson, 1921–27, C
Larry Gilbert, 1914–15, OF
Carden Gillenwater, 1945–46, OF
Billy Ging, 1899, P

Roland Gladu, 1944, 3B
Ed Glenn, 1888, OF
Al Glossop, 1940, UT
Hal Goldsmith, 1926-28, P
Mike Gonzalez, 1912, C
Gene Good, 1906, OF
Ralph Good, 1910, P
Wilbur Good, 1910-11, OF
Sid Gordon, 1950-52, OF/3B*
Hank Gowdy, 1911-17, 1919-23, 1929-30, C
Kyle Graham, 1924-26, P
Peaches Graham, 1908-11, C
Sid Graves, 1927, OF
Kent Greenfield, 1927-29, P
Ed Gremminger, 1902-3, 3B
Buddy Gremp, 1940-42, IF
Hank Griffin, 1911-12, P
Tommy Griffith, 1913-14, OF
Burleigh Grimes, 1930, P
George Grosart, 1901, OF
Tom Gunning, 1884-86, C
Dick Gyselman, 1933-34, IF
Mert Hackett, 1883-85, C
Walter Hackett, 1885, IF
Mickey Haefner, 1950, P
Hal Haid, 1931, P
Dad Hale, 1902, P
Bob Hall, 1949-50, P
Billy Hamilton, 1896-1901, OF
Jack Hannifan, 1908, IF
Lew Hardie, 1890, UT
Pinky Hargrave, 1932-33, C
Dick Harley, 1905, P
George Harper, 1929, OF
Joe Harrington, 1895-96, IF
Dave Harris, 1925, OF
Roy Hartsfield, 1950-52, 2B
Mickey Haslin, 1936, UT
Buddy Hassett, 1939-41, 1B/OF
Bill Hawes, 1879, OF/C
Scott Hawley, 1894, P
Bunny Hearn, 1918, 1926-29, P
Jeff Heath, 1948-49, OF
Heinie Heltzel, 1943, 3B
Don Hendrickson, 1945-46, P
John Henry, 1918, C
Snake Henry, 1922-23, 1B/PH
Billy Herman, 1946, IF
Al Hermann, 1923-24, IF
Frank Hershey, 1905, P
Buck Herzog, 1910-11, 1918-19, IF

Otto Hess, 1912-15, P/1B
Joe Heving, 1945, P
Jim Hickey, 1942, P
Mike Hickey, 1899, 2B
Piano Legs Hickman, 1897-99, P/OF/1B
Bill Higgins, 1888, 2B
Andy High, 1925-27, 3B
John Hill, 1939, PH
Mike Hines, 1883-85, 1888, C/OF
Paul Hines, 1890, OF/1B
John Hinton, 1901, 3B
Jim Hitchcock, 1938, SS
Ralph Hodgin, 1939, OF
George Hodson, 1894, P
Stew Hofferth, 1944-46, C
Izzy Hoffman, 1907, OF
Shanty Hogan, 1925-27, 1933-35, C
Brad Hogg, 1911-12, P
Bobby Hogue, 1948-51, P
Walter Holke 1919-22, 1B
Dutch Holland, 1932-33, OF
Bonnie Hollingsworth, 1928, P
Tommy Holmes, 1942-51, OF
Abe Hood, 1925, 2B
Dick Hoover, 1952, P
Johnny Hopp, 1946-47, OF/1B
Rogers Hornsby, 1928, 2B
Joe Hornung, 1881-88, OF
Pete Hotaling, 1882, OF
Sadie Houck, 1879-80, OF/SS
Ben Houser, 1911-12, 1B
Del Howard, 1906-7, UT
Otto Huber, 1939, IF
Tom Hughes, 1914-18, OF
Harry Hulihan, 1922, P
Bill Hunnefield, 1931, IF
Jerry Hurley, 1889, OF/C
Warren Huston, 1944, IF
Johnny Hutchings, 1941-42, 1944-46, P
Ira Hutchinson, 1937-38, 1944-45, P
Scotty Ingerton, 1911, UT
Fred Jacklitsch, 1917, C
George Jackson, 1911-13, OF
Bernie James, 1929-30, 2B
Bill James 1913-15, 1919, P
Al Javery, 1940-46, P
George Jeffcoat, 1943, P
Virgil Jester, 1952, P*
Sam Jethroe, 1950-52, OF
Art Johnson, 1940-42, P
Ernie Johnson, 1950, P*
Paul Johnson, 1918, PH

Roy Johnson, 1937–38, OF
Si Johnson, 1946–47, P
Dick Johnston, 1885–89, OF
Jimmy Johnston, 1926, UT
Bill Jones, 1911–12, OF/PH
Charley Jones, 1879–80, OF
Johnny Jones, 1920, P
Ken Jones, 1930, P
Percy Jones, 1929, P
Sheldon Jones, 1952, P
Eddie Joost, 1943, IF
Buck Jordan, 1932–37, 1B
Bob Kahle, 1938, PH
Owen Kahn, 1930, PR
Al Kaiser, 1911–12, OF
Ike Kamp, 1924–25, P
Tom Kane, 1938, 2B
Andy Karl, 1947, P
Ray Keating, 1919, P
Bill Keister, 1898, UT
John Kelleher, 1924, PH
Joe Kelley, 1891, 1908, OF/1B
Jim Kelly, 1918, OF
Joe Kelly, 1917–19, OF
King Kelly, 1887–89, 1891–92, UT
Art Kenney, 1938, P
Buddy Kerr, 1950–51, SS
Hod Kibbie, 1925, IF
John Kiley, 1891, P
Frank Killen, 1899, P
Lee King, 1919, PH
Jay Kirke, 1911–13, UT
Malachi Kittredge, 1901–3, C
Billy Klaus, 1952, SS*
Johnny Kling, 1911–12, C
Fred Klobedanz, 1896–99, 1902, P
Stan Klopp, 1944, P
Billy Klusman, 1888, 2B
Clyde Kluttz, 1942–45, C
Elmer Knetzer, 1916, P
Jack Knight, 1927, P
Fritz Knothe, 1932–33, 3B
Joe Knotts, 1907, C
Ed Konetchy, 1916–18, 1B
Jim Konstanty, 1946, P
Larry Kopf, 1922–23, IF
Fabian Kowalik, 1936, P
Clarence Kraft, 1914, 1B
Rube Kroh, 1912, P
Art Krueger, 1910, OF
Steve Kuczek, 1949, PH
Charlie Kuhns, 1899, IF
Hi Ladd, 1898, OF

Fred Lake, 1891, 1897, 1910, UT
Al Lakeman, 1949, 1B
Frank LaManna, 1940–42, P
Henry Lampe, 1894, P
Hunter Lane, 1924, IF
Walt Lanfranconi, 1947, P
Johnny Lanning, 1936–39, 1947, P
Gene Lansing, 1922, P
Swede Larsen, 1936, 2B
Bill Lauterborn, 1904–5, UT
Al Lawson, 1890, P
Bob Lawson, 1901, P
Freddy Leach, 1932, OF
Jack Leary, 1880, P/OF
Bill Lee, 1945–46, P
Hal Lee, 1933–36, OF
Wade Lefler, 1924, OF
Lou Legett, 1929, C
Andy Leonard, 1876–78, UT
Dixie Leverett, 1929, P
Bill Lewis, 1935–36, C
Fred Lewis, 1881, OF
Ted Lewis, 1896–1900, P
Fred Liese, 1910, PH
Vive Lindaman, 1907–9, P
Ernie Lindeman, 1907, P
Walt Linden, 1950, C
Carl Lindquist, 1943–44, P
Danny Litwhiler, 1946–48, OF
Mickey Livingston, 1949, C
Bobby Loane, 1940, OF
Johnny Logan, 1951–52, SS*
Ernie Lombardi, 1942, C
Herman Long, 1890–1902, SS
Red Long, 1902, SS/P
Al Lopez, 1936–40, C
Bris Lord, 1913, OF
Tom Lovett, 1894, P
Fletcher Low, 1915, 3B
Bobby Lowe, 1890–1901, 2B, UT
Red Lucas, 1924–25, P
Dolf Luque, 1914–15, P
Billy Lush, 1901–2, OF
Al Lyons, 1948, P
Danny MacFayden, 1935–39, 1943, P
Joe Mack, 1945, 1B
Max Macon, 1944, 1B/OF/P
Harry MacPherson, 1944, P
Bunny Madden, 1906, OF
Kid Madden, 1887–89, P
Sherry Magee, 1915–17, OF
Harl Maggert, 1938, OF/3B
Freddie Maguire, 1929–31, 2B

Mike Mahoney, 1897, C/P
Willard Mains, 1896, P
Hank Majeski, 1939–41, 3B
John Malarkey, 1902–3, P
Les Mallon, 1934–35, UT
Charlie Maloney, 1908, P
Leo Mangum, 1932–35, P
Les Mann, 1913–14, 1919–20,
  1924–27, OF
Jack Manning, 1876, 1878, UT/P
Jimmy Manning, 1884–85, UT
Don Manno, 1940–41, UT
Dick Manville, 1950, P
Rabbit Maranville, 1912–20,
  1929–33, 1935, SS
Jim Maroney, 1906, P
Rube Marquard, 1922–25, P
Luis Marquez, 1951, OF
Bill Marriott, 1925, 3B
Doc Marshall, 1904, UT
Willard Marshall, 1950–52, OF
Marty Martel, 1910, 1B
Bill Martin, 1914, SS
Jack Martin, 1914, IF
Ray Martin, 1943, 1947–48, P
Phil Masi, 1939–49, C
Mike Massey, 1917, 2B
Roy Massey, 1918, UT
Joe Mathes 1916, 2B
Bobby Mathews, 1881–82, P/IF
Eddie Mathews, 1952, 3B*
Al Mattern, 1908–12, P
Jim Matthews, 1922, P
Gene Mauch, 1950–51, IF
Eddie Mayo, 1937–38, IF
Bill McAfee, 1931, P
Gene McAuliffe, 1904, C
Dick McBride, 1876, P
Bill McCarthy, 1905, C, 1906, P
Johnny McCarthy, 1943, 1B
Tom McCarthy, 1908–9, P
Tommy McCarthy, 1885, 1892–95,
  OF, UT
Jeff McCloskey, 1913, 3B
Jim McCloskey, 1936, P
Hal McClure, 1882, OF
Frank McCormick, 1947–48, 1B
Mike McCormick, 1946–48, OF
Tom McCreery, 1903, OF
Ed McDonald, 1911–12, 3B
Tex McDonald, 1913, UT
Frank McElyea, 1942, OF

Dan McGann, 1896, 1908, IF
Chippy McGarr, 1890, 3B
Dan McGee, 1934, SS
Tim McGinley, 1876, OF/C
Beauty McGowan, 1937, OF
Stuffy McInnis, 1923–24, 1B
Bill McKechnie, 1913, UT
Ralph McLeod, 1938, OF
Marty McManus, 1934, IF
Dinny McNamara, 1927–28, OF
Tim McNamara, 1922–25, P
Ed McNichol, 1904, P
Hugh McQuillan, 1918–22, 1927, P
Bill McTigue, 1911–13, P
Joe Medwick, 1945, OF/1B
Jouett Meekin, 1899, P
Bill Merritt, 1893–94, C
Chief Meyers, 1917, C
Doc Miller, 1910–12, OF
Eddie Miller, 1939–42, SS
Frank Miller, 1922–23, P
Tom Miller, 1918–19, PH
Art Mills, 1927–28, P
Fred Mitchell, 1913, PH
George Mogridge, 1926–27, P
Al Montgomery, 1941, C
Eddie Moore, 1926–28, UT
Gene Moore, 1936–38, 1940–41, OF
Randy Moore, 1930–35, OF
Herbie Moran, 1908–10, 1914–15, OF
Hiker Moran, 1938–39, P
Pat Moran, 1901–05, UT/C
Forrest More, 1909, P
Cy Morgan, 1921–22, P
Gene Moriarty, 1884, UT/P
Ed Moriarty, 1884, P
Ed Moriarty, 1935–36, 2B/PH
John Morril, 1876–88, UT/P
Guy Morrison, 1927–28, P
Ray Moss, 1931, P
Joe Mowry, 1933–35, OF
Heinie Mueller, 1928–29, OF
Ray Mueller, 1935–38, 1951, C
Joe Muich, 1924, P
Dick Mulligan, 1946–47, P
Tim Murnane, 1876–77, UT
Buzz Murphy, 1918, OF
Dave Murphy, 1905, IF
Frank Murphy, 1901, OF
Amby Murray, 1936, P
Jim Murray, 1914, OF
Danny Murtaugh, 1947, 2B
Hap Myers, 1913, 1B

Billy Nash, 1885–89, 1891–95, 3B
Tom Needham, 1904–7, C
Art Nehf, 1915–19, P
Tommy Neill, 1946–47, OF
Bernie Neis, 1925–26, OF
Tom Nelson, 1945, IF
Johnny Neun, 1930–31, 1B
Charlie Nice, 1895, SS
Chet Nichols, 1951, P*
Kid Nichols, 1890–1901, P/OF
Tricky Nichols, 1876, P
Fred Nicholson, 1921–22, OF
Butch Nieman, 1943–45, OF
Johnny Niggeling, 1938, P
Al Nixon, 1921–23, OF
Lou North, 1924, P
Jake Northrop, 1918–19, P
Wynn Noyes, 1913, P
Dizzy Nutter, 1919, OF
Ken O'Dea, 1946, C
Dave Odom, 1943, P
Joe Oeschger, 1919–23, P
Joe Ogrodowski, 1925, P
Kid O'Hara, 1904, OF
Dan O'Leary, 1880, OF
Luis Olmo, 1950–51, OF
Mickey O'Neil, 1919–25, C
Jack O'Neil, 1906, C
Jess Orndorff, 1907, C
Frank O'Rourke, 1912, SS
Jim O'Rourke, 1876–78, 1800, UT
John O'Rourke, 1879–80, OF
Tom O'Rourke, 1887–88, C
Wayne Osborne, 1936, P
Jimmy Outlaw, 1939, OF
Don Padgett, 1946, C
Ernie Padgett, 1923–25, IF
Phil Paine, 1951, P*
Emilio Palmero, 1928, P
Bill Parks, 1876, OF
Jiggs Parson, 1910–11, P
Charlie Parsons, 1886, P
Gene Patton, 1944, PH
Red Peery, 1929, P
Henry Peploski, 1929, 3B
Hub Perdue, 1911–14, P
Big Jeff Pfeffer, 1906–8, 1911, P/OF
Damon Phillips, 1944, IF
Eddie Phillips, 1924, C
Wiley Piatt, 1903, P
Charlie Pick, 1919–20, UT
Dave Pickett, 1898, OF
Clarence Pickrel, 1934, P

Al Piechota, 1940–41, P
Al Pierotti, 1920–21, P
Andy Pilney, 1936, PH
Togie Pittinger, 1900–4, P
Hugh Poland, 1943–44, 1946, C
Tom Poorman, 1885–86, OF
Bill Posedel, 1939–41, 1946, P
Nels Potter, 1948–49, P
Ray Powell, 1917–24, OF
Phil Powers, 1880, C
Mel Preibisch, 1940–41, OF
Jim Prendergast, 1948, P
Hub Pruett, 1932, P
Blondie Purcell, 1885, OF
Ewald Pyle, 1945, P
Bill Quarles, 1893, P
Jack Quinn, 1913, P
Joe Quinn, 1888–89, 1891–92, IF
Paddy Quinn, 1881, C/1B
Old Hoss Radbourn, 1886–89, P
Paul Radford, 1883, OF
Pat Ragan, 1915–19, P
Bill Ramsey, 1945, OF
Newt Randall, 1907, OF
Bill Rariden, 1909–13, C
Johnny Rawlings, 1917–20, UT
Irv Ray, 1888–89, UT
Fred Raymer, 1904–5, 2B
Bill Reed, 1952, 2B
Wally Rehg, 1917–18, OF
Earl Reid, 1946, P
Bobby Reis, 1936–38, UT/P
Tommy Reis, 1938, P
Pete Reiser, 1949–50, OF
Ed Reulbach, 1916–17, P
Flint Rhem, 1934–35, P
Billy Rhiel, 1930, 3B
Woody Rich, 1944, P
Hardy Richardson, 1889, 2B/OF
Lance Richbourg, 1927–31, OF
Lew Richie, 1909–10, P
John Richmond, 1880–81, SS
Lee Richmond, 1879, P
Joe Rickert, 1901, OF
Marv Rickert, 1948–49, OF
Art Rico, 1916–17, C
Harry Riconda, 1926, 3B
Johnny Riddle, 1937–38, C
Joe Riggert, 1919, OF
Jimmy Riley, 1910, OF
Claude Ritchey, 1907–9, 2B
Skippy Roberge, 1941–42, 1946, UT
Charlie Robertson, 1927–28, P

Gene Robertson, 1929–30, 3B
Red Rollings, 1930, IF
George Rooks, 1891, OF
Bunny Roser, 1922, OF
Steve Roser, 1946, P
Chet Ross, 1939–44, OF
Bama Rowell, 1939–41, 1946–47, OF/2B
Ed Rowen, 1882, UT
Norm Roy, 1950, P
Dick Rudolph, 1913-20, 1922-23, 1927, P
Jim Russell, 1948–49, OF
Babe Ruth, 1935, OF
Connie Ryan, 1943–44, 1946–50, 2B
Cyclone Ryan, 1891, P
John Ryan, 1894–96, C
Rosy Ryan, 1925–26, P
Johnny Sain, 1942, 1946–51, P
Bill Salkeld, 1948–49, C
Manny Salvo, 1940–43, P
Ray Sanders, 1946, 1948–49, 1B
Mike Sandlock, 1942, IF
Ed Sauer, 1949, OF
Johnny Scalzi, 1931, PH
Les Scarsella, 1940, 1B
Sid Schacht, 1951, P
Hal Schacker, 1945, P
Harry Schafer, 1876–78, UT
Al Schellhasse, 1890, UT
Butch Schmidt, 1913–15, 1B
Hank Schreiber, 1917, IF
Wes Schulmerich, 1931–33, OF
Jack Schulte, 1932, SS
Johnny Schulte, 1932, C
Joe Schultz, 1912–13, UT
Bill Schuster, 1939, IF
Art Schwind, 1912, 3B
Jack Scott, 1917, 1919–21, P/OF
Socks Seibold, 1929–33, P
Rube Sellers, 1910, OF
Frank Sexton, 1895, P
Cy Seymour, 1913, OF
Joe Shannon, 1915, OF
Red Shannon, 1915, 2B
Bud Sharpe, 1905, OF
Al Shaw, 1909, C
Marty Shay, 1924, 2B
Dave Shean, 1909–10, 1912, IF
Earl Sheely, 1931, 1B
Stan Shemo, 1944–45, IF
Bill Sherdel, 1930–32, P
Art Shires, 1932, 1B
Milt Shoffner, 1937–39, P
Clyde Shoun, 1947–49, P

Vince Shupe, 1945, 1B
Oscar Siemer, 1925–26, C
Al Simmons, 1939, OF
Hosea Siner, 1909, IF
Elmer Singleton, 1945–46, P
George Sisler, 1928–30, 1B
Sibby Sisti, 1939–42, 1946–52, UT*
Jimmy Slagle, 1901, OF
Bob Smith, 1923–30, 1933–37, P/IF
Earl Smith, 1923–24, C
Edgar Smith, 1883, OF
Elmer Smith, 1901, OF
Fred Smith, 1913, IF
Harry Smith, 1908–10, C
Jack Smith, 1926–29, OF
Jimmy Smith, 1918, UT
Pop Smith, 1889–90, UT
Red Smith, 1914–19, 3B
Stub Smith, 1898, SS
Tom Smith, 1894, P
Fred Snodgrass, 1915–16, OF
Pop Snyder, 1878–79, 1881, C
Pete Sommers, 1888, C
Billy Southworth, 1921–23, OF
Bill Sowders, 1888–89, P
Warren Spahn, 1942, 1946–52, P*
Chet Spencer, 1906, OF
Ed Sperber, 1924–25, OF/PH
Al Spohrer, 1928–35, C
Jack Spratt, 1911–12, UT
Ebba St. Claire, 1951–52, C*
Bob Stafford, 1898–99, UT
Chick Stahl, 1897–1900, OF
Harry Staley, 1891–94, P
Eddie Stanky, 1948–49, 2B
Joe Stanley, 1903-4, OF/P
Charlie Starr, 1909, IF
Ray Starr, 1933, P
Harry Steinfeldt, 1911, 3B
Fred Stem, 1908-9, 1B
Bill Stemmyer, 1885–87, P
Casey Stengel, 1924–25, OF
Joe Stewart, 1904, P
Jack Stivetts, 1892–98, P/OF/1F
Otis Stocksdale, 1895, P
Allyn Stout, 1943, P
Harry Stovey, 1891–92, OF
Paul Strand, 1913–15, P/OF
Gabby Street, 1905, C
Oscar Streit, 1899, P
Nick Strincevich, 1940–41, P
Joe Stripp, 1938, 3B
Allie Strobel, 1905-6, UT

Boston Braves All-Time Roster, 1876-1952 (continued)

Dutch Stryker, 1924, P
George Stultz, 1894, P
Bobby Sturgeon, 1948, IF
Andy Sullivan, 1899-1900, C/IF
Denny Sullivan, 1880, C
Jim Sullivan, 1891, 1895-97, P
Joe Sullivan, 1939-41, P
John Sullivan, 1920-21, OF
Marty Sullivan, 1890-91, OF
Mike Sullivan, 1898-99, P
Max Surkont, 1950-52, P*
Butch Sutcliffe, 1938, C
Ezra Sutton, 1877-88, 3B/IF/OF
Bill Sweeney, 1907-13, IF
Bill Swift, 1940, P
John Taber, 1890, P
Ray Talcott, 1943, P
Pop Tate, 1885-88, C
Eddie Taylor, 1926, IF
Zack Taylor, 1926-29, C
Fred Tenney, 1894-1907, 1911,
  1B/C/OF
Bert Thiel, 1952, P
Herb Thomas, 1924-25, 1927, OF/IF
Roy Thomas, 1909, OF
Walt Thomas, 1908, SS
Don Thompson, 1949, OF
Fuller Thompson, 1911, P
Tommy Thompson, 1933-36, OF
Bob Thorpe, 1951-52, OF/PH*
Jim Thorpe, 1919, OF
Cotton Tierney, 1924, IF
John Titus, 1912-13, OF
Jim Tobin, 1940-45, P/1B
Earl Torgeson, 1947-52, 1B
Red Torphy, 1920, 1B
Lou Tost, 1942-43, P
Clay Touchstone, 1928-29, P
Ira Townsend, 1920-21, P
Walt Tragesser, 1913, 1915-19, C
Sam Trott, 1880, C
Tommy Tucker, 1890-97, 1B
Jim Turner, 1937-39, P
George Twombly, 1917, OF
Fred Tyler, 1914, C
Johnnie Tyler, 1934-35, OF
Lefty Tyler, 1910-17, P/1B
Jim Tyng, 1879, P
Mike Ulisney, 1945, C
Bill Upham, 1918, P
Luke Urban, 1927-28, C
Billy Urbanski, 1931-37, SS/3B
Bill Van Dyke, 1893, OF

Bill Vargus, 1925-26, P
Al Veigel, 1939, P
Art Veltman, 1931, PH
Emil Verban, 1950, UT
Lee Viau, 1892, P
Bill Voiselle, 1947-49, P
Jake Volz, 1905, P
Phil Voyles, 1929, OF
Bill Wagner, 1918, C
Murray Wall, 1950, P
Lefty Wallace, 1942, 1945-46, P
Norm Wallen, 1945, 3B
Ed Walsh, 1917, P
Joe Walsh, 1938, SS
Bucky Walters, 1931-32, 1950, IF
Lloyd Waner, 1941, OF
Paul Waner, 1941-42, OF
John Warner, 1895, C/UT
Rabbit Warstler, 1936-40, IF
Link Wasem, 1937, P
Mule Watson, 1920-23, P
Hal Weafer, 1936, P
Orlie Weaver, 1911, P
Charlie Weeden, 1911, PH
Roy Weir, 1936-39, P
Jimmy Welsh, 1925-27, 1929-30, OF
Stan Wentzel, 1945, OF
Johnny Wertz, 1926-29, P
Frank West, 1894, P
Max West, 1938-42, 1946, OF/1B
Oscar Westerberg, 1907, SS
Al Weston, 1929, PH
Bert Whaling, 1913-15, C
Bobby Wheelock, 1887, UT
Tom Whelan, 1920, 1B
Pete Whisenant, 1952, OF
Bob Whitcher, 1945, P
Deacon White, 1877, UT
Ernie White, 1946-48, P
John White, 1904, OF
Kirby White, 1909-10, P
Sam White, 1919, C
Steve White, 1912, P
Will White, 1877, P
Gil Whitehouse, 1912, C
Gurdon Whitely, 1885, OF
Frank Whitney, 1876, OF
Jim Whitney, 1881-85, P/OF
Pinky Whitney, 1933-36, IF
Possum Whitted, 1914, UT
Al Wickland, 1918, OF
Whitey Wietelmann, 1939-46, IF
Claude Wilborn, 1940, OF

Kaiser Wilhelm, 1904-5, P
Joe Wilhoit, 1916-17, OF
Ace Williams, 1940, P
Earl Williams, 1928, C
Pop Williams, 1903, P
Vic Willis, 1898-1905, P
Art Wilson, 1918-20, C/IF
Charlie Wilson, 1931, 3B
Frank Wilson, 1924-26, OF
Jim Wilson, 1951-52, P*
Zeke Wilson, 1895, P
Nick Wise, 1888, OF/C
Sam Wise, 1882-88, UT
Roy Witherup, 1906, P
Harry Wolverton, 1905, 3B
Sid Womack, 1926, C
George Woodend, 1944, P

Chuck Workman, 1943-46, UT
Red Worthington, 1931-34, OF
Ab Wright, 1944, OF
Al Wright, 1933, 2B
Ed Wright, 1945-48, P
George Wright, 1876-78, 1880-81, IF
Harry Wright, 1876-77, OF
Sam Wright, 1876, SS
George Yeager, 1896-99, UT
Jim Yeargin, 1922, P
Cy Young, 1911, P
Harley Young, 1908, P
Herman Young, 1911, IF
Irv Young, 1905-8, P
Tom Zachary, 1930-34, P
Guy Zinn, 1913, OF

Managers

Dave Bancroft, 1924-27
Del Bissonette, 1945
Frank Bowerman, 1909
Al Buckenberger, 1902-4
Jack Burdock, 1883
Bob Coleman, 1944-45
Judge Fuchs, 1929
Charlie Grimm, 1952
Charlie Hackett, 1889
Jim Hart, 1889
Tommy Holmes, 1951-52
Rogers Hornsby, 1928
Joe Kelley, 1908

Johnny Kling, 1912
Fred Lake, 1910
Bill McKechnie, 1930-37
Fred Mitchell, 1921-23
John Morrill, 1882-88
Frank Selee, 1890-91
Jack Slattery, 1928
Harry Smith, 1909
Billy Southworth, 1946-51
George Stallings, 1913-20
Casey Stengel, 1938-43
Fred Tenney, 1905-7, 1911
Harry Wright, 1876-81

MILWAUKEE BRAVES ALL-TIME ROSTER, 1953–1965

Henry Aaron, 1954–65, OF*
Tommie Aaron, 1962–63, 1965, 1B/OF*
Joe Adcock, 1953–62, 1B
Sandy Alomar, 1964–65, IF*
Felipe Alou, 1964–65, OF/1B*
Johnny Antonelli, 1953, P*
Ken Aspromonte, 1962, IF
Toby Atwell, 1956, C
Bobby Avila, 1959, 2B
Ed Bailey, 1964, C
Jim Beauchamp, 1965, UT*
Howie Bedell, 1962, OF
Gus Bell, 1962–64, OF
Vern Bickford, 1953, P*
Ethan Blackaby, 1962, OF
Johnny Blanchard, 1965, C/OF
Wade Blasingame, 1963–65, P*
Frank Bolling, 1962–65, 2B*
Ray Boone, 1959–60, 1B
Bob Boyd, 1961, 1B
John Braun, 1964, P
George Brunet, 1960–61, P
Bill Bruton, 1953–60, OF
Bob Buhl, 1953–62, P
Lew Burdette, 1953–63, P*
Paul Burris, 1953, C*
Cecil Butler, 1962, P
Sammy Calderone, 1954, C
Clay Carroll, 1964–65, P*
Rico Carty, 1963–65, OF*
Neil Chrisley, 1961, PH
Gino Cimoli, 1961, OF
Ty Cline, 1963–65, OF/1B*
Tony Cloninger, 1961–65, P*
Dave Cole, 1953, P*
Dick Cole, 1957, UT
Gene Conley, 1954–58, P
Jim Constable, 1962, P
Walker Cooper, 1953, C*
Chuck Cottier, 1959–60, 2B
Wes Covington, 1956–61, OF
Billy Cowan, 1965, OF/LF
Del Crandall, 1953–63, C*
Ray Crone, 1954–57, P
George Crowe, 1953, 1B*
Jack Curtis, 1962, P
Alvin Dark, 1960, UT*
Mike de la Hoz, 1964–65, UT*
John DeMerit, 1957–59, 1961, OF
Don Dillard, 1963, 1965, OF
Jack Dittmer, 1953–56, IF*

Moe Drabowsky, 1961, P
John Edelman, 1955, P
Dave Eilers, 1964–65, P
Hank Fischer, 1962–65, P*
Terry Fox, 1960, P
Frank Funk, 1963, P
Len Gabrielson, 1960, 1963–64, OF/1B
Bob Giggie, 1959–60, P
Jesse Gonder, 1965, C
Sid Gordon, 1953, OF*
Charlie Gorin, 1954–55, P
Eddie Haas, 1958, OF
Harry Hanebrink, 1953, 1957–58, UT
Bob Hartman, 1959, P
Bob Hazle, 1957–58, OF
Bob Hendley, 1961–63, P
Earl Hersh, 1956, OF
Billy Hoeft, 1964, P
Joey Jay, 1953–55, 1957–60, P
Virgil Jester, 1953, P*
Ernie Johnson, 1953–58, P
Ken Johnson, 1965, P*
Lou Johnson, 1962, OF
Dave Jolly, 1953–57, P
Mack Jones, 1961–63, 1965, OF*
Nippy Jones, 1957, 1B
Dick Kelley, 1964–65, P*
Billy Klaus, 1953, PH*
Lou Klimchock, 1962–65, UT
Gary Kolb, 1964–65, UT
Joe Koppe, 1958, SS
Dave Koslo, 1954–55, P
Mike Krsnich, 1960, UT
Norm Larker, 1963, B
Frank Lary, 1964, P
Charlie Lau, 1960–61, C*
Denny Lemaster, 1962–65, P*
Don Liddle, 1953, P
Dick Littlefield, 1958, P
Johnny Logan, 1953–61, SS*
Stan Lopata, 1959–60, C/1B
Ken MacKenzie, 1960–61, P
Bobby Malkmus, 1957, 2B
Felix Mantilla, 1956–61, UT
Billy Martin, 1961, 2B
Eddie Mathews, 1953–65, 3B*
Lee Maye, 1959–65, OF
Don McMahon, 1957–62, P
Roy McMillan, 1961–64, SS
Denis Menke, 1962–65, IF*
Catfish Metkovich, 1954, 1B/OF

---

*Indicates that man played for Braves in other city, too.

Seth Morehead, 1961, P
Joe Morgan, 1959, IF
Bubba Morton, 1963, OF
Red Murff, 1956–57, P
Chet Nichols, 1954–56, P*
Phil Niekro, 1964–65, P*
Don Nottebart, 1960–62, P
Johnny O'Brien, 1959, 2B
Danny O'Connell, 1954–57, IF
Billy O'Dell, 1965, P
Gene Oliver, 1963–65, C/UT*
Chi Chi Olivo, 1961, 1965–65, P*
Dan Osinski, 1965, P
Andy Pafko, 1953–59, OF
Phil Paine, 1964–67, P*
Jim Pendleton, 1953–56, UT
Taylor Phillips, 1956–57, P
Ron Piche, 1960–63, P
Jim Pisoni, 1959, OF
Juan Pizarro, 1957–60, P
Billy Queen, 1954, OF
Merritt Ranew, 1964, C
Claude Raymond, 1961–63, P*
Del Rice 1955–59, C
Mel Roach, 1953–54, 1957–61, UT
Humberto Robinson, 1955–56, 1958,
Phil Roof, 1961, C
Bob Roselli, 1955–56, 1958, C
Bob Rush, 1958–60, P
Bob Sadowski, 1963–65, P
Amado Samuel, 1962–63, IF
Carl Sawatski, 1957–58, C
Dan Schneider, 1963–64, P*

Red Schoendienst, 1957–60, 2B
Bob Shaw, 1962–63, P
Ray Shearer, 1957, OF
Sibby Sisti, 1953–54, UT*
Enos Slaughter, 1959, OF
Lou Sleater, 1956, P
Roy Smalley, 1954, UT
Jack Smith, 1964, P
Bill Southworth, 1964, 3B
Warren Spahn, 1953–64, P*
Al Spangler, 1959–61, OF
Ebba St. Claire, 1953, C*
Max Surkont, 1953, P*
Chuck Tanner, 1955–57, OF
Bennie Taylor, 1955, 1B
Hawk Taylor, 1957–78, 1961–63, P
Frank Thomas, 1961, OF/1B
Bobby Thomson, 1954–57, OF
Bob Thorpe, 1953, OF*
Bobby Tiefenauer, 1963–65, P
Frank Torre, 1956–60, 1B
Joe Torre, 1960–65, C/1B*
Bob Trowbridge, 1956–59, P
Bob Uecker, 1962–63, C*
Arnie Umbach, 1964, P*
Roberto Vargas, 1955, P
Mickey Vernon, 1959, 1B/OF
Charlie White, 1954–55, C
Sammy White, 1961, C
Carlton Willey, 1958–62, P
Jim Wilson, 1953–54, P
Casey Wise, 1958–59, IF
Woody Woodward, 1963–65, IF*

Managers

Bobby Bragan, 1963–65
Charlie Dressen, 1960–61
Charlie Grimm, 1953–56

Fred Haney, 1956–59
Birdie Tebbetts, 1961–62

ATLANTA BRAVES ALL-TIME ROSTER, 1966-

Henry Aaron, 1966–74, OF*
Tommie Aaron, 1968–71, 1B/OF*
Ted Abernathy, 1966, P
Jack Aker, 1974, P
Doyle Alexander, 1980, P
Sandy Alomar, 1966, 2B*
Felipe Alou, 1966–69, OF/1B*
Bob Aspromonte, 1969–70, UT
Al Autry, 1976, P
Dusty Baker, 1968–75, OF
Lee Bales, 1966, IF
Steve Barber, 1970–72, P
Bob Beall, 1975, 1978–79, 1B
Mike Beard, 1974–77, P
Jim Beauchamp, 1967, UT*
Rob Belloir, 1975–78, IF
Bruce Benedict, 1980– , C
Larvell Blanks, 1972–75, 1980– , UT
Wade Blasingame, 1966–67, P*
Tommy Boggs, 1978– , P
Frank Bolling, 1966, 2B*
Barry Bonnell, 1977–79, OF/IF
Jim Bouton, 1978, P
Clete Boyer, 1967–71, 3B
Larry Bradford, 1977, 1979– , P
Jim Breazeale, 1969, 1971–72, 1B
Jim Britton, 1967–69, P
Tony Brizzolara, 1979, P
Oscar Brown, 1969–73, OF
Bob Bruce, 1967, P
Jeff Burroughs, 1977–80, OF
Rick Camp, 1976–78, 1980, P
Dave Campbell, 1977–78, P
Buzz Capra, 1974–77, P
Don Cardwell, 1970, P
Clay Carroll, 1966–68, P*
Rico Carty, 1966–67, 1969–72,
  OF/C/IF*
Paul Casanova, 1972–74, C
Wayne Causey, 1968, IF
Orlando Cepeda, 1969–72, 1B
Chris Chambliss, 1980– , 1B
Darrell Chaney, 1976–79, LF
Dave Cheadle, 1973, P
Glen Clark, 1967, PH
Ty Cline, 1966–67, OF/1B*
Tony Cloninger, 1966–68, P*
Alan Closter, 1973, P
Don Collins, 1977, P
Gary Cooper, 1980– , OF
Vic Correll, 1974–77, C

Terry Crowley, 1976, PH
Bruce Dal Canton, 1975–77, P
Mike Davey, 1977–78, P
Ted Davidson, 1968, P
Mike de la Hoz, 1966–67, UT*
Adrian Devine, 1973, 1975–76,
  1978–79, P
Bob Dider, 1969–72, C
Dick Dietz, 1973, C
Pat Dobson, 1973, P
Paul Doyle, 1969, P
Jamie Easterly, 1974–79, P
Mike Eden, 1976, 2B
Darrell Evans, 1969–76, 3B
Hank Fischer, 1966, P*
Wenty Ford, 1973, P
Leo Foster, 1971, 1973–74, IF
Tito Francona, 1967–69, 1B/OF
Jimmy Freeman, 1972–73, P
Pepe Frias, 1979, IF
Danny Frisella, 1973–74, P
John Fuller, 1974, OF/PH
Gene Garber, 1978– , P
Ralph Garr, 1968–75, OF
Adrian Garrett, 1966, OF/PH
Gil Garrido, 1968–72, IF
Cito Gaston, 1967, 1975–78, OF
Aubrey Gatewood, 1970, P
Gary Geiger, 1966–67, OF
Gary Gentry, 1973–75, P
Rod Gilbreath, 1972–78, 2B
Chuck Goggin, 1973, IF
Luis Gomez, 1980– , IF
Tony Gonzalez, 1969–70, OF
Ed Goodson, 1975, IF
Skip Guinn, 1978, P
Jimmie Hall, 1970, OF
Preston Hanna, 1975– , P
Jim Hardin, 1972, P
Steve Hargan, 1977, P
Terry Harper, 1980– , OF
Roric Harrison, 1973–75, P
Ken Henderson, 1976, OF
Ron Herbel, 1971, P
Angel Hermoso, 1967, P
Ramon Hernandez, 1967, P
John Herrnstein, 1966, OF
Garry Hill, 1969, P
Herb Hippauf, 1966, P
Joe Hoerner, 1972–73, P
Bob Horner, 1978– , 3B
Tom House, 1971–75, P

---

*Indicates that man played for Braves in other city, too.

146

Larry Howard, 1973, C
Al Hrabosky, 1980– , P
Walt Hrniak, 1968–69, C
Glenn Hubbard, 1978, IF
Sonny Jackson, 1968–74, SS
Pat Jarvis, 1966–72, P
Larry Jaster, 1970, 1972, P
Joey Jay, 1966, P
Bob Johnson, 1968, UT
Bob Johnson, 1977, P
Dave Johnson, 1973–73, IF
Deron Johnson, 1968, 1B/3B
Ken Johnson, 1966–69, P*
Mack Jones, 1966–67, OF*
Dick Kelley, 1966–68, P*
Tom Kelley, 1971–73, P
Marty Keough, 1966, OF/1B
Rick Kester, 1968–70, P
Hal King, 1970–71, C
Ron Kline, 1970, P
Steve Kline, 1977, P
George Kopacz, 1966, 1B
Lew Krausse, 1974, P
Frank LaCorte, 1975–79, P
Lee Lacy, 1976, IF/OF
Tony LaRussa, 1971, LF
Charlie Lau, 1967, PH*
Denny Lemaster, 1966–67, P
Max Leon, 1973–78, P
Mike Lum, 1967–75, 1979– , OF
Ken Macha, 1979, IF
Jerry Maddox, 1978, 3B
Mickey Mahler, 1977– , P
Rickey Mahler, 1979, P
Mike Marshall, 1976–77, P
Marty Martinez, 1967–68, UT
Eddie Mathews, 1966, 3B*
Gary Matthews, 1977– , OF
Rick Matula, 1979– , P
Larry Maxie, 1969, P
Dave May, 1975–76, OF
Denny McLain, 1972, P
Bo McLaughlin, 1979, P
Joey McLaughlin, 1977, 1979, P
Mike McQueen, 1969–72, P
Larry McWilliams, 1978– , P
Denis Menke, 1966–67, IF*
Andy Messersmith, 1976–77, P
Felix Millan, 1966–72, 2B
Eddie Miller, 1978– , OF
Norm Miller, 1973–74, OF
Stu Miller, 1968, P
Willie Montanez, 1976–77, 1B

Junior Moore, 1976–77, IF
Rogelio Moret, 1976, P
Carl Morton, 1973–76, P
Dale Murphy, 1976– , C/1B/OF
Ivan Murrell, 1974, OF
Bill Nahorodny, 1980– , C
Jim Nash, 1970–72, P
Julio Navarro, 1970, P
Gary Neibauer, 1969–73, P
Dave Nicholson, 1967, OF
Joe Niekro, 1973–74, P
Phil Niekro, 1966– , P*
Joe Nolan, 1975, 1977–80, C
Johnny Oates, 1973–75, C
Bill O'Dell, 1966, P
Blue Moon Odom, 1975, P
Rowland Office, 1972, 1974–79, OF
Gene Oliver, 1966–67, C/UT*
Chi Chi Olivo, 1966, P*
Tom Paciorek, 1976–78, OF/1B
Mike Page, 1968, OF
Jim Panther, 1973, P
Milt Pappas, 1968–70, P
Joe Pepitone, 1973, 1B
Marty Perez, 1971–76, SS/2B
Jack Pierce, 1973–74, 1B
Biff Pocoroba, 1975– , C
Bob Priddy, 1969–71, P
Ed Rakow, 1967, P
Rafael Ramirez, 1980– , SS
Claude Raymond, 1967–69, P*
Ron Reed, 1966–75, P
Jay Ritchie, 1966–67, P
Bill Robinson, 1966, OF
Craig Robinson, 1974–77, IF
Pat Rockett, 1976–78, SS
Jerry Royster, 1976– , IF
Chico Ruiz, 1978, 1980, IF
Dick Ruthven, 1976–78, P
Ray Sadecki, 1975, P
Eddie Sadowski, 1966, C
Al Santorini, 1968, P
Dan Schneider, 1966, P*
Ron Schueler, 1972–73, P
Don Schwall, 1966–67, P
Craig Skok, 1978–79, P
Hank Small, 1978, 1B
Eddie Solomon, 1977–79, P
Elias Sosa, 1975–76, P
Charlie Spikes, 1979– , OF
Marv Staehle, 1971, 2B
George Stone, 1967–72, P
Frank Tepedino, 1973–74, 1B/PH

Atlanta Braves All-Time Roster, 1966- (continued)

Duane Theiss, 1977–78, P
Lee Thomas, 1966, 1B/OF
Mike Thompson, 1974–75, P
Bob Tillman, 1968–70, C
Joe Torre, 1966–68, C/1B
Pablo Torrealba, 1975–76, P
Bob Uecker, 1967, C*
Arnie Umbach, 1966, P*
Cecil Upshaw, 1966–69, 1971–73, P
Sandy Valdespino, 1968, OF
Pete Varney, 1976, C

Charlie Vaughan, 1966, P
Federico Velazquez, 1973, C
Zoilo Versalles, 1971, IF
Jim Wessinger, 1979, IF
Larry Whisenton, 1977–79, PH/OF
Hoyt Wilhelm, 1969–71, P
Earl Williams, 1970–72, 1975–76,
  3B/C/1B
Woody Woodward, 1966–68, IF*
Jim Wynn, 1976, OF

Managers

Bobby Bragan, 1966
Dave Bristol, 1976–77
Bobby Cox, 1978–81
Luman Harris, 1968–72
Billy Hitchcock, 1966–67

Clyde King, 1974–75
Eddie Mathews, 1972–74
Connie Ryan, 1975
Ken Silvestri, 1967
Joe Torre, 1982–
Ted Turner, 1977

GENE GARBER, the relief pitcher who stopped Pete Rose's streak at 44 games

CHRIS CHAMBLISS, who was acquired in 1980 and had an outstanding first season with the Braves.

RICO CARTY, a natural hitter whose career was interrupted by injuries and a bout with tuberculosis

TONY CLONINGER, the only pitcher to hit two grand slams in one game

JOE ADCOCK, one of the few men in baseball history to hit four homers in one game

RALPH GARR, one of the fastest runners to ever wear a Braves' uniform

LUMAN HARRIS, the manager from 1968 to 1972, skippered the Braves to their 1969 Championship Playoffs.

JIM BOUTON, author of *Ball Four Plus Ball Five*, made a valiant comeback in 1978 after eight years out of major league baseball. (*photo courtesy of* The Atlanta Journal)

DAVE JOHNSON, who holds the record for most home runs by a second baseman in a season

EDDIE MATHEWS, a Hall of Famer who is the most prolific home-run-hitting third baseman of all time

DENNY MCLAIN, a former 30-game winning pitcher who allowed personal problems to affect his skills

EARL WILLIAMS, a power-hitting catcher who had two tours of action with the Braves

HANK AARON, as he hit his 715th home run (breaking Babe Ruth's record) on April 8, 1974, in Atlanta Stadium

TED TURNER, the Braves' owner who is also known as a master yachtsman

CHIEF NOC-A-HOMA, the Braves' mascot

JEFF BURROUGHS, who clubbed 41 homers in his first season at Atlanta in 1977

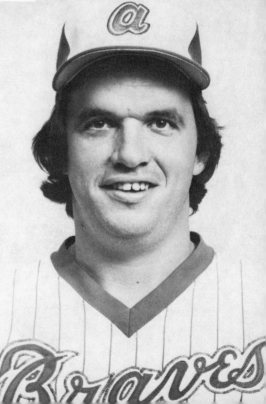

RICK CAMP, the current ace of the Braves' bullpen

PHIL NIEKRO, the knuckleballer who has logged in three 20-win seasons

DALE MURPHY, the only Brave on the 1980 National League All-Star team

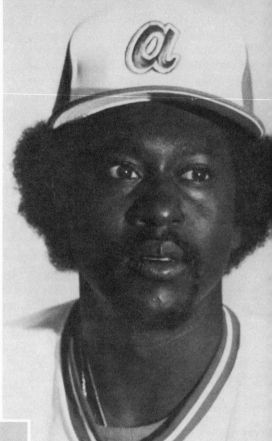

GARY MATTHEWS, signed as a free agent in 1977, was the 1979 Brave representative on the N.L. All-Stars.

MIKE LUM, the only Hawaiian native in the major leagues

Bobby Cox, the Braves' skipper since 1978

Bob Horner, who has smashed 91 homers in only three years in the majors

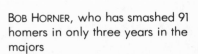

PETE VAN WIEREN, Braves' broadcaster

◀ ERNIE JOHNSON, Braves' broadcaster

FELIPE ALOU, the only one of th
three Alou brothers to appear
in a Braves' uniform

DAVE PURSLEY, Braves' trainer

The 1957 World Champion Milwaukee Braves   (Courtesy of National Baseball Hall of fame)

1980 ATLANTA BRAVES

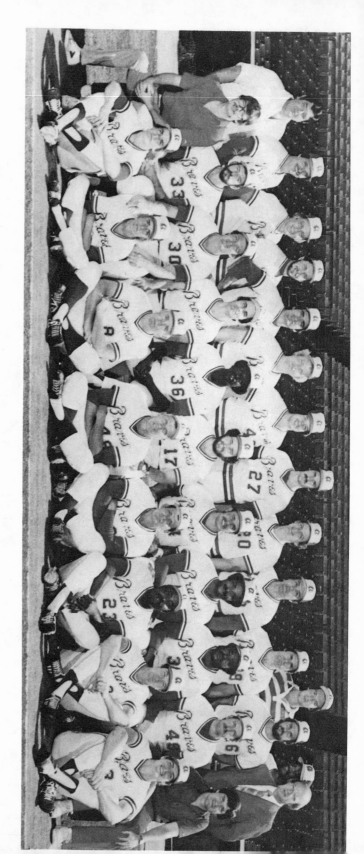

Front Row: Batboy Neil Pursley, Batboy Bill Lassiter, Coach John Sullivan, Coach Cloyd Boyer, Manager Bob Cox, Coach Tommie Aaron, Coach Bobby Dews, Dale Murphy

Second Row: Asst. Equipment Manager John Holland, Doyle Alexander, Brian Asselstine, Luis Gomez, Gary Matthews, Glenn Hubbard, Biff Pocoroba, Charlie Spikes, Larry Bradford, Preston Hanna, Equipment Manager Bill Acree

Back Row: Trainer Dave Pursley, Rich Camp, Phil Niekro, Bill Nahorodny, Rich Matula, Bob Horner, Tommy Boggs, Larry McWilliams, Bruce Benedict, Mike Lum, Al Hrabosky, Clubhouseman Steve Cowen, Gene Garber, Jerry Royster, Traveling Secretary Pete Van Wieren

BRAVES HALL OF FAME MEMBERS

Name	Position	Years with Braves	Year Elected to Hall
Henry Aaron	OF	1954–74	1982
Earl Averill	OF	1941	1975
Dan Brouthers	IF	1889	1945
John Clarkson	P	1888–1892	1963
Jimmy Collins	IF	1895–1900	1945
Hugh Duffy	OF	1892–1900	1945
Johnny Evers	IF	1914–17; 1929	1946
Burleigh Grimes	P	1930	1964
Bill Hamilton	OF	1896–1901	1961
Billy Herman	IF	1946	1975
Rogers Hornsby	IF/MGR	1928	1942
Joe Kelley	OF/MGR	1891; 1908	1971
Mike Kelly	IF/OF	1887–89; 1891–92	1945
Rabbit Maranville	IF	1912–20; 1929–33; 1935	1954
Rube Marquard	P	1922–25	1971
Eddie Mathews	IF	1952–1966	1978
Bill McKechnie	MGR	1930–37	1962
Tommy McCarthy	OF	1885; 1892–95	1946
Joe Medwick	OF	1945	1968
Kid Nichols	P	1890–1901	1949
Jim O'Rourke	OF	1876–78; 1880	1945
Old Hoss Radbourn	P	1886–89	1939
Babe Ruth	OF	1935	1936
Al Simmons	OF	1939	1953
Warren Spahn	P	1942; 1946–64	1973
Casey Stengel	MGR	1938–1943	1966
George Sisler	IF	1928–30	1939
Ed Walsh	P	1917	1946
Lloyd Waner	OF	1941	1967
Paul Waner	OF	1941–42	1952
Harry Wright	MGR	1876–1881	1953
Cy Young	P	1911	1937

BRAVES ON THE NATIONAL LEAGUE ALL-STAR TEAM, 1933-1981

1933 Wally Berger, OF
1934 Wally Berger, OF; Fred Frankhouse, P
1935 Wally Berger, OF
1936 Wally Berger, OF
1937 Gene Moore, OF
1938 Tony Cuccinello, 2B; Jim Turner, P
1939 Lou Fette, P
1940 Max West, OF
1941 Eddie Miller, SS
1942 Eddie Miller, SS; Ernie Lombardi, C
1943 Al Javery, P
1944 Nate Andrews, P; Al Javery, P; Connie Ryan, 2B
1946 Mort Cooper, P; Phil Masi, C; Johnny Hopp, OF
1947 Bob Elliott, 3B; Phil Masi, C; Warren Spahn, P; Johnny Sain, P
1948 Bob Elliott, 3B; Tommy Holmes, OF; Eddie Stanky, 2B; Johnny Sain, P
1949 Vern Bickford, P; Warren Spahn, P
1950 Walker Cooper, P; Warren Spahn, P
1951 Bob Elliott, 3B; Warren Spahn, P
1952 Warren Spahn, P
1953 Warren Spahn, P; Del Crandall, C; Eddie Mathews, 3B
1954 Warren Spahn, P; Del Crandall, C; Gene Conley, P; Jim Wilson, P
1955 Henry Aaron, OF; Gene Conley, P; Del Crandall, C; Johnny Logan, SS; Eddie Mathews, 3B
1956 Henry Aaron, OF; Del Crandall, C; Eddie Mathews, 3B; Warren Spahn, P
1957 Henry Aaron, OF; Lew Burdette, P; Johnny Logan, SS; Eddie Mathews, 3B; Red Schoendienst, 2B; Warren Spahn, P
1958 Henry Aaron, OF; Del Crandall, C; Johnny Logan, SS; Eddie Mathews, 3B; Don McMahon, P; Warren Spahn, P
1959 Henry Aaron, OF; Lew Burdette, P; Del Crandall, C; Eddie Mathews, 3B; Warren Spahn, P; Johnny Logan, 2B (second game only)
1960 Henry Aaron, OF; Joe Adcock, 1B; Bob Buhl, P; Del Crandall, C; Eddie Mathews, 3B
1961 Henry Aaron, OF; Frank Bolling, 2B; Eddie Mathews, 3B; Warren Spahn, P
1962 Henry Aaron, OF; Frank Bolling, 2B; Del Crandall, C; Eddie Mathews, 3B; Bob Shaw, P; Warren Spahn, P
1963 Henry Aaron, OF; Warren Spahn, P; Joe Torre, C
1964 Henry Aaron, OF; Joe Torre, C
1965 Henry Aaron, OF; Joe Torre, C
1966 Henry Aaron, OF; Joe Torre, C; Felipe Alou, 1B
1967 Henry Aaron, OF; Joe Torre, C; Denny Lemaster, P
1968 Henry Aaron, OF; Felipe Alou, 1B; Ron Reed, P
1969 Henry Aaron, OF; Felix Millan, 2B; Phil Niekro, P
1970 Henry Aaron, OF; Rico Carty, OF; Hoyt Wilhelm, P
1971 Henry Aaron, OF; Felix Millan, 2B
1972 Henry Aaron, OF
1973 Henry Aaron, OF; Darrell Evans, 3B; Dave Johnson, 2B
1974 Henry Aaron, OF; Ralph Garr, OF; Buzz Capra, P
1975 Phil Niekro, P
1976 Dick Ruthven, P
1977 Willie Montanez, 1B
1978 Phil Niekro, P; Biff Pocoroba, C; Jeff Burroughs, OF
1979 Gary Matthews, OF
1980 Dale Murphy, OF
1981 Bruce Bennedict, C

BRAVES BROTHERS

Last Name	First Names	Years Played Together
Aspromonte	Bob and Ken	
Aaron*	Henry and Tommie	1962–1963; 1965; 1968–1971
Barnes	Jesse and Virgil	
Clarkson*	Dad and John	1892
Cooney*	Jimmy and Johnny	1928
Cooper	Mort and Walker	
Hackett*	Mert and Walter	1885
Hitchcock	Billy and Jim	
Niekro*	Joe and Phil	1973–1977
O'Rourke	Jim and John	
Shannon*	Joe and Red (twins)	1915
Sadowski	Bob and Eddie	
Torre*	Frank and Joe	1960
Tyler*	Fred and Lefty	1914
Waner*	Lloyd and Paul	1941
White*	Deacon and Will	1877
Wright*	George, Harry, and Sam	1876
Wright	George and Harry	1877
Wright	George and Sam	1881

BRAVES NICKNAMES

Henry Aaron	Hammerin' Hank; The Hammer
Stan Andrews	Polo
Johnnie B. Baker	Dusty
Bill Bagwell	Big Bill
Dave Bancroft	Beauty
Walter Barbare	Dinty
George Barclay	Deerfoot
David Barron	Red
John Barry	Shad
Clarence Beaumont	Ginger
David Bell	Gus
Russell Blackburne	Lena; Slats
Bob Boyd	The Rope
Ralph Boyle	Buzz
George Bradley	Foghorn
James Brady	King
William Bransfield	Kitty
Clarence Bray	Buster
Sigmund Broskie	Chops
Dan Brouthers	Big Dan
Eddie Brown	Glass Arm
John Burdock	Black Jack
Bill Calhoun	Mary
Virgin Cannell	Rip
Dorsey Carroll	Dixie
Chet Chadbourne	Pop
James Chaplin	Tiny
Charles Chatham	Buster

*Brothers who played for the Braves. Asterisk indicates that the brothers played on the same Braves team.

Braves Nicknames (continued)

Barbra Chrisley	Neil
William Clarke	Boileryard
Josh Clarke	Pepper
James Carlson	Buzz
Arthur Clarkson	Dad
Pete Compton	Bash
Art Conlon	Jocko
Richard Conway	Rip
Duff Cooley	Sir Richard
Jimmy Cooney	Scoops
Bill Cronin	Crunchy
Jack Daniels	SourMash
Alvin Dark	Blackie
John Davis	Daisy
John DeMerit	Thumper
Robert Detweiler	Ducky
Patrick Dolan	Cozy
Mike Donlin	Turkey
Sylvester Donnelley	Blix
Harold Elliott	Rowdy
Anthony Fricken	Hon
John Gammons	Daff
Dennis Gearin	Dinty
George Graham	Peaches
William Hargrove	Pinky
Frederick Henry	Snake
Charles Hickman	Piano Legs
Stephen Houck	Sadie
Tom Kane	Sugar
Mike Kelly	King
John McInnis	Stuffy
Albert Moran	Hiker
Ralph Myers	Hap
Everett Nutter	Dizzy
James O'Hara	Kid
Hubbard Perdue	Squash
William Purcell	Blondie
Carvell Rowell	Bama
Edward St. Claire	Ebba
Ed Sauer	Horn
Carl Sawatski	Swats
Bob Taylor	Hawk
Bobby Thomson	The Staten Island Scot
Jim Tobin	Abba Dabba
Earl Torgeson	The Earl of Snohomish
Emil Verban	The Antelope
Joe Walsh	Tweet
Charlie Wilson	Swamp Baby
Irv Young	Cy the Second

Docs: Bass, Carney, Crandall, Farrell, Gautreau, Marshall, Miller

MEN WHO PLAYED FOR THE RED SOX AND THE BRAVES

Batters

Name	Played for Red Sox	Played for Braves
Aspromonte, Ken	1957	1962
Avila, Bobby	1959	1959
Bailey, Gene	1920	1919–20
Barbare, Walter	1918	1921–22
Boone, Ray	1960	1959–60
Cepeda, Orlando	1973	1969–72
Coffey, Jack	1918	1909
Collins, Jimmy	1901–7	1895–1900
Cooney, Jimmy	1917	1928
Correll, Vic	1972	1974–77
Dahlgren, Babe	1935–36	1941
Didier, Bob	1974	1969–72
Dugan, Joe	1922	1929
Farrell, Doc	1935	1927–29
Ferrell, Wes	1934–37	1941
Freeman, Buck	1901–7	1900
Geiger, Gary	1959–65	1966–67
Goggin, Chuck	1974	1973
Herman, Billy	1964–66 (manager)	1946
Hickman, Piano Legs	1902	1897–99
Hitchcock, Billy	1948–49	1966–67 (manager)
Hrniak, Walt	1977– (coach)	1968–69
Johnson, Deron	1974–76	1968
Johnson, Roy	1932–35	1937–38
Joost, Eddie	1955	1943; 1945
Keough, Marty	1956–60	1966
Klaus, Billy	1955–58	1952–53
Legett, Lou	1933–35	1929
Mantilla, Felix	1963–65	1956–61
Mauch, Gene	1956–57	1950–51
McInnis, Stuffy	1918–21	1923–24
McManus, Marty	1931–33	1934
Metkovich, George	1943–46	1954
Mitchell, Fred	1901–2	1913
Myers, Hap	1910–11	1913
Oliver, Gene	1968	1963–67
O'Rourke, Frank	1922	1912
Rehg, Wally	1913–15	1917–18
Riggert, Joe	1911	1919
Rollings, Red	1927–28	1930
Ruth, Babe	1914–19	1935
Sadowski, Eddie	1960	1966
Shannon, Red	1919	1915
Shaw, Al	1907	1909
Shean, Dave	1918–19	1909–10; 1912
Simmons, Al	1943	1939
Stahl, Chick	1901–6	1897–1900
Thomas, Lee	1964–65	1966
Thomson, Bobby	1960	1954–57
Tillman, Bob	1962–67	1968–70

Men Who Played for the Red Sox and the Braves, Batters (continued)

Vernon, Mickey	1956–57	1959
Walters, Bucky	1933–34	1931; 1950 (coach)
Warner, John	1902	1895
Warstler, Rabbit	1930–33	1936–40
White, Sammy	1951–59	1961
Wilhoit, Joe	1919	1916–17

Pitchers

Name	Played for Red Sox	Played for Braves
Barberich, Frank	1910	1907
Barrett, Frank	1944–45	1946
Brady, King	1908	1912
Conley, Gene	1961–63	1952; 1954–58
Cuppy, George	1901	1900
Dinneen, Bill	1902–7	1900–1901
Fischer, Hank	1966–67	1962–66
Hernandez, Ramon	1977	1967
Heving, Joe	1939–40	1945
Hoeft, Billy	1959	1964
House, Tom	1976–77	1971–75
Kline, Ron	1969	1970
Krausse, Lew	1972	1974
Kroh, Rube	1906–7	1912
Lewis, Ted	1901	1896–1900
Littlefield, Dick	1950	1958
MacFayden, Danny	1926–32	1935–39; 1943
McMahon, Don	1966–67	1957–62
Moret, Rogelio	1970–75	1976
Nichols, Chet	1960–63	1951; 1954–56
Osinski, Danny	1966–67	1965
Pizarro, Juan	1968–69	1957–60
Potter, Nelson	1941	1948–49
Quinn, John Picus	1922–25	1913
Rich, Woody	1939–41	1944
Ritchie, Jay	1964–65	1966–67
Sadowski, Bob	1966	1963–65
Schwall, Don	1961–62	1966–67
Skok, Craig	1973	1978–80
Volz, Jake	1901	1905
Wall, Murray	1957–59	1950
Wilson, Jim	1945–46	1951–54
Young, Cy	1901–8	1911

MEN WHO PLAYED FOR THE METS AND THE BRAVES

Batters

Name	Played for Mets	Played for Braves
Cowan, Billy	1965	1965
DeMerit, John	1962	1957–59; 1961
Foster, Leo	1976–77	1971; 1973–74
Gonder, Jesse	1960–61	1965
Johnson, Bob	1967	1968
Klimchock, Lou	1966	1962–65
Kolb, Gary	1965	1964–65
Mantilla, Felix	1962	1956–61
Millan, Felix	1973–77	1962–72
Montanez, Willie	1978–79	1976–77
Nolan, Joe	1972	1975; 1977–80
Samuel, Amado	1964	1962–63
Taylor, Hawk	1964–67	1957–58; 1961–63
Thomas, Frank	1962–64	1961; 1965
Torre, Joe	1975–77	1960–68

Pitchers

Name	Played for Mets	Played for Braves
Aker, Jack	1974	1974
Capra, Buzz	1971–73	1974–77
Cardwell, Don	1967–70	1970
Eilers, Dave	1965–66	1964–65
Frisella, Danny	1967–72	1973–74
Gentry, Gary	1969–72	1973–75
Hendley, Bob	1967	1961–63
Herbel, Ron	1970	1971
Johnson, Bob	1969	1977
Lary, Frank	1964–65	1964
MacKenzie, Ken	1962–63	1960–61
Sadecki, Ray	1970–74; 1977	1975
Shaw, Bob	1966–67	1962–63
Spahn, Warren	1965	1942; 1946–64
Stone, George	1973–75	1967–72
Willey, Carlton	1963–65	1958–62

REGULARS AT EACH POSITION,
PLUS PITCHING RECORDS FOR EACH YEAR, 1876–1980

1876 (Harry Wright)	BA	HR	RBI		IP	W-L	ERA
1B T. Murnane	.282	2	34	J. Borden	218	11-20	2.89
2B J. Morrill	.263	0	26	J. Manning	197	18- 5	2.14
SS G. Wright	.299	1	34	F. Bradley	173	9-10	2.49
3B H. Schafer	.252	0	35				
RF J. Manning	.264	2	25				
CF J. O'Rourke	.327	2	43				
LF A. Leonard	.281	0	27				
C L. Brown	.210	2	21				

1877 (Harry Wright)	BA	HR	RBI		IP	W-L	ERA
1B D. White	*.387*	2	*49*	T. Bond	621	*40*-17	2.11
2B G. Wright	.276	0	35				
SS E. Sutton	.292	0	39				
3B J. Morrill	.302	0	28				
RF H. Schafer	.277	0	13				
CF J. O'Rourke	.362	0	23				
LF A. Leonard	.287	0	27				
C L. Brown	.253	1	31				

1878 (Harry Wright)	BA	HR	RBI		IP	W-L	ERA
1B J. Morril	.240	0	23	T. Bond	*533*	*40*-19	2.06
2B J. Burdock	.260	0	25				
SS G. Wright	.225	0	12				
3B E. Sutton	.226	1	29				
RF J. Manning	.254	0	23				
CF J. O'Rourke	.278	1	29				
LF A. Leonard	.260	0	16				
C P. Snyder	.212	0	14				

1879 (Harry Wright)	BA	HR	RBI		IP	W-L	ERA
1B E. Cogswell	.322	1	18	T. Bond	555	43-19	1.96
2B J. Burdock	.240	0	36	C. Foley	162	9- 9	2.51
SS E. Sutton	.248	0	34				
3B J. Morrill	.282	0	49				
RF S. Houck	.267	2	49				
CF J. O'Rourke	.341	6	*62*				
C P. Snyder	.237	2	35				

1880 (Harry Wright)	BA	HR	RBI		IP	W-L	ERA
1B J. Morrill	.237	2	44	T. Bond	493	26-29	2.67
2B J. Burdock	.253	2	35	C. Foley	238	14-14	3.89
SS E. Sutton	.250	0	25				
3B J. O'Rourke	.275	*6*	45				
RF C. Foley	.292	2	31				
CF J. O'Rourke	.275	3	36				
LF C. Jones	.300	5	37				
C P. Powers	.143	0	10				

1881	(Harry Wright)	BA	HR	RBI		IP	W-L	ERA
1B	J. Morrill	.289	1	39	J. Whitney	*522*	*31-33*	2.48
2B	J. Burdock	.238	1	24	J. Fox	124	6- 8	3.33
SS	R. Barnes	.271	0	17				
3B	E. Sutton	.291	0	31				
RF	F. Lewis	.219	0	9				
CF	B. Crowley	.254	0	31				
LF	J. Hornung	.241	2	25				
C	P. Snyder	.228	0	16				

1882	(John Morrill)	BA	HR	RBI		IP	W-L	ERA
1B	J. Morrill	.289	2	54	J. Whitney	420	24-21	2.64
2B	J. Burdock	.238	0	27	B. Mathews	285	19-15	2.87
SS	S. Wise	.221	4	34				
3B	E. Sutton	.251	2	38				
RF	E. Rowen	.248	1	43				
CF	P. Hotaling	.259	0	28				
LF	J. Hornung	.302	1	50				
C	P. Deasley	.265	0	29				

1883	(Jack Burdock) (John Morrill)	BA	HR	RBI		IP	W-L	ERA
1B	J. Morrill	.319	6	68	J. Whitney	514	37-21	2.24
2B	J. Burdock	.330	5	88	C. Buffinton	333	24-13	3.03
SS	S. Wise	.271	4	58				
3B	E. Sutton	.324	3	73				
RF	P. Radford	.205	0	14				
CF	E. Smith	.217	0	16				
LF	J. Hornung	.278	8	66				
C	M. Hines	.225	0	16				

1884	(John Morrill)	BA	HR	RBI		IP	W-L	ERA
1B	J. Morrill	.260	3	*	C. Buffinton	587	47-16	2.15
2B	J. Burdock	.269	6		J. Whitney	336	24-17	2.09
SS	S. Wise	.214	4					
3B	E. Sutton	.346	3					
RF	B. Crowley	.270	6					
CF	J. Manning	.241	2					
LF	J. Hornung	.268	7					
C	M. Hackett	.205	1					

1885	(John Morrill)	BA	HR	RBI		IP	W-L	ERA
1B	J. Morrill	.226	4	44	J. Whitney	441	18-*32*	2.98
2B	J. Burdock	.142	0	7	C. Buffinton	434	22-27	2.88
SS	S. Wise	.283	4	46	D. Davis	94	5- 6	4.29
3B	E. Sutton	.313	4	47				
RF	T. Poorman	.238	3	25				
CF	J. Manning	.206	2	27				
LF	T. McCarthy	.182	0	11				
C	T. Gunning	.184	0	15				

*None listed in the *Macmillan Baseball Encyclopedia* for 1884.
Italics indicate led league.

157

1886 (John Morrill)	BA	HR	RBI		IP	W-L	ERA
1B S. Wise	.289	4	72	O. Radbourn	509	27-30	3.00
2B J. Burdock	.217	0	25	B. Stemmyer	349	22-18	3.02
SS J. Morrill	.247	7	69	C. Buffinton	151	8-10	4.59
3B B. Nash	.281	1	45				
RF T. Poorman	.261	3	41				
CF D. Johnston	.240	1	57				
LF J. Hornung	.257	2	40				
C C. Daily	.239	0	21				

1887 (John Morrill)	BA	HR	RBI		IP	W-L	ERA
1B J. Morrill	.280	12	81	O. Radbourn	425	24-23	4.55
2B J. Burdock	.257	0	29	K. Madden	321	22-14	3.79
SS S. Wise	.334	9	92	D. Conway	222	9-15	4.66
3B B. Nash	.295	7	94	B. Stemmyer	119	6- 8	5.20
RF K. Kelly	.322	8	63				
CF D. Johnston	.258	5	77				
LF J. Hornung	.270	5	49				
C P. Tate	.260	0	27				

1888 (John Morrill)	BA	HR	RBI		IP	W-L	ERA
1B J. Morrill	.198	4	39	J. Clarkson	*483*	*33*-20	2.76
2B J. Quinn	.301	4	29	B. Sowders	317	19-15	2.07
SS S. Wise	.240	4	40	O. Radbourn	207	7-16	2.87
3B B. Nash	.283	4	75	K. Madden	165	7-11	2.95
RF T. Brown	.248	9	49				
CF D. Johnston	.296	12	68				
LF J. Hornung	.239	3	53				
C K. Kelly	.318	9	71				

1889 (Jim Hart)	BA	HR	RBI		IP	W-L	ERA
1B D. Brouthers	*.373*	7	118	J. Clarkson	*620*	*49-19*	*2.73*
2B H. Richardson	.304	7	79	O. Radbourn	277	20-11	3.67
SS J. Quinn	.261	2	69	K. Madden	178	10-10	4.40
3B B. Nash	.274	3	76				
RF K. Kelly	.294	9	78				
CF D. Johnston	.228	5	67				
LF T. Brown	.232	2	24				
C C. Bennett	.231	4	28				

1890 (Frank Selee)	BA	HR	RBI		IP	W-L	ERA
1B T. Tucker	.295	1	62	K. Nichols	427	27-19	2.21
2B P. Smith	.229	1	53	J. Clarkson	383	25-18	3.27
SS H. Long	.251	8	52	C. Getzein	350	23-17	3.19
3B C. McGarr	.236	1	51				
RF S. Brodie	.296	0	67				
CF P. Hines	.264	2	48				
LF M. Sullivan	.285	6	61				
C C. Bennett	.214	3	40				

1891 (Frank Selee)	BA	HR	RBI		IP	W-L	ERA
1B T. Tucker	.270	2	69	J. Clarkson	461	33-19	2.79
2B J. Quinn	.240	3	63	K. Nichols	426	30-17	2.39
SS H. Long	.288	10	75	H. Staley	252	20- 8	2.50
3B B. Nash	.276	5	95				
RF H. Stovey	.279	16	95				
CF S. Brodie	.260	2	78				
LF B. Lowe	.260	6	74				
C C. Bennett	.215	5	39				

1892 (Frank Selee)	BA	HR	RBI		IP	W-L	ERA
1B T. Tucker	.282	1	62	K. Nichols	454	35-16	2.83
2B J. Quinn	.218	1	59	J. Stivetts	415	35-16	3.04
SS H. Long	.286	6	77	H. Staley	300	22-10	3.03
3B B. Nash	.260	4	95	J. Clarkson	146	8- 6	2.35
RF T. McCarthy	.242	4	63				
CF H. Duffy	.301	5	81				
LF B. Lowe	.242	3	57				
C K. Kelly	.189	2	41				

1893 (Frank Selee)	BA	HR	RBI		IP	W-L	ERA
1B T. Tucker	.284	7	91	K. Nichols	425	33-13	3.52
2B B. Lowe	.298	13	89	J. Stivetts	284	19-13	4.41
SS H. Long	.288	6	58	H. Staley	263	18-10	5.13
3B B. Nash	.291	10	123	H. Gastright	156	12- 4	5.13
RF C. Carroll	.224	2	54				
CF H. Duffy	.363	6	118				
LF T. McCarthy	.346	5	111				
C C. Bennett	.209	4	27				

1894 (Frank Selee)	BA	HR	RBI		IP	W-L	ERA
1B T. Tucker	.330	3	100	K. Nichols	407	32-13	4.75
2B B. Lowe	.346	17	115	J. Stivetts	338	28-13	4.90
SS H. Long	.324	12	79	H. Staley	209	13-10	6.81
3B B. Nash	.289	8	87	T. Lovett	104	8- 6	5.97
RF J. Bannon	.336	13	114				
CF H. Duffy	*.438*	*18*	*145*				
LF T. McCarthy	.349	13	126				
C C. Ganzel	.278	3	56				

1895 (Frank Selee)	BA	HR	RBI		IP	W-L	ERA
1B T. Tucker	.249	3	73	K. Nichols	394	30-14	3.29
2B B. Lowe	.296	7	62	J. Stivetts	291	17-17	4.64
SS H. Long	.319	9	75	C. Dolan	198	11- 7	4.27
3B B. Nash	.289	10	108	J. Sullivan	179	11- 9	4.82
RF J. Bannon	.350	6	74				
CF J. Bannon							
LF T. McCarthy	.290	2	73				
C C. Ganzel	.264	1	52				

Regulars at Each Position, Plus Pitching Records for Each Year, 1876-1980 (continued)

1896 (Frank Selee)	BA	HR	RBI		IP	W-L	ERA
1B T. Tucker	.304	2	72	K. Nichols	375	30-15	2.81
2B B. Lowe	.321	2	48	J. Stivetts	329	21-13	4.10
SS H. Long	.339	6	100	J. Sullivan	225	11-12	4.03
3B J. Collins	.296	1	46	F. Klobedanz	81	6- 4	3.01
RF J. Bannon	.251	0	50				
CF B. Hamilton	.365	3	52				
LF B. Hamilton							
C M. Bergen	.269	4	37				

1897 (Frank Selee)	BA	HR	RBI		IP	W-L	ERA
1B F. Tenney	.325	1	85	K. Nichols	368	30-11	2.64
2B B. Lowe	.309	5	106	F. Klobedanz	309	26- 7	4.60
SS H. Long	.327	3	69	T. Lewis	290	21-12	3.85
3B J. Collins	.346	6	132	J. Stivetts	129	12- 5	3.41
RF C. Stahl	.358	4	97	J. Sullivan	89	4- 5	3.94
CF B. Hamilton	.343	3	61				
LF H. Duffy	.340	11	129				
C M. Bergen	.248	2	45				

1898 (Frank Selee)	BA	HR	RBI		IP	W-L	ERA
1B F. Tenney	.334	0	62	K. Nichols	388	29-12	2.13
2B B. Lowe	.272	4	94	T. Lewis	313	26- 8	2.90
SS H. Long	.265	6	99	V. Willis	311	24-13	2.84
3B J. Collins	.329	15	111	F. Klobedanz	271	19-10	3.89
RF C. Stahl	.311	3	52				
CF B. Hamilton	.369	3	50				
LF H. Duffy	.315	8	108				
C M. Bergen	.280	3	60				

1899 (Frank Selee)	BA	HR	RBI		IP	W-L	ERA
1B F. Tenney	.347	1	67	K. Nichols	349	21-17	2.94
2B B. Lowe	.272	4	88	V. Willis	343	27-10	2.50
SS H. Long	.265	6	100	T. Lewis	235	17-11	3.49
3B J. Collins	.277	4	91	J. Meekin	208	7- 6	2.83
RF C. Stahl	.351	8	53	F. Killen	99	7- 5	4.26
CF B. Hamilton	.310	1	33	H. Bailey	87	6- 4	3.95
LF H. Duffy	.279	5	102				
C M. Bergen	.258	1	34				

1900 (Frank Selee)	BA	HR	RBI		IP	W-L	ERA
1B F. Tenney	.279	1	56	B. Dinneen	321	10-14	3.12
2B B. Lowe	.278	3	71	V. Willis	236	10-17	4.19
SS H. Long	.261	12	66	K. Nichols	231	13-15	3.07
3B J. Collins	.304	6	95	T. Lewis	209	13-12	4.13
RF B. Freeman	.301	6	65	T. Pittinger	114	2- 9	5.13
CF B. Hamilton	.333	1	47	N. Cuppy	105	8- 4	3.08
LF C. Stahl	.295	5	82				
C B. Clarke	.315	1	30				

1901	(Frank Selee)	BA	HR	RBI			IP	W-L	ERA
1B	F. Tenney	.282	1	22	K. Nichols		326	18-15	3.17
2B	DeMontreville	.300	5	72	B. Dinneen		309	16-19	2.94
SS	H. Long	.228	3	68	V. Willis		305	20-17	2.36
3B	B. Lowe	.255	3	47	T. Pittinger		281	13-16	3.01
RF	J. Slagle	.271	0	7					
CF	B. Hamilton	.287	3	38					
LF	D. Cooley	.258	0	27					
C	M. Kittredge	.252	2	40					

1902	(Al Buckenberger)	BA	HR	RBI			IP	W-L	ERA
1B	F. Tenney	.315	2	30	V. Willis		*410*	27-*20*	2.20
2B	DeMontreville	.268	0	53	T. Pittinger		389	27-16	2.52
SS	H. Long	.228	2	44	M. Eason		206	9-11	2.75
3B	E. Gremminger	.257	1	66	J. Malarkey		170	8-10	2.59
RF	P. Carney	.270	2	65					
CF	B. Lush	.223	2	19					
LF	D. Cooley	2.96	0	58					
C	M. Kittredge	.235	2	30					

1903	(Al Buckenberger)	BA	HR	RBI			IP	W-L	ERA
1B	F. Tenney	.313	3	41	T. Pittinger		352	19-*23*	3.48
2B	Abbaticchio	.227	1	46	V. Willis		278	12-18	2.98
SS	H. Aubrey	.212	0	27	J. Malarkey		253	11-16	3.09
3B	E. Gremminger	.264	5	59	W. Piatt		181	8-13	3.18
RF	P. Carney	.240	1	49					
CF	C. Dexter	.223	3	34					
LF	D. Cooley	.289	1	70					
C	P. Moran	.262	7	54					

1904	(Al Buckenberger)	BA	HR	RBI			IP	W-L	ERA
1B	F. Tenney	.270	1	37	V. Willis		350	18-*25*	2.85
2B	F. Raymer	.210	1	27	T. Pittinger		335	15-21	2.66
SS	Abbaticchio	.256	3	54	K. Wilhelm		288	14-22	3.69
3B	J. Delahanty	.285	3	60	T. Fisher		214	6-15	4.25
RF	R. Cannell	.234	0	18	E. McNichol		122	2-12	4.28
CF	P. Geier	.243	1	27					
LF	D. Cooley	.272	5	70					
C	T. Needham	.260	4	19					

1905	(Fred Tenney)	BA	HR	RBI			IP	W-L	ERA
1B	F. Tenney	.288	0	28	I. Young		*378*	20-21	2.90
2B	F. Raymer	.211	0	31	V. Willis		342	11-*29*	3.21
SS	Abbaticchio	.279	3	41	C. Fraser		334	15-22	3.29
3B	H. Wolverton	.225	2	55	K. Wilhelm		242	4-22	4.54
RF	C. Dolan	.275	3	48					
CF	R. Cannell	.247	0	36					
LF	J. Delahanty	.258	5	55					
C	P. Moran	.240	2	22					

1906	(Fred Tenney)	BA	HR	RBI		IP	W-L	ERA
1B	F. Tenney	.283	1	28	I. Young	358	16-25	2.91
2B	A. Strobel	.202	1	24	V. Lindaman	307	12-23	2.43
SS	A. Bridwell	.227	0	22	B. Pfeffer	302	13-22	2.95
3B	D. Brain	.250	5	45	G. Dorner	257	8-25	3.88
RF	C. Dolan	.248	0	39				
CF	J. Bates	.252	6	54				
LF	D. Howard	.261	1	54				
C	T. Needham	.189	1	12				

1907	(Fred Tenney)	BA	HR	RBI		IP	W-L	ERA
1B	F. Tenney	.273	0	26	G. Dorner	271	12-17	3.12
2B	C. Titchey	.255	2	51	V. Lindaman	260	11-15	3.63
SS	A. Bridwell	.218	0	26	I. Young	245	10-23	3.96
3B	D. Brain	.279	10	56	P. Flaherty	217	12-15	2.70
RF	J. Bates	.260	2	49	B. Pfeffer	144	6- 8	3.00
CF	G. Beaumont	.322	4	62	J. Boultes	140	5- 8	2.71
LF	N. Randall	.213	0	15				
C	T. Needham	.196	1	19				

1908	(Joe Kelley)	BA	HR	RBI		IP	W-L	ERA
1B	D. McGann	.240	2	55	V. Lindaman	271	12-15	2.36
2B	C. Ritchey	.273	2	36	P. Flaherty	244	12-18	3.25
SS	B. Dahleen	.239	3	48	G. Dorner	216	8-20	3.54
3B	B. Sweeney	.244	0	40	G. Ferguson	208	12-11	2.47
RF	G. Browne	.228	1	34	T. McCarthy	94	6- 4	1.63
CF	G. Beaumont	.267	2	52	I. Young	85	4- 7	2.86
LF	J. Bates	.258	1	29				
C	F. Bowerman	.228	1	25				

1909	(Frank Bowerman)	BA	HR	RBI		IP	W-L	ERA
1B	F. Stern	.208	0	11	A. Mattern	316	16-20	2.85
2B	D. Shean	.247	1	29	G. Ferguson	227	5-25	3.73
SS	J. Coffey	.187	0	20	K. White	148	6-13	3.22
3B	B. Sweeney	.243	1	36	L. Richie	132	7- 7	2.32
RF	B. Becker	.246	6	24	B. Brown	123	4-11	3.14
CF	G. Beaumont	.263	0	60				
LF	R. Thomas	.263	0	11				
C	P. Graham	.240	0	17				

1910	(Fred Lake)	BA	HR	RBI		IP	W-L	ERA
1B	B. Sharpe	.239	0	29	A. Mattern	305	15-19	2.98
2B	D. Shean	.239	3	36	B. Brown	263	8-22	2.67
SS	B. Sweeney	.267	5	46	S. Frock	255	10-20	3.21
3B	B. Herzog	.250	3	32	C. Curtis	251	6-24	3.55
RF	D. Miller	.286	3	55	G. Ferguson	123	8- 7	3.80
CF	F. Beck	.275	10	64				
LF	B. Collins	.241	3	40				
C	P. Graham	.282	0	21				

1911 (Fred Tenney)

		BA	HR	RBI		IP	W-L	ERA
1B	F. Tenney	.263	1	36	B. Brown	241	7-18	4.29
2B	B. Sweeney	.314	3	63	A. Mattern	186	4-15	4.97
SS	B. Herzog	.310	5	41	L. Tyler	165	7-10	5.06
3B	S. Ingerton	.250	5	61	H. Perdue	137	6- 9	4.98
RF	D. Miller	.333	7	91	O. Weaver	121	3-13	6.47
CF	M. Donin	.315	2	34	B. Pfeffer	97	7- 5	4.73
LF	A. Kaiser	.203	2	15	C. Curtis	77	1- 8	4.44
C	J. Kling	.224	2	24				

1912 (Johnny Kling)

		BA	HR	RBI		IP	W-L	ERA
1B	B. Houser	.286	8	52	L. Tyler	256	11-*22*	4.18
2B	B. Sweeney	.344	1	100	O. Hess	254	12-17	3.76
SS	F. O'Rourke	.122	0	16	H. Perdue	249	13-16	3.80
3B	E. McDonald	.259	2	34	W. Dickson	189	4-19	3.86
RF	J. Titus	.325	2	48	E. Donnelly	184	5-10	4.35
CF	V. Campbell	.296	3	48	B. Brown	168	3-15	4.01
LF	G. Jackson	.262	4	48				
C	J. Kling	.317	2	30				

1913 (George Stallings)

		BA	HR	RBI		IP	W-L	ERA
1B	H. Myers	.273	2	50	L. Tyler	290	16-17	2.79
2B	B. Sweeney	.257	0	47	D. Rudolph	249	14-13	2.92
SS	R. Maranville	.247	2	48	O. Hess	218	7-17	3.83
3B	A. Devlin	.229	0	12	H. Perdue	212	16-13	3.26
RF	J. Titus	.297	5	38	B. James	136	6-10	2.79
CF	L. Mann	.253	3	51	W. Dickson	128	6- 7	3.23
LF	J. Connolly	.281	5	57				
C	B. Rariden	.236	3	30				

1914 (George Stallings)

		BA	HR	RBI		IP	W-L	ERA
1B	B. Schmidt	.285	1	71	D. Rudolph	336	*27*-10	2.35
2B	J. Evers	.279	1	40	B. James	332	26- 7	1.90
SS	R. Maranville	.246	4	78	L. Tyler	271	16-14	2.69
3B	C. Deal	.210	0	23	D. Crutcher	159	5- 6	3.46
RF	L. Gilbert	.268	5	25	O. Hess	89	5- 6	3.03
CF	L. Mann	.247	4	40				
LF	J. Connolly	.306	9	65				
C	H. Gowdy	.243	3	46				

1915 (George Stallings)

		BA	HR	RBI		IP	W-L	ERA
1B	B. Schmidt	.251	2	60	D. Rudolph	341	21-*19*	2.37
2B	J. Evers	.263	1	22	T. Hughes	280	20-14	2.12
SS	R. Maranville	.244	2	43	P. Ragan	227	14-12	2.46
3B	R. Smith	.264	2	65	L. Tyler	205	9- 9	2.86
RF	H. Moran	.200	0	21				
CF	S. Magee	.280	2	87				
LF	J. Connolly	.298	0	23				
C	H. Gowdy	.247	2	30				

1916 (George Stallings)	BA	HR	RBI		IP	W-L	ERA
1B E. Konetchy	.260	3	70	D. Rudolph	312	19-12	2.16
2B J. Evers	.216	0	15	L. Tyler	249	17-10	2.02
SS R. Maranville	.235	4	38	P. Ragan	182	9- 9	2.08
3B R. Smith	.259	3	60	J. Barnes	163	6-14	2.37
RF J. Wilhoit	.230	2	38	T. Hughes	161	16- 3	2.35
CF F. Snodgrass	.249	1	32	A. Nehf	121	7- 5	2.01
LF S. Magee	.241	3	54	F. Allen	113	8- 2	2.07
C H. Gowdy	.252	1	34	E. Reulbach	109	7- 6	2.47

1917 (George Stallings)	BA	HR	RBI		IP	W-L	ERA
1B E. Konetchy	.272	2	54	J. Barnes	295	13-*21*	2.68
2B J. Rawlings	.256	2	31	D. Rudolph	243	13-13	3.41
SS R. Maranville	.260	3	43	L. Tyler	239	14-12	2.52
3B R. Smith	.295	2	62	A. Nehf	233	17- 8	2.16
RF W. Rehg	.270	1	31	P. Ragan	148	7- 9	2.93
CF R. Powell	.272	4	30	F. Allen	112	3-11	3.94
LF J. Kelly	.222	3	36				
C W. Tragesser	.222	0	25				

1918 (George Stallings)	BA	HR	RBI		IP	W-L	ERA
1B E. Konetchy	.236	2	56	A. Nehf	284	9-15	2.69
2B B. Herzog	.228	0	26	P. Ragan	206	9-14	2.31
SS J. Rawlings	.207	0	21	D. Rudolph	154	6-12	2.71
3B R. Smith	.298	2	65	B. Hearn	126	12-12	3.50
RF A. Wickland	.262	4	32	D. Fillingim	113	8-14	3.59
CF R. Powell	.213	0	20			5- 6	3.83
LF R. Massey	.291	0	18				
C A. Wilson	.246	0	19				

1919 (George Stallings)	BA	HR	RBI		IP	W-L	ERA
1B W. Holke	.292	0	48	D. Rudolph	274	13-18	2.17
2B B. Herzog	.280	1	25	D. Fillingim	186	5-13	3.38
SS R. Maranville	.267	5	43	A. Nehf	169	8- 9	3.09
3B T. Boeckel	.249	1	26	R. Keating	136	6-11	2.98
RF R. Powell	.236	2	33	A. Demaree	128	7- 6	3.80
CF J. Riggert	.283	4	17	J. Scott	104	6- 6	3.13
LF W. Cruise	.216	1	21				
C H. Gowdy	.279	1	22				

1920 (George Stallings)	BA	HR	RBI		IP	W-L	ERA
1B W. Holke	.294	3	64	J. Oeschger	299	15-13	3.46
2B C. Pick	.297	2	28	J. Scott	291	10-21	3.53
SS R. Maranville	.266	1	43	D. Fillingim	272	12-21	3.11
3B T. Boeckel	.268	3	62	H. McQuillan	226	11-15	3.55
RF W. Cruise	.278	1	21	D. Rudolph	89	4- 8	4.04
CF R. Powell	.225	6	29				
LF L. Mann	.276	3	32				
C M. O'Neil	.283	0	28				

1921 (Fred Mitchell)	BA	HR	RBI		IP	W-L	ERA
1B W. Holke	.261	3	63	J. Oeschger	299	20-14	3.52
2B H. Ford	.279	2	61	M. Watson	259	14-13	3.85
SS W. Barbare	.302	0	49	H. McQuillan	250	13-17	4.00
3B T. Boeckel	.313	10	84	D. Fillingim	240	15-10	3.45
RF B. Southworth	.308	7	79	J. Scott	234	15-13	3.70
CF R. Powell	.306	12	74				
LF W. Cruise	.346	8	55				
C M. O'Neil	.249	2	29				

1922 (Fred Mitchell)	BA	HR	RBI		IP	W-L	ERA
1B W. Holke	.291	0	46	M. Watson	201	8-14	4.70
2B L. Kopf	.266	1	37	F. Miller	200	11-13	3.51
SS H. Ford	.272	2	60	R. Marquard	198	11-15	5.09
3B T. Boeckel	.289	6	47	J. Oeschger	196	6-21	5.06
RF W. Cruise	.278	4	46	H. McQuillan	136	5-10	4.24
CF R. Powell	.296	6	37	D. Fillingim	117	5- 9	4.54
LF A. Nixon	.264	2	22				
C M. O'Neil	.223	0	26				

1923 (Fred Mitchell)	BA	HR	RBI		IP	W-L	ERA
1B S. McInnis	.315	2	95	R. Marquard	239	11-14	3.73
2B H. Ford	.271	2	50	J. Genewich	227	13-14	3.72
SS B. Smith	.251	0	40	J. Barnes	195	10-14	2.76
3B T. Boeckel	.298	7	79	J. Oeschger	166	5-15	5.68
RF B. Southworth	.319	6	78	T. McNamara	139	3-13	4.91
CF R. Powell	.302	4	38	L. Benton	128	5- 9	4.99
LF G. Felix	.273	6	44	D. Filingim	100	1- 9	5.20
C M. O'Neil	.212	0	20				

1924 (Dave Bancroft)	BA	HR	RBI		IP	W-L	ERA
1B S. McInnis	.291	1	59	J. Barnes	268	15-20	3.23
2B C. Tierney	.259	6	58	J. Genewich	200	10-19	5.21
SS B. Smith	.228	2	38	J. Cooney	181	8- 9	3.18
3B E. Padgett	.255	1	46	T. McNamara	179	8-12	5.18
RF C. Stengel	.280	5	39	J. Yeargin	141	1-11	5.09
CF F. Wilson	.237	1	15	L. Benton	128	5- 7	4.15
LF B. Cunningham	.272	1	40	D. Stryker	73	3- 8	6.01
C M. O'Neil	.246	0	22				

1925 (Dave Bancroft)	BA	HR	RBI		IP	W-L	ERA
1B D. Burrus	.340	5	87	J. Cooney	246	14-14	3.48
2B D. Gautreau	.262	0	23	J. Barnes	216	11-16	4.53
SS D. Bancroft	.319	2	49	L. Benton	183	14- 7	3.09
3B B. Marriott	.268	1	40	J. Genewich	169	12-10	3.99
RF J. Welsh	.312	7	63	K. Graham	157	7-12	4.41
CF G. Felix	.307	2	66	R. Ryan	123	2- 8	6.31
LF B. Neis	.285	5	45	R. Marquard	72	2- 8	5.75
C F. Gibson	.278	2	50				

Regulars at Each Position, Plus Pitching Records for Each Year, 1876–1980 (continued)

1926	(Dave Bancroft)	BA	HR	RBI		IP	W-L	ERA
1B	D. Burrus	.270	3	61	L. Benton	232	14-14	3.85
2B	D. Gautreau	.267	0	8	J. Genewich	216	8-16	3.88
SS	D. Bancroft	.311	1	44	B. Smith	193	10-13	3.91
3B	A. High	.296	2	66	J. Wertz	189	11- 9	3.28
RF	J. Welsh	.278	3	57	G. Mogridge	142	6-10	4.50
CF	J. Smith	.311	2	25	B. Hearn	117	4- 9	4.22
LF	E. Brown	.328	2	84	H. Goldsmith	101	5- 7	4.37
C	Z. Taylor	.255	0	42				

1927	(Dave Bancroft)	BA	HR	RBI		IP	W-L	ERA
1B	J. Fournier	.283	10	53	B. Smith	261	10-18	3.76
2B	D. Gautreau	.246	0	20	K. Greenfield	190	11-14	3.84
SS	D. Bancroft	.243	1	31	J. Genewich	181	11- 8	3.83
3B	A. High	.302	4	46	J. Wertz	164	4-10	4.55
RF	L. Richbourg	.309	2	34	C. Robertson	154	7-17	4.72
CF	J. Welsh	.288	9	54	F. Edwards	92	2- 8	4.99
LF	E. Brown	.306	2	75	G. Modridge	49	6- 4	3.70
C	S. Hogan	.288	3	32				

1928	(Jack Slattery) (Rogers Hornsby)	BA	HR	RBI		IP	W-L	ERA
1B	G. Sisler	.340	4	68	B. Smith	244	13-17	3.87
2B	R. Hornsby	*.387*	21	94	E. Brandt	225	9-*21*	5.07
SS	D. Farrell	.215	3	43	A. Delaney	192	9-11	3.79
3B	L. Bell	.277	10	91	K. Greenfield	144	3-11	5.32
RF	L. Richbourg	.337	2	52	J. Cooney	90	3- 7	4.32
CF	J. Smith	.280	1	32	J. Genewich	81	3- 7	4.13
LF	E. Brown	.268	2	59				
C	Z. Taylor	.251	2	30				

1929	(Bill Carrigan)	BA	HR	RBI		IP	W-L	ERA
1B	P. Todt	.262	4	64	R. Ruffing	244	9-*22*	4.86
2B	B. Regan	.288	1	54	M. Gaston	244	12-19	3.73
SS	H. Rhyne	.251	0	38	J. Russell	226	6-18	3.94
3B	B. Reeves	.248	2	28	MacFayden	221	10-18	3.62
RF	B. Barrett	.270	3	35	E. Morris	208	14-14	4.45
CF	J. Rothrock	.300	6	59	B. Bayne	84	5- 5	6.72
LF	R. Scarritt	.294	1	71				
C	C. Berry	.242	1	21				

1930	(Bill McKechnie)	BA	HR	RBI		IP	W-L	ERA
1B	G. Sisler	.309	3	67	S. Seibold	251	15-16	4.12
2B	F. Maguire	.267	0	52	B. Smith	220	10-14	4.26
SS	R. Maranville	.281	2	43	B. Cantwell	173	9-15	4.88
3B	B. Chatham	.267	5	56	T. Zachary	151	11- 5	4.58
RF	L. Richbourg	.304	3	54	E. Brandt	147	4-11	5.01
CF	J. Welsh	.275	3	36	B. Sherdel	119	6- 5	4.75
LF	W. Berger	.310	38	119	F. Frankhouse	111	7- 6	5.61
C	A. Spohrer	.317	2	37	B. Cunningham	107	5- 6	5.48

166

1931	(Bill McKechnie)	BA	HR	RBI		IP	W-L	ERA
1B	E. Sheely	.273	1	77	E. Brandt	250	18-11	2.92
2B	F. Maguire	.228	0	26	T. Zachary	229	11-15	3.10
SS	R. Maranville	.260	0	33	S. Seibold	206	10-18	4.67
3B	B. Urbanski	.238	0	17	B. Cantwell	156	7- 9	3.63
RF	Schulmerich	.309	2	43	B. Sherdel	138	6-10	4.25
CF	W. Berger	.323	19	84	B. Cunningham	137	3-12	4.48
LF	Worthington	.291	4	44	F. Frankhouse	127	8- 8	4.03
C	A. Spohrer	.240	0	27				

1932	(Bill McKechnie)	BA	HR	RBI		IP	W-L	ERA
1B	A. Shires	.238	5	30	E. Brandt	254	16-16	3.97
2B	R. Maranville	.235	0	37	H. Betts	222	13-11	2.80
SS	B. Urbanski	.272	8	46	B. Brown	213	14- 7	3.30
3B	R. Knothe	.238	1	36	T. Zachary	212	12-11	3.10
RF	Schulmerich	.260	11	57	B. Cantwell	146	13-11	2.96
CF	W. Berger	.307	17	73	S. Seibold	137	3-10	4.68
LF	Worthington	.303	8	61	F. Frankhouse	109	4- 6	3.56
C	A. Spohrer	.269	0	33				

1933	(Bill McKechnie)	BA	HR	RBI		IP	W-L	ERA
1B	B. Jordan	.286	4	46	E. Brandt	288	18-14	2.60
2B	R. Maranville	.218	0	38	B. Cantwell	255	20-10	2.62
SS	B. Urbanski	.251	0	35	F. Frankhouse	245	16-15	3.16
3B	P. Whitney	.246	8	49	H. Betts	242	11-11	2.79
RF	R. Moore	.302	8	70	T. Zachary	125	7- 9	3.53
CF	W. Berger	.313	27	106				
LF	H. Lee	.221	1	28				
C	S. Hogan	.253	3	30				

1934	(Bill McKechnie)	BA	HR	RBI		IP	W-L	ERA
1B	B. Jordan	.311	2	58	E. Brandt	255	16-14	3.53
2B	M. McManus	.276	8	47	F. Frankhouse	234	17- 9	3.20
SS	B. Urbanski	.293	7	53	H. Betts	213	17-10	4.06
3B	P. Whitney	.259	12	79	F. Rhem	153	8- 8	3.60
RF	T. Thompson	.265	0	37	B. Cantwell	143	5-11	4.33
CF	W. Berger	.298	34	121	B. Smith	122	6- 9	4.66
LF	H. Lee	.292	8	79				
C	A. Spohrer	.223	0	17				

1935	(Bill McKechnie)	BA	HR	RBI		IP	W-L	ERA
1B	B. Dahlgren	.263	9	63	W. Ferrell	322	25-14	3.52
2B	O. Melilo	.261	1	39	L. Grove	273	20-12	2.70
SS	J. Cronin	.295	9	95	G. Rhodes	146	2-10	5.41
3B	B. Werber	.255	14	61	J. Welch	143	10- 9	4.47
RF	D. Cooke	.306	3	34	R. Walberg	143	5- 9	3.91
CF	M. Almada	.290	3	59	Ostermueller	138	7- 8	3.92
LF	R. Johnson	.315	3	66				
C	R. Ferrell	.310	3	61				

1936 (Bill McKechnie)	BA	HR	RBI		IP	W-L	ERA
1B B. Jordan	.323	3	66	MacFayden	267	17-13	2.87
2B T. Cuccinello	.308	7	86	T. Chaplin	231	10-15	4.12
SS B. Urbanski	.261	0	26	J. Lanning	153	7-11	3.65
3B J. Coscarart	.254	2	44	B. Reis	139	6- 5	4.48
RF G. Moore	.290	13	67	B. Smith	136	6- 7	3.77
CF W. Berger	.288	25	91	B. Cantwell	133	9- 9	3.04
LF H. Lee	.253	3	64	R. Benge	115	7- 9	5.79
C A. Lopez	.242	8	50				

1937 (Bill McKechnie)	BA	HR	RBI		IP	W-L	ERA
1B E. Fletcher	.247	1	38	L. Fette	259	20-10	2.88
2B T. Cuccinello	.271	11	80	J. Turner	257	20-11	2.38
SS R. Warstler	.223	3	36	MacFayden	246	14-14	2.93
3B G. English	.290	2	37	G. Bush	181	8-15	3.54
RF G. Moore	.283	16	70	J. Lanning	117	5- 7	3.93
CF V. DiMaggio	.256	13	69	I. Hutchinson	92	4- 6	3.73
LF D. Garms	.259	2	37	F. Gabler	76	4- 7	5.09
C A. Lopez	.204	3	38				

1938 (Casey Stengel)	BA	HR	RBI		IP	W-L	ERA
1B E. Fletcher	.272	6	48	J. Turner	268	14-18	3.46
2B T. Cuccinello	.265	9	76	L. Fette	240	11-13	3.15
SS R. Warstler	.231	0	40	MacFayden	220	14- 9	2.95
3B J. Stripp	.275	1	19	I. Hutchinson	151	9- 8	2.74
RF J. Cooney	.271	0	17	M. Shoffner	140	8- 7	3.54
CF V. DiMaggio	.228	14	61	J. Lanning	138	8- 7	3.72
LF M. West	.234	10	63	D. Errickson	123	9- 7	3.15
C R. Mueller	.237	4	35				

1939 (Casey Stengel)	BA	HR	RBI		IP	W-L	ERA
1B B. Hassett	.308	2	60	B. Posedel	221	15-13	3.92
2B T. Cuccinello	.306	2	40	MacFayden	192	8-14	3.90
SS E. Miller	.267	4	31	J. Turner	158	4-11	4.28
3B H. Majeski	.272	7	54	L. Fette	146	10-10	2.96
RF D. Garms	.298	2	37	M. Shoffner	132	4- 6	3.13
CF J. Cooney	.274	2	27	J. Lanning	129	5- 6	3.42
LF M. West	.285	19	82	D. Errickson	128	6- 9	4.00
C A. Lopez	.272	8	49	J. Sullivan	114	6- 9	3.64

1940 (Casey Stengel)	BA	HR	RBI		IP	W-L	ERA
1B B. Hassett	.234	0	27	D. Errickson	236	12-13	3.16
2B B. Rowell	.305	3	58	B. Posedel	233	12-17	4.13
SS E. Miller	.276	14	79	J. Sullivan	177	10-14	3.55
3B S. Sisti	.251	6	34	M. Salvo	161	10- 9	3.08
RF M. West	.261	7	72	Strincevich	129	4- 8	5.53
CF J. Cooney	.318	0	21	J. Tobin	96	7- 3	3.83
LF C. Ross	.281	17	89				
C R. Berres	.192	0	14				

1941	(Casey Stengel)	BA	HR	RBI		IP	W-L	ERA
1B	B. Hassett	.296	1	33	J. Tobin	238	12-12	3.10
2B	B. Rowell	.267	7	60	M. Salvo	195	7-16	4.06
SS	E. Miller	.239	6	68	A. Johnson	183	7-15	3.53
3B	S. Sisti	.259	1	45	D. Errickson	166	6-12	4.78
RF	G. Moore	.272	5	43	A. Javery	161	10-11	4.31
CF	J. Cooney	.319	0	29	T. Earley	139	6- 8	2.53
LF	M. West	.277	12	68	F. LaManna	73	5- 4	5.33
C	R. Berres	.201	1	19				

1942	(Casey Stengel)	BA	HR	RBI		IP	W-L	ERA
1B	M. West	.254	16	56	J. Tobin	*288*	12-*21*	3.97
2B	S. Sisti	.211	4	35	A. Javery	261	12-16	3.03
SS	E. Miller	.243	6	47	L. Tost	148	10-10	3.53
3B	N. Fernandez	.255	6	55	M. Salvo	131	7- 8	3.03
RF	P. Waner	.258	1	39	T. Earley	113	6-11	4.71
CF	T. Holmes	.278	4	41	J. Sain	97	4- 7	3.90
LF	C. Ross	.195	5	19				
C	E. Lombardi	*.330*	11	46				

1943	(Casey Stengel)	BA	HR	RBI		IP	W-L	ERA
1B	J. McCarthy	.304	2	33	A. Javery	*303*	17-16	3.21
2B	C. Ryan	.212	1	24	N. Andrews	284	14-*20*	2.57
SS	Wietelmann	.215	0	39	R. Barrett	255	12-18	3.18
3B	E. Joost	.185	2	20	J. Tobin	250	14-14	2.66
RF	C. Workman	.249	10	67	M. Salvo	93	5- 6	3.28
CF	T. Holmes	.270	5	41				
LF	B. Nieman	.251	7	46				
C	P. Masi	.273	2	28				

1944	(Bob Coleman)	BA	HR	RBI		IP	W-L	ERA
1B	B. Etchison	.214	8	33	J. Tobin	299	18-19	3.01
2B	C. Ryan	.295	4	25	N. Andrews	257	16-15	3.22
SS	W. Wietelmann	.240	2	32	A. Javery	254	10-19	3.54
3B	D. Phillips	.258	1	53	R. Barrett	230	9-16	4.06
RF	C. Workman	.208	11	53	I. Hutchinson	120	9- 7	4.21
CF	T. Holmes	.309	13	73				
LF	B. Nieman	.265	16	65				
C	P. Masi	.275	3	23				

1945	(Bob Coleman) (Del Bissonette)	BA	HR	RBI		IP	W-L	ERA
1B	V. Shupe	.269	0	15	J. Tobin	197	9-14	3.84
2B	W. Wietelmann	.271	4	33	B. Logan	187	7-11	3.18
SS	D. Culler	.262	2	30	J. Hutchings	185	7- 6	3.75
3B	C. Workman	.274	25	87	N. Andrews	138	7-12	4.58
RF	T. Holmes	.352	*28*	117	E. Wright	111	8- 3	2.51
CF	C. Gillenwater	.288	7	72	B. Lee	106	6- 3	2.79
LF	B. Nieman	.247	14	56	M. Cooper	78	7- 4	3.35
C	P. Masi	.272	7	46	D. Hendrickson	73	4- 8	4.91

Regulars at Each Position, Plus Pitching Records for Each Year, 1876-1980 (continued)

1946 (Billy Southworth)		BA	HR	RBI		IP	W-L	ERA
1B	R. Sanders	.243	6	35	J. Sain	265	20-14	2.21
2B	C. Ryan	.241	1	48	M. Cooper	199	13-11	3.12
SS	D. Culler	.255	0	33	E. Wright	176	12- 9	3.52
3B	N. Fernandez	.255	2	42	B. Lee	140	10- 9	4.18
RF	T. Holmes	.310	6	79	S. Johnson	127	6- 5	2.76
CF	C. Gillenwater	.228	1	14	W. Spahn	126	8- 5	2.94
LF	B. Rowell	.280	3	31				
C	P. Masi	.267	3	62				

1947 (Billy Southworth)		BA	HR	RBI		IP	W-L	ERA
1B	E. Torgeson	.281	16	78	W. Spahn	290	21-10	2.33
2B	C. Ryan	.265	5	69	J. Sain	266	21-12	3.52
SS	D. Culler	.248	0	19	R. Barrett	211	11-12	3.55
3B	B. Elliott	.317	22	113	B. Voiselle	131	8- 7	4.32
RF	T. Holmes	.309	9	53	S. Johnson	113	6- 8	4.23
CF	J. Hopp	.288	2	32				
LF	B. Rowell	.276	5	40				
C	P. Masi	.304	9	50				

1948 (Billy Southworth)		BA	HR	RBI		IP	W-L	ERA
1B	E. Torgeson	.253	10	67	J. Sain	315	24-15	2.60
2B	E. Stanky	.320	2	29	W. Spahn	257	15-12	3.71
SS	A. Dark	.322	3	48	B. Voiselle	216	13-13	3.63
3B	B. Elliott	.283	23	100	V. Bickford	146	11- 5	3.27
RF	T. Holmes	.325	6	61	R. Barrett	128	7- 8	3.65
CF	M. McCormick	.303	1	39	B. Hogue	86	8- 2	3.23
LF	J. Heath	.319	20	76	C. Shoun	74	5- 1	4.01
C	P. Masi	.253	5	44				

1949 (Billy Southworth)		BA	HR	RBI		IP	W-L	ERA
1B	E. Fletcher	.262	11	51	W. Spahn	302	21-14	3.07
2B	E. Stanky	.285	1	42	J. Sain	243	10-17	4.81
SS	A. Dark	.276	3	53	V. Bickford	231	16-11	4.25
3B	B. Elliott	.280	17	76	B. Voiselle	169	7- 8	4.04
RF	T. Holmes	.266	8	59	N. Potter	97	6-11	4.19
CF	J. Russell	.231	8	54	J. Antonelli	96	3- 7	3.56
LF	M. Rickert	.292	6	49	B. Hall	74	6- 4	4.36
C	B. Salkeld	.255	5	25				

1950 (Billy Southworth)		BA	HR	RBI		IP	W-L	ERA
1B	E. Torgeson	.290	23	87	V. Bickford	312	19-14	3.47
2B	R. Hartsfield	.277	7	24	W. Spahn	293	21-17	3.16
SS	B. Kerr	.227	2	46	J. Sain	278	20-13	3.94
3B	B. Elliott	.305	24	107	B. Chipman	124	7- 7	4.43
RF	T. Holmes	.298	9	51	B. Hogue	63	34- 5	5.03
CF	S. Jethroe	.273	18	58				
LF	S. Gordon	.304	27	103				
C	W. Cooper	.329	14	60				

1951	(Billy Southworth)(Tommy Holmes)	BA	HR	RBI		IP	W-L	ERA
1B	E. Torgeson	.263	24	92	W. Spahn	311	22-14	2.98
2B	R. Hartsfield	.271	6	31	M. Surkont	237	12-16	3.99
SS	B. Kerr	.186	1	18	V. Bickford	165	11- 9	3.12
3B	B. Elliott	.285	15	70	J. Sain	160	5-13	4.21
RF	W. Marshall	.281	11	62	C. Nichols	156	11- 8	*2.88*
CF	S. Jethroe	.280	18	65	J. Wilson	110	7- 7	5.40
LF	S. Gordon	.287	29	109	B. Chipman	52	4- 3	4.85
C	W. Cooper	.313	18	59				

1952	(Billy Southworth)(Charlie Grimm)	BA	HR	RBI		IP	W-L	ERA
1B	E. Torgeson	.230	5	34	W. Spahn	290	14-19	2.98
2B	J. Dittmer	.193	7	41	J. Wilson	234	12-14	4.23
SS	J. Logan	.283	4	42	M. Surkont	215	12-13	3.77
3B	E. Mathews	.242	25	58	V. Bickford	161	7-12	3.74
RF	B. Thorpe	.260	3	26	L. Burdette	137	6-11	3.61
CF	S. Jethroe	.232	13	58	E. Johnson	92	6- 3	4.11
LF	S. Gordon	.289	25	75				
C	W. Cooper	.235	10	55				

1953	(Charlie Grimm)	BA	HR	RBI		IP	W-L	ERA
1B	J. Adcock	.285	18	80	W. Spahn	266	*23-7*	*2.10*
2B	J. Dittmer	.266	9	63	L. Burdette	175	15- 5	3.24
SS	J. Logan	.273	11	73	J. Antonelli	175	12-12	3.18
3B	E. Mathews	.302	*47*	135	M. Surkont	170	11- 5	4.18
RF	A. Pafko	.297	17	72	B. Buhl	154	13- 8	2.97
CF	B. Bruton	.250	1	41	D. Liddle	129	7- 6	3.08
LF	S. Gordon	.274	19	75	J. Wilson	114	4- 9	4.34
C	D. Crandall	.272	15	51				

1954	(Charlie Grimm)	BA	HR	RBI		IP	W-L	ERA
1B	J. Adcock	.308	23	87	W. Spahn	283	21-12	.314
2B	D. O'Connell	.279	2	37	L. Burdette	238	15-14	2.76
SS	J. Logan	.275	8	66	G. Conley	194	14- 9	2.96
3B	E. Mathews	.290	40	103	J. Wilson	128	8- 2	3.52
RF	A. Pafko	.286	14	69	C. Nichols	122	9-11	4.41
CF	B. Bruton	.284	4	30	D. Jolly	111	11- 6	2.43
LF	H. Aaron	.280	13	69	B. Buhl	110	2- 7	4.00
C	D. Crandall	.242	21	64				

1955	(Charlie Grimm)	BA	HR	RBI		IP	W-L	ERA
1B	G. Crowe	.281	15	55	W. Spahn	246	17-14	3.26
2B	D. O'Connell	.225	6	40	L. Burdette	230	13- 8	4.03
SS	J. Logan	.297	14	83	B. Buhl	202	12-11	3.21
3B	E. Mathews	.289	41	101	G. Conley	158	11- 7	4.16
RF	H. Aaron	.314	27	106	C. Nichols	144	9- 8	4.00
CF	B. Bruton	.275	9	47	R. Crone	140	10- 9	3.46
LF	B. Thompson	.257	12	56	E. Johnson	92	5- 7	3.42
C	D. Crandall	.236	26	62				

1956	(Charlie Grimm) (Fred Haney)	BA	HR	RBI		IP	W-L	ERA
1B	J. Adcock	.291	38	103	W. Spahn	281	20-11	2.78
2B	D. O'Connell	.239	2	42	L. Burdette	256	19-10	2.70
SS	J. Logan	.281	15	46	B. Buhl	217	18- 8	3.32
3B	E. Mathews	.272	37	95	R. Crone	170	11-10	3.87
RF	H. Aaron	.328	26	92	G. Conley	158	8- 9	3.13
CF	B. Bruton	.272	8	56	T. Phillips	88	5- 3	2.26
LF	B. Thompson	.235	20	74	E. Johnson	51	4- 3	3.71
C	D. Crandall	.238	16	48	D. Jolly	46	2- 3	3.74

1957	(Fred Haney)	BA	HR	RBI		IP	W-L	ERA
1B	F. Torre	.272	5	40	W. Spahn	271	21-11	2.69
2B	Schoendienst	.310	6	32	L. Burdette	257	17- 9	3.72
SS	J. Logan	.273	10	49	B. Buhl	217	18- 7	2.74
3B	E. Mathews	.292	32	94	G. Conley	148	9- 9	3.16
RF	H. Aaron	.322	44	132	B. Trowbridge	126	7- 5	3.64
CF	B. Bruton	.278	5	30	J. Pizarro	99	5- 6	4.62
LF	W. Covington	.284	21	65	E. Johnson	65	7- 3	3.88
C	D. Crandall	.253	15	46	D. McMahon	47	2- 3	1.54

1958	(Fred Haney)	BA	HR	RBI		IP	W-L	ERA
1B	F. Torre	.309	6	55	W. Spahn	290	22-11	3.07
2B	Schoendienst	.262	1	24	L. Burdette	275	20-10	2.91
SS	J. Logan	.226	11	53	B. Rush	147	10- 6	3.42
3B	E. Mathews	.251	31	77	C. Willey	140	9- 7	2.70
RF	H. Aaron	.326	30	95	J. Pizarro	97	6- 4	2.70
CF	B. Bruton	.280	3	28	J. Jay	97	7- 5	2.14
LF	W. Covington	.330	24	74	D. McMahon	59	7- 2	3.68
C	D. Crandall	.272	18	63				

1959	(Fred Haney)	BA	HR	RBI		IP	W-L	ERA
1B	J. Adcock	.292	25	76	W. Spahn	292	21-15	2.96
2B	F. Mantilla	.215	3	19	L. Burdette	290	21-15	4.07
SS	J. Logan	.291	13	50	B. Buhl	198	15- 9	2.86
3B	E. Mathews	.306	46	114	J. Jay	136	6-11	4.09
RF	H. Aaron	.355	39	123	J. Pizarro	134	6- 2	3.77
CF	B. Bruton	.289	6	41	C. Willey	117	5- 9	4.15
LF	W. Covington	.279	7	45	B. Rush	101	5- 6	2.40
C	D. Crandall	.257	21	72	D. McMahon	81	5- 3	2.57

1960	(Chuck Dressen)	BA	HR	RBI		IP	W-L	ERA
1B	J. Adcock	.298	25	91	L. Burdette	276	19-13	3.36
2B	C. Cottier	.277	3	19	W. Spahn	268	21-10	3.50
SS	J. Logan	.245	7	42	B. Buhl	239	16- 9	3.09
3B	E. Mathews	.277	39	124	C. Willey	145	6- 7	4.35
RF	H. Aaron	.292	40	126	J. Jay	133	9- 8	3.24
CF	B. Bruton	.286	12	54	J. Pizarro	115	6- 7	4.55
LF	W. Covington	.249	10	35	D. McMahon	64	3- 6	5.94
C	D. Crandall	.294	19	77	R. Piche	48	3- 5	3.56

1961 (Chuck Dressen) (Birdie Tebbetts)	BA	HR	RBI		IP	W-L	ERA
1B J. Adcock	.285	35	108	L. Burdette	272	18-11	4.00
2B F. Bolling	.262	15	56	W. Spahn	263	21-13	3.02
SS R. McMillan	.220	7	48	B. Buhl	188	9-10	4.11
3B E. Mathews	.306	32	91	C. Willey	160	6-12	3.83
RF L. Maye	.271	14	41	D. Nottebart	126	6- 7	4.06
CF H. Aaron	.327	34	120	B. Hendley	97	5- 7	3.90
LF F. Thomas	.284	25	67	D. McMahon	92	6- 4	2.84
C J. Torre	.278	10	42				

1962 (Birdie Tebbetts)	BA	HR	RBI		IP	W-L	ERA
1B J. Adcock	.248	29	78	W. Spahn	269	18-14	3.04
2B F. Bolling	.271	9	43	B. Shaw	225	15- 9	2.80
SS R. McMillan	.246	12	41	B. Hendley	200	11-13	3.60
3B E. Mathews	.265	29	90	L. Burdette	144	10- 9	4.89
RF M. Jones	.255	10	36	T. Cloninger	111	8- 3	4.30
CF H. Aaron	.323	45	128	C. Raymond	43	5- 5	2.74
LF L. Maye	.244	10	41				
C D. Crandall	.297	8	45				

1963 (Bobby Bragan)	BA	HR	RBI		IP	W-L	ERA
1B G. Oliver	.250	11	47	W. Spahn	260	23- 7	2.60
2B F. Bolling	.244	5	43	D. Lemaster	237	11-14	3.04
SS R. McMillan	.250	4	29	B. Hendley	169	9- 9	3.93
3B E. Mathews	.263	23	84	B. Shaw	159	7-11	2.66
RF H. Aaron	.319	44	130	T. Cloninger	145	9-11	3.78
CF M. Jones	.219	3	22	B. Sadowski	117	5- 7	2.62
LF L. Maye	.271	11	34	L. Burdette	84	6- 5	3.63
C. J. Torre	.293	14	71	C. Raymond	53	4- 6	5.40

1964 (Bobby Bragan)	BA	HR	RBI		IP	W-L	ERA
1B G. Oliver	.276	13	49	T. Cloninger	243	19-14	3.56
2B F. Bolling	.199	5	34	D. Lemaster	221	17-11	4.15
SS D. Menke	.283	20	65	W. Spahn	174	6-13	5.29
3B E. Mathews	.233	23	74	H. Fischer	168	11-10	4.01
RF H. Aaron	.328	24	95	B. Sadowski	167	9-10	4.10
CF L. Maye	.304	10	74	W. Blasingame	117	9- 5	4.24
LF R. Carty	.330	22	88	B. Tiefenauer	73	4- 6	3.21
C J. Torre	.321	20	109				

1965 (Bobby Bragan)	BA	HR	RBI		IP	W-L	ERA
1B G. Oliver	.270	21	58	T. Cloninger	279	24-11	3.29
2B F. Bolling	.264	7	50	W. Blasingame	225	16-10	3.77
SS W. Woodward	.208	0	11	K. Johnson	180	13- 8	3.21
3B E. Mathews	.251	32	95	D. Lemaster	146	7-13	4.43
RF H. Aaron	.318	32	89	B. Sadowski	123	5- 9	4.32
CF M. Jones	.262	31	75	H. Fischer	123	8- 9	3.89
LF F. Alou	.297	23	78	B. O'Dell	111	10- 6	2.18
C J. Torre	.291	27	80	P. Niekro	75	2- 3	2.89

1966	(Bobby Bragan) (Billy Hitchcock)	BA	HR	RBI		IP	W-L	ERA
1B	F. Alou	.327	31	74	T. Cloninger	258	14-11	4.12
2B	W. Woodward	.264	0	43	K. Johnson	216	14- 8	3.30
SS	D. Menke	.251	15	60	D. Lemaster	171	11- 8	3.74
3B	E. Mathews	.250	16	53	C. Carroll	144	8- 7	2.37
RF	H. Aaron	.279	44	127	D. Kelley	81	7- 5	3.22
CF	M. Jones	.264	23	66	W. Blasingame	68	3- 7	5.32
LF	R. Carty	.326	15	76	C. Olivo	66	5- 4	4.23
C	J. Torre	.315	36	101	T. Abernathy	65	4- 4	3.86

1967	(Billy Hitchcock) (Ken Silvestri)	BA	HR	RBI		IP	W-L	ERA
1B	F. Alou	.274	15	43	D. Lemaster	215	9- 9	3.34
2B	W. Woodward	.226	0	25	K. Johnson	210	13- 9	2.74
SS	D. Menke	.227	7	39	P. Niekro	207	11- 9	1.87
3B	C. Boyer	.245	26	96	P. Jarvis	194	15-10	3.66
RF	H. Aaron	.307	39	109	D. Kelley	98	2- 9	3.77
CF	M. Jones	.253	17	50	C. Carroll	93	6-12	5.52
LF	R. Carty	.255	15	64	J. Ritchie	82	4- 6	3.17
C	J. Torre	.277	20	68	T. Cloninger	77	4- 7	5.17

1968	(Lum Harris)	BA	HR	RBI		IP	W-L	ERA
1B	D. Johnson	.208	8	33	P. Niekro	257	14-12	2.59
2B	F. Millan	.289	1	33	P. Jarvis	256	16-12	2.60
SS	S. Jackson	.226	1	19	R. Reed	202	11-10	3.35
3B	C. Boyer	.227	4	17	K. Johnson	135	5- 8	3.47
RF	H. Aaron	.287	29	86	M. Pappas	121	10- 8	2.37
CF	F. Alou	.317	11	57	C. Upshaw	117	8- 7	2.47
LF	M. Lum	.224	3	21	J. Britton	90	4- 6	3.09
C	J. Torre	.271	10	55	G. Stone	75	7- 4	2.76

1969	(Lum Harris)	BA	HR	RBI		IP	W-L	ERA
1B	O. Cepeda	.257	22	88	P. Niekro	284	23-13	2.57
2B	F. Millan	.267	6	57	R. Reed	241	18-10	3.47
SS	S. Jackson	.239	1	27	P. Jarvis	217	13-11	4.44
3B	C. Boyer	.250	14	57	G. Stone	165	13-10	3.65
RF	H. Aaron	.300	44	97	M. Pappas	144	6-10	3.63
CF	F. Alou	.282	5	32	C. Upshaw	105	6- 4	2.91
LF	T. Gonzalez	.294	10	50	J. Britton	88	7- 5	3.78
C	B. Didier	.256	0	32				

1970	(Lum Harris)	BA	HR	RBI		IP	W-L	ERA
1B	O. Cepeda	.305	34	111	P. Jarvis	254	16-16	3.61
2B	F. Millan	.310	2	37	P. Nieko	230	12-18	4.27
SS	S. Jackson	.259	0	20	J. Nash	212	13- 9	4.08
3B	C. Boyer	.246	16	62	G. Stone	207	11-11	3.87
RF	H. Aaron	.298	38	118	R. Reed	135	7-10	4.40
CF	T. Gonzalez	.265	7	55	H. Wilhelm	78	6- 4	3.10
LF	R. Carty	.366	25	101	B. Priddy	73	5- 5	5.42
C	B. Tillman	.238	11	30				

174

1971 (Lum Harris)	BA	HR	RBI		IP	W-L	ERA
1B H. Aaron	.327	47	118	P. Niekro	269	15-14	2.98
2B R. Millan	.289	2	45	R. Reed	222	13-14	3.73
SS M. Perez	.227	4	32	G. Stone	173	6- 8	3.59
3B D. Evans	.242	12	38	P. Jarvis	162	6-14	4.11
RF M. Lum	.269	13	55	T. Kelley	143	9- 5	2.96
CF S. Jackson	.258	2	25	J. Nash	133	9- 7	4.94
LF R. Garr	.343	9	44	C. Upshaw	82	11- 6	3.51
C E. Williams	.260	33	87	B. Priddy	64	4- 9	4.22

1972 (Lum Harris) (Eddie Mathews)	BA	HR	RBI		IP	W-L	ERA
1B H. Aaron	.265	34	77	P. Niekro	282	16-12	3.06
2B F. Millan	.257	1	38	R. Reed	213	11-15	3.93
SS M. Perez	.228	1	28	R. Schueler	145	5- 8	3.66
3B D. Evans	.254	19	71	T. Kelley	116	5- 7	4.58
RF M. Lum	.228	9	38	G. Stone	111	6-11	5.51
CF D. Baker	.321	17	76	P. Jarvis	99	11- 7	4.09
LF R. Garr	.325	12	53	C. Upshaw	54	3- 5	3.67
C E. Williams	.258	28	87				

1973 (Eddie Mathews)	BA	HR	RBI		IP	W-L	ERA
1B M. Lum	.294	16	82	C. Morton	256	15-10	3.41
2B D. Johnson	.270	43	99	P. Niekro	245	13-10	3.31
SS M. Perez	.250	8	57	R. Schueler	186	8- 7	3.86
3B D. Evans	.281	41	104	R. Harrison	177	11- 8	4.16
RF H. Aaron	.301	40	96	R. Reed	116	4-11	4.42
CF D. Baker	.288	21	99	G. Gentry	87	4- 6	3.41
LF R. Garr	.299	11	55	T. House	67	4- 2	4.70
C J. Oates	.248	4	27	P. Dobson	58	3- 7	4.97

1974 (Eddie Mathews) (Clyde King)	BA	HR	RBI		IP	W-L	ERA
1B D. Johnson	.251	15	62	P. Niekro	*302*	*20*-13	2.38
2B M. Perez	.260	2	34	C. Morton	275	16-12	3.14
SS C. Robinson	.230	0	29	B. Capra	217	16- 8	*2.28*
3B D. Evans	.240	25	79	R. Reed	186	10-11	3.39
RF D. Baker	.256	20	69	R. Harrison	126	6-11	4.71
CF R. Office	.246	3	31	T. House	103	6- 2	1.92
LF R. Garr	*.353*	11	54	M. Leon	75	4- 7	2.64
C J. Oates	.223	1	21	D. Frisella	42	3- 4	5.14

1975 (Clyde King) (Connie Ryan)	BA	HR	RBI		IP	W-L	ERA
1B E. Williams	.240	11	50	C. Morton	278	17-16	3.50
2B M. Perez	.275	2	34	P. Niekro	276	15-15	3.20
SS L. Blanks	.234	3	38	T. House	79	7- 7	3.19
3B D. Evans	.243	22	73	B. Capra	78	4- 7	4.27
RF D. Baker	.261	19	72	J. Easterly	69	2- 9	4.96
CF R. Office	.290	3	20	B. DalCanton	67	2- 7	2.26
LF R. Garr	.278	6	31				
C V. Correll	.215	11	39				

1976 (Dave Bristol)		BA	HR	RBI		IP	W-L	ERA
1B	W. Montanez	.321	9	64	P. Niekro	271	17-11	3.29
2B	R. Gilbreath	.251	1	32	D. Ruthven	240	14-17	4.20
SS	D. Chaney	.252	1	50	A. Messersmith	207	11-11	3.04
3B	J. Royster	.248	5	45	C. Morton	140	4- 9	4.18
RF	K. Henderson	.262	13	61	F. LaCorte	105	3-12	4.71
CF	R. Office	.281	4	34	A. Devine	73	5- 6	3.21
LF	J. Wynn	.207	17	66	E. Sosa	34	5- 5	5.35
C	V. Correll	.225	5	16				

1977 (Dave Bristol) (Ted Turner)		BA	HR	RBI		IP	W-L	ERA
1B	W. Montanez	.287	20	68	P. Niekro	330	16-20	4.04
2B	R. Gilbreath	.243	8	43	D. Ruthven	151	7-13	4.23
SS	P. Rockett	.254	1	24	B. Capra	139	6-11	5.37
3B	J. Moore	.260	5	34	A. Messersmith	102	5- 4	4.41
RF	G. Matthews	.283	17	64	E. Solomon	89	6- 6	4.55
CF	R. Office	.241	5	39	D. Campbell	89	0- 6	3.03
LF	J. Burroughs	.271	41	114	R. Camp	79	6- 3	3.99
C	B. Pocoroba	.290	8	44	D. Collins	71	3- 9	5.07

1978 (Bobby Cox)		BA	HR	RBI		IP	W-L	ERA
1B	D. Murphy	.226	23	79	P. Niekro	334	19-18	2.88
2B	J. Foyster	.259	2	35	P. Hanna	140	7-13	5.14
SS	D. Chaney	.224	3	20	M. Mahler	135	4-11	4.67
3B	B. Horner	.266	23	63	E. Solomon	106	4- 6	4.08
RF	G. Matthews	.285	18	62	L. McWilliams	99	9- 3	2.82
CF	R. Office	.250	9	40	J. Easterly	78	3- 6	5.65
LF	J. Burroughs	.301	23	77	G. Garber	78	4- 4	2.53
C	B. Pocoroba	.242	6	34	A. Devine	65	5- 4	5.95
					T. Boggs	59	2- 8	6.71

1979 (Bobby Cox)		BA	HR	RBI		IP	W-L	ERA
1B	D. Murphy	.276	21	57	P. Niekro	342	21-20	3.39
2B	G. Hubbard	.231	3	29	E. Solomon	186	7-14	4.21
SS	J. Royster	.273	3	51	R. Matula	171	8-10	4.16
3B	B. Horner	.314	33	98	T. Brizzolara	107	6- 9	5.30
RF	G. Matthews	.304	27	90	G. Garber	106	6-16	4.33
CF	R. Office	.249	2	37	M. Mahler	100	5-11	5.85
LF	J. Burroughs	.224	11	47	J. McLaughlin	69	5- 3	2.48
C	J. Nolan	.248	4	21				

1980 (Bobby Cox)		BA	HR	RBI		IP	W-L	ERA
1B	C. Chambliss	.282	18	72	P. Niekro	275	15-18	3.63
2B	G. Hubbard	.248	9	43	D. Alexander	231	14-11	4.19
SS	J. Royster	.242	1	20	T. Boggs	192	12- 9	3.42
3B	B. Horner	.265	35	89	R. Matula	177	11-13	4.58
RF	G. Matthews	.278	19	75	L. McWilliams	164	9-14	4.94
CF	D. Murphy	.281	33	89	R. Camp	108	6- 4	1.92
LF	J. Burroughs	.263	13	51	G. Garber	82	5- 5	3.84
C	B. Benedict	.253	2	34	P. Hanna	79	2- 0	3.19

ODDMENTS

Henry Aaron, No. 44, hit 44 home runs in four years in his career: 1957, 1963, 1966, and 1969. He led the league in all but the latter year.

In 1889, the team's attendance was 295,000; profits were $100,000.

In 1973, Henry Aaron hit 10 home runs while Carl Morton was pitching for the Braves.

Hugh Duffy, while playing for Boston of the American Association, once scored from second base on a sacrifice fly.

The Braves' current emblem was first conceived and drawn in the 1948 pennant year by *Boston Record-American/Sunday Advertiser* artist Charlie Schmidt. He used a Mohawk as the model. The club first became known as the Braves in 1911 when a New York politician bought the club and used the Tammany Hall Indian head as a logo.

When Gabe Paul was general manager at Cincinnati, he offered Andy Seminick straight up for Henry Aaron. The Braves' John Quinn (obviously) refused.

In 1962, Joe Adcock hit only .249, but against the Phillies he was murder: he hit nine of his 29 homers, and knocked in 24 of his 78 runs in 18 games against Philadelphia.

August was usually a good month for Warren Spahn. In 1954, 1960, and 1961 he was 6-0 and in 1957 he was 7-0.

In 1966, Henry Aaron and Willie McCovey, both of whom wore No. 44, tied for the league lead in home runs with 44.

Biff Pocoroba's real first name is Biff.

Milwaukee has had its share of major league teams in addition to the Braves and the current Brewers. In 1884, the Union Association had a franchise there. In 1878, the National League had a team there. In 1891, the American Association had a franchise there, and in 1901 the American League had a club there.

Babe Ruth and Cy Young, both of whom spent the majority of their careers with American League clubs, finished out their baseball days with the Braves, in 1935 and 1911, respectively.

Andre Rodgers, an infielder in the mid-1950s, was born in the Bahamas, and played cricket until he was 17.

The "Nuf Ced" McGreevy Tavern, a late-nineteenth- and early-twentieth-century clubhouse for the Royal Rooters, one of the earliest fan clubs in baseball history, was located at the corner of Columbus Avenue and Ruggles Street in Boston.

Tommy McCarthy, a Braves outfielder at the turn of the century, was partly responsible for a rule change. It seems that McCarthy developed a habit of intentionally bobbling balls hit to him on a fly, bobbling them as he ran toward the infield, thus keeping runners on their bases. Because of him, the rule was changed so that runners could leave the base as soon as the outfielder *touched* the ball.

In the 1890s Tommy McCarthy and Hugh Duffy were partners in a combination bowling alley and saloon at 603 Washington Street in Boston.

In 1905 the Braves had four 20-game losers: Irv Young (20-21), Vic Willis (11-29), Chick Fraser (15-22), and Kaiser Wilhelm (4-22). All but Wilhelm had ERAs under 3.30. The club finished seventh, 54½ games out.

Ted Turner is not the first Southerner to own the Braves. The Dovey brothers from South Carolina owned them from 1906 through 1909. The team was called the Doves then.

George Stallings, the manager of the 1914 Miracle Team, had a habit of sliding up and down the length of the bench during games; he allegedly wore out five pairs of pants a year in the process. Stallings also had a paper fetish, and Heinie Zimmerman used to taunt him by ripping pieces of paper into shreds and dumping them into the Boston dugout when he ran by.

Braves Field in Boston opened in 1915 on the site of the Allston Golf Club. It cost $600,000 to build. The original dimensions were 402' to left field, 402' to right field, and 550' (!) to center.

Oddments (continued)

In the May 1, 1920, record-setting 26-inning game, only three balls were used.

While in Boston, the Braves had a promotional film called "Take Me Out to the Wigwam."

After spring training in 1916, the Braves embarked on a 20-day exhibition tour during which they slept on a train which carried them from city to city. Most of the cars didn't have dining facilities and, in general, the players were rather disgusted with the arrangement. They complained to management, but to no avail. Rabbit Maranville finally led a rebellion of sorts. They continued to play, but they refused to shave, and wore nothing but blue work shirts, loud neckties, and flashy caps. Maranville, and two others, were chased out of a Georgia store when the owner telephoned the police, thinking they were jailbreakers on the prowl.

In the 1940s, the "Troubadors," or "Three Little Earaches," led by trumpeter Hy Brenner, serenaded the Braves and their opponents. They played "Has Anybody Here Seen Kelly" for Tommy Holmes's at-bats, and blew funeral dirges for shower-bound enemy pitchers.

On opening day, 1946, approximately 5,000 people left the park with green paint on their clothes. The freshly painted seats hadn't quite dried. In the following day's newspapers the club ran "An Apology to Braves Fans." "The management," it said, "will reimburse any of its patrons for any expense to which they may be put for necessary cleansing of clothing as a result of paint damage." Thirteen thousand claims came in, some from as far away as California, Nebraska, and Florida. Five thousand were paid. The average claim was settled for $1.50, the highest was $50. The Braves opened a paint account at a local bank to handle the claims. Red Sox owner Tom Yawkey loaned Fenway Park until the paint dried.

In the Braves' later years in Boston, one of the biggest fans was Mrs. Lolly Hopkins of Providence, Rhode Island, who used to yell exhortations through a big megaphone.

Larvell Blanks is the nephew of former Boston Patriot running back Sid Blanks.

After the 1935 season, the club decided to change its name from the Braves; hoping to change its luck in the process (the Braves finished 1935 with a 38-115 record, good for 61½ games behind the pennant-winning Cubs). So they solicited suggestions from the fans (some of the more unkind ones were "Sacred Cods" and "Bankrupts") and had the 26 sportswriters who covered baseball vote for their favorite. "Bees" won with 14 votes. Other suggestions (with vote totals in parentheses) were: Bluebirds (4), Beacons (3), Colonials (2), Bulldogs (1), Blues, (1) and Bulls (1). Thirteen fans suggested the nickname "Bees" and the winning contestant was Arthur J. Rockwood of East Weymouth, Mass., whose name was chosen out of a hat.

Chris Chambliss is the cousin of ex-Celtic JoJo White.

Gene Mauch has the distinction of having played in the Braves organization in the three cities that the franchise was located, but not all with the parent club. He played in Boston with the parent club in 1951, but then played in the minors with Milwaukee of the American Association in 1952, and with Atlanta of the Southern League in 1953.

Hugh Duffy managed in Milwaukee and in Boston, but he never managed the Braves. He was the pilot of the 1901 American League Milwaukee club, and he managed the Red Sox in 1921 and 1922.

Miguel Gonzalez became Boston's first Latin player ever in 1912. He was later the first Latin coach and manager (with other clubs), and was credited with coining the "good field, no hit" tag so common in baseball jargon.

Bob Shaw, a Braves' pitcher in 1962–63, is the man whom Gaylord Perry credits for having taught him the spitter while both men were with the Giants in 1964.

During the 1980 season there were seven major league managers who were either ex-Braves or former Braves farmhands. They were Bobby Cox, Jim Frey, Tony LaRussa, Billy Martin, Gene Mauch, Chuck Tanner, and Joe Torre.

The 1897 club had a mascot by the name of Darkhue White, who was once quoted as saying "Ah'll voodoo dat man Anson," referring apparently to Cap Anson of Chicago.

BOX SCORES

1914 World Series Composite

Team Totals

	W	AB	H	2B	3B	HR	R	RBI	BA	BB	SO	ERA
BOS N	4	135	33	6	2	1	16	14	.244	15	18	1.15
PHI A	0	128	22	9	0	0	6	5	.172	13	28	3.65

Individual Batting

Boston (NL)

	AB	H	2B	3B	HR	R	RBI	BA
B. Schmidt, 1b	17	5	0	0	0	2	1	.294
C. Deal, 3b	16	2	2	0	0	1	0	.125
J. Evers, 2b	16	7	0	0	0	2	2	.438
P. Whitted, of	14	3	0	1	0	2	4	.214
R. Maranville, ss	13	4	0	0	0	1	3	.308
H. Moran, of	13	1	1	0	0	2	0	.077
H. Gowdy, c	11	6	3	1	1	3	3	.545
J. Connolly, of	9	1	0	0	0	1	1	.111
L. Mann, of	7	2	0	0	0	1	0	.286
D. Rudolph, p	6	2	0	0	0	1	0	.333
T. Cather, of	5	0	0	0	0	0	0	.000
B. James, p	4	0	0	0	0	0	0	.000
L. Tyler, p	3	0	0	0	0	0	0	.000
J. Devore	1	0	0	0	0	0	0	.000
L. Gilbert	0	0	0	0	0	0	0	—

Errors: J. Connolly, J. Evers, R. Maranville, H. Moran. Stolen bases: C. Deal (2), R. Maranville (2), H. Moran, H. Gowdy, P. Whitted, B. Schmidt, J. Evers.

Philadelphia (AL)

	AB	H	2B	3B	HR	R	RBI	BA
F. Baker, 3b	16	4	2	0	0	0	2	.250
E. Murphy, of	16	3	2	0	0	2	0	.188
R. Oldring, of	15	1	0	0	0	0	0	.067
E. Collins, 2b	14	3	0	0	0	0	1	.214
S. McInnis, 1b	14	2	1	0	0	2	0	.143
J. Barry, ss	14	1	0	0	0	1	0	.071
W. Schang, c	12	2	1	0	0	1	0	.167
A. Strunk, of	7	2	0	0	0	0	0	.286
J. Walsh, of	6	2	1	0	0	0	1	.333
J. Bush, p	5	0	0	0	0	0	0	.000
C. Bender, p	2	0	0	0	0	0	0	.000
E. Plank, p	2	0	0	0	0	0	0	.000
B. Shawkey, p	2	1	1	0	0	0	1	.500
H. Pennock, p	1	0	0	0	0	0	0	.000
J. Lapp, c	1	0	0	0	0	0	0	.000
J. Wyckoff, p	1	1	1	0	0	0	0	1.000

Errors: W. Schang, S. McInnis, J. Bush. Stolen bases: J. Barry, E. Collins.

Individual Pitching

Boston (NL)

	W	L	ERA	IP	H	BB	SO	SV
D. Rudolph	2	0	0.50	18	12	4	15	0
B. James	2	0	0.00	11	2	6	9	0
L. Tyler	0	0	3.60	10	8	3	4	0

Philadelphia (AL)

	W	L	ERA	IP	H	BB	SO	SV
J. Bush	0	1	3.27	11	9	4	4	0
E. Plank	0	1	1.00	9	7	4	6	0
C. Bender	0	1	10.13	3.1	8	2	3	0
B. Shawkey	0	1	5.40	5	4	2	0	0
H. Pennock	0	0	0.00	3	2	2	3	0
J. Wyckoff	0	0	2.45	3.2	3	1	2	0

1948 World Series Composite

Team Totals

	W	AB	H	2B	3B	HR	R	RBI	BA	BB	SO	ERA
CLE A	4	191	38	7	0	4	17	16	.199	12	26	2.72
BOS N	2	187	43	6	0	4	17	16	.230	16	19	2.60

Individual Batting

Cleveland (AL)

	AB	H	2B	3B	HR	R	RBI	BA
D. Mitchell, of	23	4	1	0	1	4	1	.174
L. Doby, of	22	7	1	0	1	1	2	.318
J. Gordon, 2b	22	4	0	0	1	3	2	.182
L. Boudreau, ss	22	6	4	0	0	1	3	.273
K. Keitner, 3b	21	2	0	0	0	3	0	.095
E. Robinson, 1b	20	6	0	0	0	0	1	.300
J. Hegan, c	19	4	0	0	1	2	5	.211
W. Judnich, of	13	1	0	0	0	1	1	.077
B. Lemon, p	7	0	0	0	0	0	0	.000
B. Feller, p	4	0	0	0	0	0	0	.000
G. Bearden, p	4	2	1	0	0	1	0	.500
A. Clark, of	3	0	0	0	0	0	0	.000
T. Tucker, of	3	1	0	0	0	1	0	.333
S. Gromek, p	3	0	0	0	0	0	0	.000
B. Kennedy, of	2	1	0	0	0	0	1	.500
J. Tipton	1	0	0	0	0	0	0	.000
A. Rosen	1	0	0	0	0	0	0	.000
R. Boone	1	0	0	0	0	0	0	.000
H. Peck, of	0	0	0	0	0	0	0	—

Errors: K. Keitner, J. Gordon, L. Doby. Stolen bases: J. Gordon, J. Hegan.

Boston (NL)

	AB	H	2B	3B	HR	R	RBI	BA
T. Holmes, of	26	5	0	0	0	3	1	.192
A. Dark, ss	24	4	1	0	0	2	0	.167
M. McCormick, of	23	6	0	0	0	1	2	.261
B. Elliott, 3b	21	7	0	0	2	4	5	.333
M. Rickert, of	19	4	0	0	1	2	2	.211
E. Torgeson, 1b	18	7	3	0	0	2	1	.389
E. Stanky, 2b	14	4	1	0	0	0	1	.286
B. Saikeld, c	9	2	0	0	1	2	1	.222
P. Masi, c	8	1	1	0	0	1	1	.125
J. Sain, p	5	1	0	0	0	0	0	.200
F. McCormick, 1b	5	1	0	0	0	0	0	.200
W. Spahn, p	4	0	0	0	0	0	1	.000
C. Conatser, of	4	0	0	0	0	0	1	.000
N. Potter, p	2	1	0	0	0	0	0	.500
B. Voiselle, p	2	0	0	0	0	0	0	.000
R. Sanders	1	0	0	0	0	0	0	.000
S. Sisti, 2b	1	0	0	0	0	0	0	.000
C. Ryan	1	0	0	0	0	0	0	.000

Errors: B. Elliott (3), A. Dark (3). Stolen bases: E. Torgeson.

Individual Pitching

Cleveland (AL)

	W	L	ERA	IP	H	BB	SO	SV
B. Lemon	2	0	1.65	16.1	16	7	6	0
B. Feller	0	2	5.02	14.1	10	5	7	0
G. Bearden	1	0	0.00	10.2	6	1	4	1
S. Gromek	1	0	1.00	9	7	1	2	0
B. Muncrief	0	0	0.00	2	1	0	0	0
S. Paige	0	0	0.00	0.2	0	0	0	0
E. Klieman	0	0	0.00	0.0	1	2	0	0
Christopher	0	0	0.00	0.0	2	0	0	0

Boston (NL)

	W	L	ERA	IP	H	BB	SO	SV
J. Sain	1	1	1.06	17	9	0	9	0
W. Spahn	1	1	3.00	12	10	3	12	0
B. Voiselle	0	1	2.53	10.2	8	2	2	0
N. Potter	0	0	8.44	5.1	6	2	1	0
R. Barrett	0	0	0.00	3.2	1	0	1	0
V. Bickford	0	1	2.70	3.1	4	5	1	0

1957 World Series Composite

Team Totals

	W	AB	H	2B	3B	HR	R	RBI	BA	BB	SO	ERA
MIL N	4	225	47	6	1	8	23	22	.209	22	40	3.48
NY A	3	230	57	7	1	7	25	25	.248	22	34	2.89

Individual Batting

Milwaukee (NL)

	AB	H	2B	3B	HR	R	RBI	BA
H. Aaron, of	28	11	0	1	3	5	7	.393
J. Logan, ss	27	5	1	0	1	5	2	.185
W. Covington, of	24	5	1	0	0	1	1	.208
E. Mathews, 3b	22	5	3	0	1	4	4	.227
D. Crandall, c	19	4	0	0	1	1	1	.211
Schoendienst, 2b	18	5	1	0	0	0	2	.278
J. Adcock, 1b	15	3	0	0	0	1	2	.200
A. Pafko, of	14	3	0	0	0	1	0	.214
B. Hazle, of	13	2	0	0	0	2	0	.154
F. Mantilla, 2b	10	0	0	0	0	1	0	.000
F. Torre, 1b	10	3	0	0	2	2	3	.300
L. Burdette, p	8	0	0	0	0	0	0	.000
D. Rice, c	6	1	0	0	0	0	0	.167
W. Spahn, p	4	0	0	0	0	0	0	.000
C. Sawatski	2	0	0	0	0	0	0	.000
N. Jones	2	0	0	0	0	0	0	.000
B. Buhl, p	1	0	0	0	0	0	0	.000
J. Pizarro, p	1	0	0	0	0	0	0	.000
E. Johnson, p	1	0	0	0	0	0	0	.000
J. DeMerit	0	0	0	0	0	0	0	—

Errors: J. Adcock, E. Mathews, B. Buhl. Stolen bases: W. Covington.

New York (AL)

	AB	H	2B	3B	HR	R	RBI	BA
H. Bauer, of	31	8	2	1	2	3	6	.258
T. Kubek, of, 3b	28	8	0	0	2	4	4	.286
Y. Berra, c	25	8	1	0	1	5	2	.320
G. McDougald, ss	24	6	0	0	0	3	2	.250
J. Coleman, 2b	22	8	2	0	0	2	2	.364
M. Mantle, of	19	5	0	0	1	3	2	.263
J. Lumpe, 3b	14	4	0	0	0	0	2	.286
H. Simpson, 1b	12	1	0	0	0	0	1	.083
E. Slaughter, of	12	3	1	0	0	2	0	.250
E. Howard, 1b	11	3	0	0	1	2	3	.273
A. Carey, 3b	7	2	1	0	0	0	1	.286
W. Ford, p	5	0	0	0	0	0	0	.000
J. Collins, 1b	5	0	0	0	0	0	0	.000
B. Turley, p	4	0	0	0	0	0	0	.000
B. Skowron, 1b	4	0	0	0	0	0	0	.000
D. Larsen, p	2	0	0	0	0	1	0	.000
T. Bryne, p	2	1	0	0	0	0	0	.500
T. Sturdivant, p	1	0	0	0	0	0	0	.000
A. Ditmar, p	1	0	0	0	0	0	0	.000
B. Shantz, p	1	0	0	0	0	0	0	.000
B. Richardson, 2b	0	0	0	0	0	0	0	—

Errors: T. Kubek (2), G. McDougald, M. Mantle, Y. Berra, E. Howard. Stolen bases: G. McDougald.

Individual Pitching

Milwaukee (NL)

	W	L	ERA	IP	H	BB	SO	SV
L. Burdette	3	0	0.67	27	21	4	13	0
W. Spahn	1	1	4.70	15.1	18	2	2	0
E. Johnson	0	1	1.29	7	2	1	8	0
D. McMahon	0	0	0.00	5	3	3	5	0
B. Buhl	0	1	10.80	3.1	6	6	4	0
B. Trowbridge	0	0	45.00	1	2	3	1	0
J. Pizarro	0	0	10.80	1.2	3	2	1	0
G. Conley	0	0	10.80	1.2	2	1	0	0

New York (AL)

	W	L	ERA	IP	H	BB	SO	SV
W. Ford	1	1	1.13	16	11	5	7	0
B. Turley	1	0	2.31	11.2	7	6	12	0
D. Larsen	1	1	3.72	9.2	8	5	6	0
B. Shantz	0	1	4.05	6.2	8	2	7	0
T. Sturdivant	0	0	6.00	6	6	1	2	0
A. Ditmar	0	0	0.00	6	2	0	2	0
T. Byrne	0	0	5.40	3.1	1	2	1	0
B. Grim	0	1	7.71	2.1	3	0	2	0
J. Kucks	0	0	0.00	0.2	1	1	1	0

1958 World Series Composite

Team Totals

	W	AB	H	2B	3B	HR	R	RBI	BA	BB	SO	ERA
NY A	4	233	49	5	1	10	29	29	.210	21	42	3.39
MIL N	3	240	60	10	1	3	25	24	.250	27	56	3.71

Individual Batting

New York (AL)

	AB	H	2B	3B	HR	R	RBI	BA
H. Bauer, of	31	10	0	0	4	6	8	.323
G. McDougald, 2b	28	9	2	0	2	5	4	.321
Y. Berra, c	27	6	3	0	0	3	2	.222
B. Skowron, 1b	27	7	0	0	2	3	7	.259
M. Mantle, of	24	6	0	1	2	4	3	.250
T. Kubek, ss	21	1	0	0	0	0	1	.048
E. Howard, of	18	4	0	0	0	4	2	.222
J. Lumpe, 3b, ss	12	2	0	0	0	0	0	.167
A. Carey, 3b	12	1	0	0	0	1	0	.083
N. Siebern, of	8	1	0	0	0	1	0	.125
B. Richardson, 3b	5	0	0	0	0	0	0	.000
B. Turley, p	5	1	0	0	0	0	2	.200
W. Ford, p	4	0	0	0	0	1	0	.000
E. Slaughter	3	0	0	0	0	1	0	.000
R. Duren, p	3	0	0	0	0	0	0	.000
D. Larsen, p	2	0	0	0	0	0	0	.000
M. Throneberry	1	0	0	0	0	0	0	.000
A. Ditmar, p	1	0	0	0	0	0	0	.000
J. Kucks, p	1	1	0	0	0	0	0	1.000

Errors: T. Kubek (2), A. Ditmar. Stolen bases: E. Howard.

Milwaukee (NL)

	AB	H	2B	3B	HR	R	RBI	BA
R. Schoendienst, 2b	30	9	3	1	0	5	0	.300
H. Aaron, of	27	9	2	0	0	3	2	.333
W. Covington, of	26	7	0	0	0	2	4	.269
E. Mathews, 3b	25	4	2	0	0	3	3	.160
D. Crandall, c	25	6	0	0	1	4	3	.240
J. Logan, ss	25	3	2	0	0	3	2	.120
B. Bruton, of	17	7	0	0	1	2	2	.412
F. Torre, 1b	17	3	0	0	0	0	1	.176
J. Adcock, 1b	13	4	0	0	0	1	0	.308
W. Spahn, p	12	4	0	0	0	0	3	.333
A. Pafko, of	9	3	1	0	0	0	1	.333
L. Burdette, p	9	1	0	0	1	1	3	.111
B. Rush, p	2	0	0	0	0	0	0	.000
H. Hanebrink	2	0	0	0	0	0	0	.000
C. Wise	1	0	0	0	0	0	0	.000
F. Mantilla, ss	0	0	0	0	0	1	0	—

Errors: F. Torre (2), J. Logan (2), B. Bruton, R. Schoendienst, E. Mathews. Stolen bases: E. Mathews.

Individual Pitching

New York (AL)

	W	L	ERA	IP	H	BB	SO	SV
B. Turley	2	1	2.76	16.1	10	7	13	1
W. Ford	0	1	4.11	15.1	19	5	16	0
R. Duren	1	1	1.93	9.1	7	6	14	1
D. Larsen	1	0	0.96	9.1	9	6	9	0
M. Dickson	0	0	4.50	4	4	0	1	0
J. Kucks	0	0	2.08	4.1	4	1	0	0
A. Ditmar	0	0	0.00	3.2	2	0	2	0
Z. Monroe	0	0	27.00	1	3	1	1	0
D. Maas	0	0	81.00	0.1	2	1	0	0

Milwaukee (NL)

	W	L	ERA	IP	H	BB	SO	SV
W. Spahn	2	1	2.20	28.2	19	8	18	0
L. Burdette	1	2	5.64	22.1	22	4	12	0
B. Rush	0	1	3.00	6	3	5	2	0
D. McMahon	0	0	5.40	3.1	3	3	5	0
J. Pizarro	0	0	5.40	1.2	2	1	3	0
C. Willey	0	0	0.00	1	0	0	2	0

Playoff Game, September 28, 1959

Los Angeles	ab	r	h	rbi		*Milwaukee*	ab	r	h	rbi
Gilliam, 3b	4	0	0	0		Avila, 2b	5	0	0	1
Neal, 2b	5	1	3	0		Matthews, 3b	4	0	0	0
Moon, lf	4	1	1	0		Aaron, rf	2	0	0	0
Larker, rf	4	0	3	1		Adcock, 1b	3	0	0	0
cLillis	0	0	0	0		Pafko, lf	2	0	0	0
Fairly, rf	0	0	0	0		aMaye, lf	2	0	1	0
Hodges, 1b	3	0	1	1		Logan, ss	3	1	1	0
Demeter, cf	4	0	1	0		Crandall, c	4	1	2	0
Roseboro, c	4	1	1	1		Bruton, cf	4	0	1	1
Wills, ss	4	0	0	0		Willey, p	2	0	1	0
McDevitt, p	1	0	0	0		bSlaughter	1	0	0	0
Sherry, p	2	0	0	0		McMahon, p	0	0	0	0
Total	35	3	10	3		dTorre	1	0	0	0
						Total	33	2	6	2

aSingled for Pafko in 5th; bGrounded out for Wiley in 6th; cRan for Larker in 7th; dFlied out for McMahon in 9th.

Los Angeles	1 0 1	0 0 1	0 0 0—3
Milwaukee	0 2 0	0 0 0	0 0 0—2

E—Wills. DP—Gilliam, Neal and Hodges; Matthews, Avila and Adcock 2. LOB—Los Angeles 8, Milwaukee 8.

PO—Los Angeles 27; Gilliam, Neal 3, Moon 2, Fairly, Hodges 7, Demeter 2, Roseboro 8, Wills 3. Milwaukee 27; Avila 4, Matthews 2, Aaron 3, Adcock 6, Pafko, Maye, Logan, Crandall 5, Bruton 4. A—Los Angeles 9; Gilliam, Neal 4, Hodges, Wills 3. Milwaukee 11; Avila 3, Matthews 3, Logan 3, Willey, McMahon.

HR—Roseboro

	IP	H	R	ER	BB	SO
McDevitt	1 1/3	2	2	2	2	2
Sherry (W, 7–2)	7 2/3	4	0	0	2	4
Willey (L, 5–9)	6	8	3	3	2	3
McMahon	3	2	0	0	1	0

Umpires—Conlan, Donatelli, Gorman, Barlick, Boggess and Jackowski. Time: 2:40. Attendance—18,297.

Playoff Game, September 29, 1959

Milwaukee	ab	r	h	rbi	Los Angeles	ab	r	h	rbi
Bruton, cf	6	0	0	0	Gilliam, 3b	5	0	1	0
Matthews, 3b	4	2	2	1	Neal, 2b	6	2	2	1
Aaron, rf	4	1	2	0	Moon, rf, lf	6	1	3	1
Torre, 1b	3	0	1	2	Snider, cf	4	0	1	0
Maye, lf	2	0	0	0	eLillis	0	1	0	0
aPafko, lf	1	0	0	0	Williams, p	2	0	0	0
bSlaughter, lf	1	0	0	0	Hodges, 1b	5	2	2	0
DeMerit, lf	0	0	0	0	Larker, rf	4	0	2	2
kSpangler, lf	0	0	0	0	fPignatano, c	1	0	1	0
Logan, ss	3	1	2	0	Roseboro, c	3	0	0	0
Schoendienst, 2b	1	0	0	0	gFurillo, rf	2	0	2	1
dVernon	1	0	0	0	Wills, ss	5	0	1	0
Cottier, 2b	0	0	0	0	Drysdale, p	1	0	0	0
lAdcock	1	0	0	0	Podres, p	1	0	0	0
Avila, 2b	0	0	0	0	Churn, p	0	0	0	0
Crandall, c	6	1	1	0	cDemeter	1	0	0	0
Mantilla, 2b, ss	5	0	1	1	Koufax, p	0	0	0	0
Burdette, p	4	0	1	0	Labine, p	0	0	0	0
McMahon, p	0	0	0	0	hEsseglan	0	0	0	0
Spahn, p	0	0	0	0	jFairly, cf	2	0	0	0
Jay, p	1	0	0	0	Total	48	6	15	5
Rush, p	1	0	0	0					
Total	44	5	10	4					

aFlied out for Maye in 5th; bPopped out for Pafko in 7th; cLined out for Churn in 8th; Struck out for Schoendienst in 9th; eRan for Snider in 9th; fRan for Larker in 9th; gHit sacrifice fly for Roseboro in 9th; hAnnounced for Labine in 9th; jHit into forceout for Essegian in 9th; kWalked for DeMerit in 11th; lHit into forceout for Cottier in 11th.

Milwaukee	2 1 0	0 1 0	0 1 0	0 0 0—5
Los Angeles	1 0 0	1 0 0	0 0 3	0 0 1—6

Two out when winning run was scored.

E—Snider, Neal, Mantilla 2. DP—Willis, Neal, Hodges; Torre, Logan, Torre. LOB—Milwaukee 13, Los Angeles 11.

PO—Milwaukee 35; Bruton 4, Matthews 2, Aaron 3, Torre 10, Maye 2, DeMerit, Spangler 3, Logan 2, Avila, Crandall 6, Mantilla, Los Angeles 36; Gilliam 4, Neal 3, Moon 3, Snider, Hodges 11, Larker 2, Pignatano 3, Roseboro 5, Willis 2, Drysdale, Fairly. A—Milwaukee 13; Matthews 2, Torre 2, Logan 5, Crandall, Mantilla, Burdette

2. Los Angeles 14; Gilliam 3, Neal 2, Moon, Roseboro, Wills 5, Drysdale, Churn.
2B Hit—Aaron, 38—Neal, Crandall. HR—Neal, Matthews, SF—Mantilla, Furillo.

	IP	H	R	ER	BB	SO
*Burdette	8	10	5	5	0	4
McMahon	0	1	0	0	0	0
Spahn	1/3	1	0	0	0	0
Jay	2 1/3	1	0	0	1	1
Rush (L, 5-6)	1	2	1	0	1	0
Drysdale	4 1/3	6	4	3	2	3
Podres	2 1/3	3	0	0	1	1
Churn	1 1/3	1	1	1	0	0
Koufax	2/3	0	0	0	3	1
Labine	1/3	0	0	0	0	1
Williams (W, 5-5)	3	0	0	0	3	3

HBP—By Jay (Pignatano). Wild pitch—Podres. PB—Pignatano. Umpires—Barlick, Boggess, Donatelli, Conlan, Jackowski, Gorman. Time—4:06. Attendance—36,528.

1969 Playoff Game Box Scores

Game of Saturday, Oct. 4

New York	ab	r	h	rbi	Atlanta	ab	r	h	rbi
Agee, cf	5	0	0	0	Millan, 2b	5	1	2	0
Garrett, 3b	4	1	2	0	Gonzalez, cf	5	2	2	2
Jones, lf	5	1	1	1	H. Aaron, rf	5	1	2	2
Shamsky, rf	4	1	3	0	Carty, lf	3	1	1	0
Weis, pr, 2b	0	0	0	0	Lum, lf	1	0	1	0
Boswell, 2b	3	2	0	0	Cepeda, 1b	4	0	1	0
Gaspar, rf	0	0	0	0	Boyer, 3b	1	0	0	1
Kranep'l, 1b	4	2	1	0	Didier, c	4	0	0	0
Grote, c	3	1	1	1	Garrido, ss	4	0	1	0
Har'lson, ss	3	1	1	2	Niekro, p	3	0	0	0
Seaver, p	3	0	0	0	Aspro'nte, ph	1	0	0	0
Martin, ph	1	0	1	2	Upshaw, p	0	0	0	0
Taylor, p	0	0	0	0	Totals	36	5	10	5
Totals	35	9	10	6					

New York   0 2 0 2 0 0 0 5 0—9
Atlanta   0 1 2 0 1 0 1 0 0—5

New York	IP	H	R	ER	BB	SO
Seaver (Winner)	7	8	5	5	4	2
Taylor (Save)	2	2	0	0	0	1

Atlanta	IP	H	R	ER	BB	SO
Niekro (Loser)	8	9	9	4	4	4
Upshaw	1	1	0	0	0	1

*Faced 3 batters in 9th; Faced 1 batter in 9th.

E—Boswell, Cepeda, Gonzalez. DP—Atlanta 2. LOB—New York 3, Atlanta 9.
2B—Carty, Millan, Gonzalez, H. Aaron, Garrett, Lum. 3B—Harrelson. HR—
Gonzalez, H. Aaron. SB—Cepeda, Jones. SF—Boyer, PB—Didier, Grote. U—Barlick,
Donatelli, Sudol, Vargo, Pelekoudas and Steiner. T—2:37. A—50,122.

Game of Sunday, October 5

New York	ab	r	h	rbi		Atlanta	ab	r	h	rbi
Agee, cf	4	3	2	2		Millan, 2b	2	1	2	0
Garrett, 3b	5	1	2	1		Gonzalez, cf	4	1	1	0
Jones, lf	5	2	3	3		H. Aaron, rf	5	1	1	3
Shamsky, rf	5	1	3	1		Carty, lf	4	2	1	0
Gasp'r, pr-rf	0	0	0	0		Cepeda, 1b	4	1	2	1
Boswell, 2b	5	1	1	2		Boyer, 3b	4	0	1	2
McGraw, p	0	0	0	0		Didier, c	4	0	0	0
Kranep'l, 1b	4	0	1	1		Garrido, ss	4	0	1	0
Grote, c	5	1	0	0		Reed, p	0	0	0	0
Har'lson, ss	5	1	1	1		Doyle, p	0	0	0	0
Koosman, p	2	1	0	0		Pappas, p	1	0	0	0
Taylor, p	0	0	0	0		T. Aaron, ph	1	0	0	0
Martin, ph	1	0	0	0		Britton, p	0	0	0	0
Weis, 2b	1	0	0	0		Upshaw, p	1	0	0	0
						Aspro'nte, ph	1	0	0	0
						Neibauer, p	0	0	0	0
Totals	42	11	13	11		Totals	35	6	9	6

```
New York        1 3 2   2 1 0   2 0 0—11
Atlanta         0 0 0   1 5 0   0 0 0— 6
```

New York	IP	H	R	ER	BB	SO
Koosman	4 2/3	7	6	6	4	5
Taylor (Winner)	1 1/3	1	0	0	0	2
McGraw (Save)	3	1	0	0	1	1

Atlanta	IP	H	R	ER	BB	SO
Reed (Loser)	1 2/3	5	4	4	3	3
Doyle	1	2	2	0	1	3
Pappas	2 1/3	4	3	3	0	4
Britton	1/3	0	0	0	1	0
Upshaw	2 2/3	2	2	2	1	1
Neibauer	1	0	0	0	0	1

E—H. Aaron, Cepeda, Harrelson, Boyer. DP—New York 2, Atlanta 1. LOB—New
York 10, Atlanta 7. 2B—Jones, Harrelson, Carty, Garrett, Cepeda. HR—Agee, Bos-
well. H. Aaron, Jones. SB—Agee 2, Garrett, Jones. U—Donatelli, Sudol, Vargo,
Pelekoudas, Steiner and Barlick. T—3:10. A—50,270.

Game of Monday, October 6

Atlanta	ab	r	h	rbi
Millan, 2b	5	0	0	0
Gonzalez, cf	5	1	2	0
H. Aaron, rf	4	1	2	2
Carty, lf	3	1	1	0
Cepeda, 1b	3	1	2	2
Boyer, 3b	4	0	0	0
Didier, c	3	0	0	0
Lum, ph	1	0	1	0
Jackson, ss	0	0	0	0
Garrido, ss	2	0	0	0
Alou, ph	1	0	0	0
Tillman, c	0	0	0	0
Jarvis, p	2	0	0	0
Stone, p	1	0	0	0
Upshaw, p	0	0	0	0
Aspro'te, ph	1	0	0	0
Totals	35	4	8	4

New York	ab	r	h	rbi
Agee, cf	5	1	3	2
Garrett, 3b	4	1	1	2
Jones, lf	4	1	2	0
Shamsky, rf	4	1	1	0
Gaspar, pr, rf	0	0	0	0
Boswell, 2b	4	1	3	3
Weis, 2b	0	0	0	0
Kranep'l, 1b	4	0	1	0
Grote, c	4	1	1	0
Harrelson, ss	3	0	0	0
Gentry, p	0	0	0	0
Ryan, p	4	1	2	0
Totals	36	7	14	7

Atlanta	2 0 0	0 2 0	0 0 0—4
New York	0 0 1	2 3 1	0 0 x—7

Atlanta	IP	H	R	ER	BB	SO
Jarvis (Loser)	4 1/3	10	6	6	0	6
Stone	1	2	1	1	0	0
Upshaw	2 2/3	2	0	0	0	2

New York	IP	H	R	ER	BB	SO
Gentry	2*	5	2	2	1	1
Ryan (Winner)	7	3	2	2	2	7

E—Millan. DP—Atlanta 1. LOB—Atlanta 7, New York 6. 2B—Cepeda, Agee, H. Aaron, Kranepool, Jones, Grote. HR—H. Aaron, Agee, Boswell, Cepeda, Garrett. SH—Harrelson. U—Sudol, Vargo, Pelekoudas, Stevens, Barlick and Donatelli. T—2:24. A—53,195.

---

*Pitched to three batters in third.

All-Star Game at Boston July 7, 1936

American League

	ab	r	h	tb	2b	3b	hr	bb	so	sh	sb	po	a	e
Appling, Chic., ss	4	0	1	1	0	0	0	1	0	0	0	2	2	0
Gehringer, Det., 2b	3	0	2	3	1	0	0	2	0	0	0	2	1	0
DiMaggio, N.Y., rf	5	0	0	0	0	0	0	0	0	0	0	1	0	1
Gehrig, N.Y., 1b	2	1	1	4	0	0	1	2	0	0	0	7	0	0
Averill, Cleve., cf	3	0	0	0	0	0	0	0	0	0	0	3	1	0
Chapman, Wash., cf	1	0	0	0	0	0	0	0	0	0	0	0	0	0
R. Ferrell, Bost., c	2	0	0	0	0	0	0	0	2	0	0	4	0	0
Dickey, N.Y., c	2	0	0	0	0	0	0	0	0	0	0	2	0	0
Radcliff, Chi. lf	2	0	1	1	0	0	0	0	0	0	0	2	0	0
Goslin, Det., lf	1	1	1	1	0	0	0	1	0	0	0	1	0	0
Higgins, Phila., 3b	2	0	0	0	0	0	0	0	2	0	0	0	1	0
Foxx, Bost., 3b	2	1	1	1	0	0	0	0	1	0	0	0	1	0
Grove, Bost., p	1	0	0	0	0	0	0	0	1	0	0	0	0	0
Rowe, Det., p	1	0	0	0	0	0	0	0	0	0	0	0	0	0
aSelkirk, N.Y.	0	0	0	0	0	0	0	1	0	0	0	0	0	0
Harder, Clev., p	0	0	0	0	0	0	0	0	0	0	0	0	1	0
bCrosetti, N.Y.	1	0	0	0	0	0	0	0	1	0	0	0	0	0
Total	32	3	7	11	1	0	1	7	7	0	0	24	7	1

National League

	ab	r	h	tb	2b	3b	hr	bb	so	sh	sb	po	a	e
Galan, Chic., cf	4	1	1	4	0	0	1	0	2	0	0	1	0	0
W. Herman, Chic., 2b	3	1	2	2	0	0	0	1	0	0	0	3	4	0
Collins, St. L., 1b	2	0	0	0	0	0	0	2	0	0	0	9	1	0
Medwick, St. L., lf	4	0	1	1	0	0	0	0	0	0	0	0	0	0
Demaree, Chic., rf	3	1	1	1	0	0	0	0	0	0	0	1	0	0
Ott, N.Y., rf	1	0	1	1	0	0	0	0	0	0	0	0	0	0
Hartnett, Chic., c	4	1	1	3	0	1	0	0	0	0	0	7	0	0
Whitney, Phila., 3b	3	0	1	1	0	0	0	0	1	0	0	0	2	0
Riggs, Cinc., 3b	1	0	0	0	0	0	0	0	1	0	0	0	0	0
Durocher, St. L., ss	3	0	1	1	0	0	0	0	1	0	0	4	0	0
J. Dean, St. L., p	1	0	0	0	0	0	0	0	1	0	0	0	2	0
Hubbell, N.Y., p	1	0	0	0	0	0	0	0	0	0	0	2	1	0
Davis, Chic., p	0	0	0	0	0	0	0	0	0	0	0	0	1	0
Warneke, Chic., p	1	0	0	0	0	0	0	0	0	0	0	0	0	0
Total	31	4	9	14	0	1	1	3	6	0	0	27	11	0

aBatted for Rowe in seventh. bBatted for Harder in ninth.

Score by Innings

American League	0 0 0 0 0 0 3 0 0	—3
National League	0 2 0 0 2 0 0 0 0	—4

Runs batted in—National League: Hartnett, Whitney, Galan, Medwick. American League: Gehrig, Appling 2.

Left on bases—American League 9, National League 6, Double plays—Whitney,

190

Herman and Collins; Higgins, Gehringer and Gehrig. Struck out—By J. Dean 3, Hubbell 2, Warneke 2, Grove 2, Rowe 2, Harder 2. Bases on balls—Off J. Dean 2, Hubbell 1, Davis 1, Warneke 3, Grove 2, Rowe 1. Passed ball—Hartnett. Hits—Off J. Dean 0 in 3 innings, Hubbell 2 in 3, Davis 4 in 2/3, Warneke 1 in 2 1/3, Grove 3 in 3, Rowe 4 in 3, Harder 2 in 2. Winning pitcher—J. Dean. Losing pitcher—Grove. Umpires—Reardon (NL) at plate, Summers (AL) at first base, Stewart (NL) at second and Kolls (AL) at third for first four and a half innings; Summers at plate, Stewart at first, Kolls at second and Reardon at third for remainder of game. Time of game—2 hours.

All-Star Game at Milwaukee, July 12, 1955

American League

	ab	r	h	po	a	e
Kuenn, ss	3	1	1	1	0	0
Carrasquel, ss	3	0	2	1	3	1
Fox, 2b	3	1	1	2	0	0
Avila, 2b	1	0	0	1	2	0
Williams, lf	3	1	1	1	0	0
Smith, lf	1	0	0	0	0	0
Mantle, cf	6	1	2	3	0	0
Berra, c	6	1	1	8	2	0
Kaline, rf	4	0	1	6	0	0
Vernon, 1b	5	0	1	8	0	0
Finigan, 3b	3	0	0	2	0	0
Rosen, 3b	2	0	0	0	0	1
Pierce, p	0	0	0	0	0	0
bJensen	1	0	0	0	0	0
Wynn, p	0	0	0	0	1	0
gPower	1	0	0	0	0	0
Ford, p	1	0	0	0	1	0
Sullivan, p	1	0	0	0	0	0
Total	44	5	10	*33	9	2

National League

	ab	r	h	po	a	e
Schoendienst, 2b	6	0	2	3	2	0
Ennis, lf	1	0	0	1	0	0
cMusial, lf	4	1	1	0	0	0
Snider, cf	2	0	0	3	0	0
Mays, cf	3	2	2	3	0	0
Kluszewski, 1b	3	1	2	9	1	0
Mathews, 3b	2	0	0	0	3	1
Jackson, 3b	3	1	1	0	0	0
Mueller, rf	2	0	1	0	0	0
dAaron, rf	2	1	2	0	0	0
Banks, ss	2	0	0	2	1	0
Logan, ss	3	0	1	1	1	0
Crandall, c	1	0	0	1	0	0
eBurgess, c	1	0	0	2	0	0
hLopata, c	3	0	0	10	0	0
Roberts, p	0	0	0	1	1	0
aThomas	1	0	0	0	0	0
Haddix, p	0	0	0	0	2	0
fHodges	1	0	1	0	0	0
Newcombe, p	0	0	0	0	0	0
aBaker	1	0	0	0	0	0
Jones, p	0	0	0	0	0	0
Nuxhall, p	2	0	0	0	1	0
Conley, p	0	0	0	0	0	0
Total	45	6	13	36	12	1

aPopped out for Roberts in third. bPopped out for Pierce in fourth. cStruck out for Ennis in fourth. dRan for Mueller in fifth. eHit into force out for Crandall in fifth. fSingled for Haddix in sixth. gPopped out for Wynn in seventh. hSafe on error for Burgess in seventh. iFlied out for Newcombe in seventh.

American	4 0 0	0 0 1	0 0 0	0 0 0—5
National	0 0 0	0 0 0	2 3 0	0 0 1—6

Runs batted in—Mantle 3, Vernon, Logan, Jackson, Aaron, Musial.
Two base hits—Kluszewski, Kaline.
Home runs—Mantle, Musial. Sacrifices—Pierce, Avila. Double plays—Kluszewski, Banks and Roberts; Wynn, Carrasquel and Vernon. Left on bases—American 12,

*None out when winning run was scored.

All-Star Game at Milwaukee, July 12, 1955 (continued)

National 8. Bases on balls—Roberts 1 (Williams), Ford 1 (Aaron), Jones 2 (Vernon, Rosen), Nuxhall 3 (Smith, Kaline, Avila), Sullivan 1 (Musial). Strike outs—Pierce 3 (Ennis, Snider, Banks), Haddix 2 (Kaline, Finnigan), Wynn 1 (Musial), Newcombe 1 (Avila), Jones 1 (Mantle), Nuxhall 5 (Ford, Vernon, Rosen, Sullivan, Smith), Sullivan 4 (Mays, Jackson, Logan, Lopata), Conley 3 (Kaline, Vernon, Rosen).

Hits—Off Roberts 4 in 3 innings, Pierce 1 in 3, Haddix 3 in 3, Wynn 3 in 3, Newcombe 1 in 1, Jones 0 in 2/3, Ford 5 in 1 2/3, Nuxhall 2 in 3 1/3. Sullivan 4 in 3 1/3 (faced one batter in twelfth), Conley 0 in 1. Runs, earned runs—Roberts 4 and 4, Haddix 1 and 1, Ford 5 and 5, Sullivan 1 and 1. Hit by pitcher—By Jones (Kaline). Wild pitch—Roberts. Passed ball—Crandall. Winning pitcher—Conley. Losing pitcher—Sullivan. Umpire— Barlick (N), Soar (A), Boggess (N), Summers (A), Secory (N) Runge (A). Time—3:17. Attendance—45,314. Receipts (gross)—$179,545.50.

All-Star Game at Atlanta July 25, 1972

American League	ab	r	h	bi	National League	ab	r	h	bi
Carew, 2b	2	0	1	1	J. Morgan, 2b	4	0	1	1
Rojas, 2b	1	1	1	2	Mays, cf	2	0	0	0
Murcer, cf	3	0	0	0	Cedeno, cf	2	1	1	0
Scheinblum, rf	1	0	0	0	H. Aaron, rf	3	1	1	2
R. Jackson, rf	4	0	2	0	A. Oliver, rf	1	0	0	0
D. Allen, 1b	3	0	0	0	Stargell, lf	1	0	0	0
Cash, 1b	1	0	0	0	B. Williams, lf	2	1	1	0
Yastrzemski, lf	3	0	0	0	Bench, c	2	0	1	0
Rudi, lf	1	0	1	0	Sanguillen, c	2	0	1	0
Grich, ss	4	0	0	0	L. May, 1b	4	0	1	1
B. Robinson, 3b	2	0	0	0	Torre, 3b	3	0	1	0
Bando, 3b	2	0	0	0	Santo, 3b	1	0	0	0
Freehan, c	1	1	0	0	Kessinger, ss	2	0	0	0
Fisk, c	2	1	1	0	Carlton, p	0	0	0	0
Palmer, p	0	0	0	0	Stoneman, p	1	0	0	0
Lolich, p	1	0	0	0	McGraw, p	0	0	0	0
G. Perry, p	0	0	0	0	Colbert, ph	0	1	0	0
R. Smith, ph	1	0	0	0	Gibson, p	0	0	0	0
Wood, p	0	0	0	0	Blass, p	0	0	0	0
Piniella, ph	1	0	0	0	Beckert, ph	1	0	0	0
McNally, p	0	0	0	0	Sutton, p	0	0	0	0
Total	33	3	6	3	Speier, ss	2	0	0	0
					Total	33	4	8	4

```
American    0 0 1   0 0 0   0 2 0   0—3
National    0 0 0   0 0 2   0 0 1   1—4
```

DP—American 2, National 2. LOB—American 3, National 5. 2B—R. Jackson, Rudi. HRS—H. Aaron (1), Rojas (1). SB—Morgan. S—Palmer, Speier.

	IP	H	R	ER	BB	SO	HBP	WP	BLK
Palmer	3	1	0	0	1	2	0	0	0
Lolich	2	1	0	0	0	1	0	0	0
G. Perry	2	3	2	2	0	1	0	0	0
Wood	2	2	1	1	1	1	0	0	0
McNally (L, 0-1)	*1/3	1	1	1	1	0	0	0	0
Gibson	2	1	0	0	0	0	0	0	0
Blass	1	1	1	1	1	0	0	0	0
Sutton	2	1	0	0	0	2	0	0	0
Carlton	1	0	0	0	1	0	0	0	0
Stoneman	2	2	2	2	0	2	0	0	0
McGraw (W, 1-0)	2	1	0	0	0	4	0	0	0

T—2:26. A—53,107

Warren Spahn: No-Hitter Box Scores

Sept. 16, 1960

Philadelphia	AB	R	H	TB	PO	A	E
Callison, lf	3	0	0	0	1	0	0
dDel Greco	1	0	0	0	0	0	0
Malkmus, 2b	4	0	0	0	4	6	0
Walters, rf	2	0	0	0	4	0	0
Herrera, 1b	3	0	0	0	9	1	0
Gonzalez, cf	3	0	0	0	4	0	0
Naeman, c	2	0	0	0	2	1	0
Woods, 3b	2	0	0	0	0	0	0
aTaylor	1	0	0	0	0	0	0
Lepcio, 3b	0	0	0	0	0	0	0
Amaro, ss	2	0	0	0	0	2	0
bWalls	1	0	0	0	0	0	0
Koppe, ss	0	0	0	0	0	0	0
Buzhardt, p	2	0	0	0	0	2	0
cSmith	1	0	0	0	0	0	0
Totals	27	0	0	0	24	12	0

Milwaukee	AB	R	H	TB	PO	A	E
Bruton, cf	3	1	2	2	4	0	0
Crandall, c	4	0	2	2	15	0	0
Mathews, 3b	4	0	2	2	0	1	0
Aaron, rf	3	1	1	1	1	0	0
Dark, lf	4	1	1	3	1	0	0
Adcock, 1b	2	0	1	1	4	1	0
Logan, ss	3	0	0	0	1	2	0
Cottier, 2b	3	0	0	0	0	0	0
SPAHN, p	3	1	1	1	1	2	0
Totals	29	4	10	12	27	6	0

Philadelphia	0 0 0 0 0 0 0 0 0—0
Milwaukee	0 0 0 2 1 0 1 0 x—4

*One out when winning run was scored.

aStruck out for Woods in eighth. bStruck out for Amaro in eighth. cStruck out for Buzhardt in ninth. dStruck out for Callison in ninth. Runs batted in—Crandall, Dark, Mathews, Adcock. Three-base hit—Dark. Stolen base—Bruton. Sacrifice hit—Logan. Sacrifice fly—Adcock. Double plays—Amaro, Malkmus and Herrera 2. Left on bases— Philadelphia 2, Milwaukee 6. Bases on balls—Off Buzhardt 3 (Bruton, Aaron, Adcock), off SPAHN 2 (Walters, Neeman). Struck out—By Buzhardt 1 (Logan), by SPAHN 15 (Callison, Del Greco, Walters, Herrera 2, Gonzalez 3, Neeman, Woods 2, Taylor, Walls, Buzhardt, Smith). Runs and earned runs—Off Buzhardt 4-4. Winning pitcher—SPAHN (20-9). Losing pitcher—Buzhardt (4-16). Umpires—Gorman, Smith, Sudol and Boggess. Time—2:02. Attendance—6,117.

April 28, 1961

San Francisco	AB	R	H	TB	PO	A	E
Hiller, 2b	2	0	0	0	2	0	0
Kuenn, 3b	3	0	0	0	1	0	0
Mays, cf	3	0	0	0	4	0	0
McCovey, 1b	2	0	0	0	3	1	1
Cepeda, lf	3	0	0	0	2	0	0
F. Alou, rf	3	0	0	0	1	0	0
Bailey, c	3	0	0	0	11	0	0
Pagan, ss	2	0	0	0	0	1	0
aM. Alou	1	0	0	0	0	0	0
Jones, p	2	0	0	0	0	0	0
bAmalfitano	1	0	0	0	0	0	0
Totals	25	0	0	0	24	2	1

Milwaukee	AB	R	H	TB	PO	A	E
McMillan, ss	3	0	0	0	3	6	0
Bolling, 2b	3	1	2	2	2	0	0
Mathews, 3b	3	0	0	0	1	0	0
Aaron, cf	3	0	1	1	1	0	0
Roach, lf	4	0	1	1	1	0	0
Spangler, lf	0	0	0	0	0	0	0
Adcock, 1b	3	0	1	1	10	0	0
Lau, c	2	0	0	0	5	0	1
DeMerit, rf	4	0	0	0	4	0	0
SPAHN, p	4	0	0	0	0	5	0
Totals	29	1	5	5	27	11	1

San Francisco	0 0 0 0 0 0 0 0 0—0
Milwaukee	1 0 0 0 0 0 0 0 x—1

aGrounded out for Pagan in ninth. bGrounded out for Jones in ninth. Runs batted in—McMillan. Double plays—SPAHN, McMillan and Adcock 2. Passed balls—Bailey 2. Left on bases—San Francisco 0, Milwaukee 11. Bases on balls—Off Jones 5 (Mathews, Aaron, Adcock, Lau 2), off SPAHN 2 (Hiller, McCovey). Struck out—By Jones 10 (McMillan, Mathews 2, Aaron, Roach, Lau, DeMerit 3, SPAHN), by SPAHN 5 (Mays 2, McCovey, Bailey, Jones). Runs and earned runs—Off Jones 1-1. HBP—Bolling (by Jones). Winning pitcher—SPAHN (2-1). Losing pitcher—Jones (2-1). Umpires—Donatelli, Burkhart, Pelekoudas, Forman and Conlan. Time—2:16. Attendance—8,513.